JFK: Satyr, Sinner, Saint!

Les Plosia

JFK: SATYR, SINNER, SAINT!

Copyright © 2014 LES PLOSIA

All rights reserved.

ISBN: 1620181525

DEDICATION

For my mother, Kathryn O'Donnell Plosia
and librarians around the world.

CONTENTS

Introduction	9
Prologue	19
JFK and his LSD Gal Pal	39
The Assassination and the Warren Commission	43
Cherchez la Femme	61
CIA and El Indio	93
Chicago Hit Squad	109
Satyriasis or Just Horny?	123
The Race Card	153
The Plots Converge	163
Mary Redux	185
The Texas Lynch Mob	229
John F. Kennedy: A Great Life	255
The Honey Trap	263

ACKNOWLEDGMENTS

This book is uniquely my own but the brew owes its aroma to discoveries, research, investigative skills, tenacity and selfless courage by a multitude of mythbusters to whom with awe and gratitude I exercise my precious pup, doff my tattered cap and wave my Irish blackthorn stick in salute.

INTRODUCTION

Like brainstorming a Tribune Media Services Sunday crossword puzzle, or solving one of Will Shortz's *New York Times* twisters, fitting final pieces to the John F. Kennedy assassination riddle was an epiphany.

The JFK mystery fades with time. It is dissolved by sequential disclosures and mountains of fragmented facts pulled together to form a mosaic that in retrospect can be seen as obvious. Reduced to wispy memories are spidery shreds of disinformation seemingly planted to lead through overgrown forests to dead-end glades of darkness. The Warren Commission Report? A paradigm on how to confuse people with facts. While shrouding realities of what occurred in Dallas in November 1963, the report issued in the fall of 1964 in all its fictional fulsomeness, factual selectivity, and clever non-sequiturs, admirably served its intended purpose. It was a foil of history. The context was admitted to years later by Lyndon Johnson, the sponsor of the Warren Commission Report. Johnson said such a report was necessary in order to divert public wrath away from the Soviet Union and Cuba so as to avoid a war with all of its horrible possibilities in a nuclear age. The explanation's superficial plausibility allowed LBJ to avoid facing less innocent truths.

We now have the perspective of fifty years, replete with confessions, time-layered revelations, a body of knowledge so immense that one wonders how any serious person can persist in believing the obsessional skewed original version of how and why first term President Kennedy was shot in broad daylight noontime in Dallas, Texas on Nov. 22, 1963 while he was ending the five-city weeklong opening leg of his reelection campaign.

Who killed Kennedy, you ask?

"Everybody," responds my muse. At least four separate assassination teams from four cities – Dallas, Chicago, Miami and Marseilles – each with different motivations, converged for what a renegade CIA master spy, E. Howard Hunt, called "The Big Event." "There were so many plots," he added in a deathbed confession. "Thank God one of them worked."

The poignant question was not "who," but "why." Why was Jack Kennedy shot? Ask yourself that question. And why the big lie cover up?

Commission member Allen Dulles, the retired director of the Central Intelligence Agency, publicly proclaimed and was quoted in a banner *Washington Post* headline early in 1964 that if the Warren Commission subpoenaed CIA and FBI witnesses, "THEY WILL LIE". Dulles hit the nail on the head.

As years went by truth seeped out. When FBI Director J. Edgar Hoover testified before the Warren Commission he "lied through his teeth", according to a public accusation in 1970 on the floor of Congress by Hale Boggs, the Democratic majority leader from Louisiana. The falsity of the Oswald story as the years went by was affirmed by LBJ, and by JFK superloyalists Ken O'Donnell and David Powers. A son of the slain president's brother, Robert F. Kennedy Jr., said his father RFK never accepted the Warren Commission version. The Commission itself was split, with three of the seven members dissenting, all evidence of their dissent destroyed, according to a lion of the upper house, Sen. Richard Russell, D-Georgia, a Commission member and ally of LBJ himself.

Why was the public not told that even the Warren Commission was split down the middle?

A massive conspiracy has been documented in deathbed confessions, mea culpas, books and memoirs as years went by and state statutes of limitation expired for everything except personally pulling the murder triggers in Dealey Plaza.

Assassination literature, for all of its forensic diligence and tracking of dramatis personae, is lamentably weak on vital and indispensable national security issues, foreign policy backlash, dynastic drift, and personality foibles of the president himself, as this book will show. Internal turmoil invisible to the public dominated the relatively brief Kennedy incumbency, a mere 1,037 days from inauguration until sudden end. The drama was not unfolded on a starkly empty stage, like a Sherwood Anderson play. The scenery and orchestration were indispensable to understand the denouement. In the sweep of history, Kennedy was not shot for no reason. His shaping dynasty, tag-lined Camelot by his widow after the Arthurian fantasy then playing on Broadway, was brutally cut off not because people did not like Jack Kennedy personally, but because those who orchestrated his demise saw no alternative way.

There is precious little attention given to the perilous times or to the realities of cause and effect which usually color history, and which certainly were prevalent in the case of JFK.

The assassination struck barely more than a year after the international saber-rattling nuclear Cuban Missile Crisis, which had threatened to end the world. If JFK finally extricated our nation from the crisis, he did so not without misgivings about how he had allowed the situation to reach such a crisis in the first place. The assassination occurred two months after Cuban freedom fighters run by the CIA were choked off and legally attacked by the Kennedys and other government agencies including, on orders, the FBI due to a change of plans which would suddenly exempt Fidel Castro from American aggression, an offshoot of a nuclear deal with Moscow. The assassination occurred 30 months after the CIA, with JFK's backing, assassinated longtime Dominican dictator Raphael Trujillo and then deposed his elected reformist successor, Orlando Bosch, also by the Dominican army with help from the CIA with JFK's green light.

In sharpest focus of all was the double cross on Nov. 1 – only three weeks earlier – by the U.S. of President Diem in Vietnam, propped up nine years earlier by the CIA to serve as bulwark against Ho Chi Minh's Communist incursions into South Vietnam. A coup engineered by CIA agent Lou Conein out of the U.S. Embassy in Saigon ended in the murder of Diem and his brother, whose fiery and vocal widow Madame Nhu was touring the United States denouncing President Kennedy in weeks prior to the Dallas ambush.

Less fully known was that the Kennedys and J. Edgar Hoover were battling about JFK's whoring with prostitutes in the European sexpionage ring that had toppled the British MacMillen conservative government over the Profumo Affair. The scandal involved British War Minister John Profumo being pumped for nuclear secrets by a prostitute named Christine Keeler who was alternately shacking up with a Soviet NKVD agent. Adding insult to injury, the FBI had just learned that JFK and his mistress, blond divorcee Mary Pinchot, had been promoting a secret cell on the Potomac to brainwash D.C. leaders by use of LSD – the FBI's espionage investigation deeply involved the president, strange as that may sound.

Outside inner circles in Washington D.C. there was no common knowledge that President John F. Kennedy was a compulsive womanizer, reckless and indiscreet, code-named 'Lancer' by his Secret Service security details, who despite their friendship toward him privately expressed alarm that he would often risk his own security and their protective responsibility by canoodling with unvetted harlots from New York City who might be murdering him, for all they knew.

What made such a seemingly fine president such as Jack Kennedy tick? I was surprised and disappointed by what I learned. He allowed his weakness for women to interfere with what I see as the nearly monastic obligation of anyone lucky enough to be gifted four or eight years in the White House to leave his excess libido at the doorstep. It seems to me that after fifty years, we ought to have truth instead of hagiography. Kennedy partisans may shrink from certain observations in this book. If any are unfair, I apologize. I met Kennedy face-to-face at Teterboro Airport that spring when he was all smiles, vibrant and so very alive.

When Grandpa Jimmy O'Donnell heard that Jack Kennedy would be running for president he was quick to join the cause. "He's a good Irishman and goddamn it that's good enough for me," the 71-year-old Greenwich Village truckman said, smarting still from the Tammany label hung on NY Governor Al Smith in the 1928 presidential election together with the Rum, Romanism and Rebellion's anti-Catholic tag.

I am not Arthur Conan Doyle and do not pretend to possess forensic skills. My investigative analysis and conclusions are free of bias and are solely my own, a residue of wide reading, research and life experience.

The blitz of books, bios, blurbs and blogs (the four Bs, needing only bourbon and beer to make it an even half dozen) recalls an old quote I first read in one of those dull green pad-type texts written by Mark Heald, that kindly bald-pated professor of the extremely popular freshman Contemporary Civilization course at Rutgers University back in the mid-20th Century. The quote from Alexander Pope's 1709 "Essay on Criticism": "A little learning is a dangerous thing. Drink deep, or taste not the Pierian spring."

Even the muses of Greek mythology at Macedonia's Pierian spring would be challenged to make sense of the Kennedy assassination. We do find, however, that violence in the post-World War II years was endemic. Coups were common, assassinations and abdications just another form of statecraft.

"In Asia," Chinese Communist insurrectionist Mao Tse Tung had proclaimed, "political power proceeds from the barrel of a gun." And in the United States?

As the French colonial empire collapsed, French Foreign Legion types, livid at loss of Algerian vacation and estate properties to the south on the Mediterranean Sea, repeatedly targeted President Charles DeGaulle, most recently in 1962 in the

'Day of the Jackal' episode made into a popular movie. It showed the weakness of an approach that relied on a single "sniper on a tall building with a high-powered rifle." Lone snipers often took potshots at DeGaulle and always missed.

In Guatemala in 1954, the CIA coordinated a military coup, driving Communist agrarian reformer Jacob Arbenz into exile by use of a clever mix of propaganda and Army insurrection. Arbenz failed to read the poker bluff.

In the Caribbean, Raphael Trujillo had wielded dictatorial control for well over a generation in the Dominican Republic until May of 1961, when a rifle assault team assassinated him as he drove in a motorcade on a major boulevard of Santo Domingo on outskirts of the capital city. Authorized by JFK, the CIA engineered the hit, telephoning the president in Paris where his French-speaking wife was creating a sensation while the Kennedys met with DeGaulle en route to Austria for JFK's admittedly less than successful sit-down with Soviet Premier Nikita Khrushchev.

Within a year, reformist Orlando Bosch, after winning the presidential election, was deposed with an okay from the Kennedys and the CIA by a military junta that objected to Bosch's constitutional changes and reforms. Infuriated, Bosch exited to Florida where he provided a safe house and arms to the delegation from Miami that drove to Dallas for the assassination, according to former Castro girlfriend Marita Lorenz, who was active with the Operation 40 plot to kill Castro that finally killed Kennedy out of exasperation with White House yoyoing of its get-Castro campaign.

"The Kennedys were running a goddamn Mafia operation in the Caribbean but Castro got Kennedy before Kennedy got him," LBJ told his aide Jack Valenti in 1965. With everyone gun shy toward Castro over fear of another nuclear cliffhanger, Castro has been given a free pass by assassination researchers even though he had every reason to eliminate JFK. The Cuban dictator knew that Kennedy agents were trying to kill him. He had clued in an Associated Press correspondent at an embassy party in Havana in September 1963 that those who would assassinate another head of state "are not themselves safe." Castro and his brother Raul had an estimated 200 Cuban G-2 spies and double agents, trained by the Soviet KGB, floating around among the roiling Cuban exile communities in Miami, the American Sun Belt and even Union City, NJ in 1963. With Mafia insider Santo Trafficante of Tampa and its "Little Havana" enclave Ybor City – seat of his bolita numbers racket – double-dealing with Castro, and with double agents talking out of both sides of their mouths, vengeful mutineers and recidavistas were running wild. They infiltrated the Operation 40 gangs in Miami and No Name Key and the superpatriot minutemen who seemed to be coming out of the woodwork in Texas, Louisiana and everywhere in the Deep South.

A Cuban named John Martino, who had been imprisoned by Castro shortly after Cuban revolutionaries took over Havana on New Year's Day of 1959, was now free and had foreknowledge in November 1963 that the president was doomed.

Listening on the radio to a report on JFK's election tour, Martino suddenly blurted out to his wife, "... they're going to kill him when he gets to Texas," Martino's wife told author Anthony Summers shortly before her death as Summers first reported in his article in Vanity Fair in 1994. Martino's son Edward later verified for the author that his father knew and had helped one of the Cuban exiles from Miami, and that Martino had spent the afternoon of the assassination making a flurry of frantic phone calls to Cuban contacts from whom he wanted to disassociate for fear they might tie him in to the killing. The widow opened up after having denied before the House Select Committee on Assassinations in 1978 that her late husband knew anything about it. Martino's prior writings about his arrest and experiences in the Cuban prison and escape from death had mentioned that among those helpful to him was David "El Indio" Morales, a CIA agent undercover in Havana in 1959. Evidence would later identify Morales and fellow CIA renegade E. Howard Hunt as spearheads of the Miami end of "the Big Event", as Hunt code worded the assassination conspiracy. Martino died mysteriously after he confided to a business associate in Texas his foreknowledge of the assassination.

The Cuban misadventures were trumped by an even more sulphurous explosion in November 1963. In Saigon on Nov. 1, the lid blew off America's seven-year struggle to save Indochina from Ho Chi Minh's Communist armies from the north. Faced with a Buddhist uprising against United States ally Ngo Dinh Diem and his hierarchal Catholic regime, the White House authorized a CIA-orchestrated soft coup that backfired, resulting in the murder of President Diem and his brother, Ngo Dinh Nhu. Madame Nhu was on a speaking tour in the United States at the time, which she immediately converted into fiery denunciations of President Kennedy in weeks just prior to his assassination. Furthermore, the Pentagon chief of the CIA's Operation Mongoose, Florida's major industry funded at $50,000,000 a year, legendary CIA superspy Gen. Edward G. Lansdale, was so upset by the killing of protégés and close friends Diem and Nhu that he wound up his business late that night at his Pentagon desk and immediately filed his pension papers, as he revealed in the last words of his autobiography. No one has hard evidence what he did next during the three weeks leading to the business of assassination that he knew so well, but Sam Giancana said in his book Doublecross that some Pentagon colonel - Lansdale's true rank - was seen mixing with Chicago Sam and Outfit bigwigs during that time period. Furthermore, Colonel J. Fletcher Prouty, one of Lansdale's aides at the Pentagon and a technical adviser to Oliver Stone for the movie JFK, saw photos of unidentified people who were in Dealey Plaza on Nov. 22, 1963 and, although seen only from the rear and side near the famous 'three tramps', swears that one of them was Ed Lansdale.

Out of Chicago came the documented story of The Outfit's ace hit man, Chuck Nicoletti, a veteran of 21 murders, picked to retaliate for the doublecross of the mob by JFK and his father after the old man had twice dined in New York City with top Mafia godfathers, taken big bucks in contributions and cash and promised to curb headstrong Robert F. Kennedy, who would later as attorney general hound, eavesdrop on and prosecute top Cosa Nostra bosses.

The lynch mob from Dallas organized by oil tycoons, superpatriots, rednecks and racists saw replacement of JFK by LBJ as an unmixed blessing. Some old-time Texans still had one foot in the state's post-Civil War tradition of lawlessness, shoot-outs and frontier justice and saw no reason for serious apology for just another killing.

The Marseilles hiring of Corsican hit men was an outcropping of what CIA roughneck Louis "Black Luigi" Conein described as trained international hit men who would go anywhere in the world for the right price to dispassionately kill anyone, and never say a word about it even if tortured. It was unlike the Mafia that functioned within borders, he explained. French-speaking Conein was proud to be an honorary member of the Corsican Brotherhood. He was privy to Marseilles waterfront Corsican boss Antonin Guerini's recruiting of an international killer to hit "the biggest vegetable", a contract financed by Sun Belt Mafiosi Trafficante and New Orleans boss Carlo Marcello, indirectly by Teamster boss James R. Hoffa and, after the Saigon coup and murder of her husband, by wealthy Madame Nhu, the 'dragon lady' of Vietnam. She had relocated to Rome where William King 'Two Gun" Harvey, exiled by Bobby Kennedy, promoted assassination plans. Author Steve Rivelle identified the Corsican hit man as Lucien Sarti, 32 at time of the assassination, an international heroin dealer who was gunned down April 27, 1972 outside a Mexico City disco, while Sarti's wife and some beauties ran around screaming. He was killed by a squad of hit men organized by President Richard Nixon and headed by ex-CIA honcho Lou Conein of the aforementioned Corsican Brotherhood. While the hit promoted the president's 'war on drugs', it did not escape the notice of insiders that it also silenced forever an assassin of President Kennedy.

Legendary spy-thriller author Tom Clancy died at age 66 on Oct. 1, 2013 so we will never hear from the CIA's classic Mr. Insider his take on what the agency did to muzzle the JFK assassination story, and specifically, why? – outside its institutional obsession with secrecy for secrecy's sake. Clancy's masterful *Clear and Present Danger*, turned into a movie starring Harrison Ford, depicts a superbureaucratic CIA Director of Plans who, amid a carpeted office fight to save or destroy computer entries, sarcastically preaches to CIA colleague Jack Ryan:

"Gray, Jack. The world is gray."

This book seeks to add a blush of color to that grayness.

Les Plosia
November, 2013

PROLOGUE

APPOINTMENT IN SAMARRA

The conspiracy that ended the shaping Kennedy dynasty was not an oddball event, nor a Luciferian raid against righteousness. It was not a bush league plot so much as a major league orchestration by at least four separate and distinct conspiratorial networks to take down an imperial pretender who, like Caesar, had gone too far and whose obsession with change seemed overly skewed toward his own preferences.

The world is forever memorializing tragedy, celebrating infamy and doting fondly on murder and mayhem. Mention Tammerlane or Genghis Khan and the blood boils faster. We are transfixed by the madness of Caligula and Adolph Hitler. The slaughter at Gettysburg goes into our history books as a proud meridian in American history and we erect in our national mall a memorial statue to the president who caused it. JFK may have been remembered as little more than a footnote in history had his murder not made him a martyr. Details of his macabre death pall in comparison to the spaghetti bowl of solutions to the greatest whodunit of the Twentieth Century. Anyone who wants to know who killed Jack Kennedy oversimplifies because the culprit is plural, culpability plausibly deniable.

The world of 1963 was a perfect backdrop for violence. It festered in a post-military culture schooled in the methods and moods of global warfare. The attempted or successful assassination of a head of state was neither unpredictable nor rare. In France, DeGaulle had conceded to anti-Colonialism in Algeria, making him a chronic target of French legionnaire types in the O.A.S. In Cuba, romanticized revolutionary Fidel Castro had compromised liberation by going to bed with the Kremlin despite global hemispheric antipathy between America and the Sino-Soviet Communist bloc, making him number one on the homicide hit parade. Indochina was in turmoil, Indonesia on the verge of an internal blood bath. East and West Europe were split physically and ideologically, nuclear cannons pointed at one another.

In decades to come, and even in JFK's time, a number of successful leaders who were anything but dumb and who were not necessarily superstitious believed firmly in a version of fate as forecast by, no, not tea leaves or shaman, but the supposedly quack science of astrology. In Indochina, Ho Chi Minh, instead of living in a castle, occupied a modest cottage and would not leave it until he checked his horoscope. His bête noire, CIA hero Colonel Edward Geary Lansdale, a Detroit native, did the same and parlayed his insights into defeating the bloody Huk rebellions in the Philippines and fighting Minh to a standoff in Vietnam. Although both were highly successful leaders, neither could match President Ronald Reagan's counterintuitive and widely ridiculed genius in bringing to an end the forty-year-old Cold War in 1988. We didn't find out until later that his celebrated "hunches" originated at least partially from his wife's consultations with an astrologer. Was it all in the stars?

Destiny may be preordained, its fatalist philosophy captured neatly in a parable from The Middle East worth citing to illustrate the point that if JFK weren't killed in Dallas, he would certainly have been murdered in some other city in much the same way. American novelist John O'Hara expropriated the title, "Appointment in Samarra" and quoted from British novelist W. Somerset Maugham's 1933 retelling of this tale:

THE SPEAKER IS DEATH

There was a merchant in Baghdad who sent his servant to market to buy provisions and in a little while the servant came back, white and trembling, and said, Master, just now when I was in the marketplace I was jostled by a woman in the crowd and when I turned I saw it was Death that jostled me. She looked at me and made a threatening gesture. Now, lend me your horse, and I will ride away from this city and avoid my fate. I will go to Samarra and there Death will not find me. The merchant lent him his horse, and the servant mounted it, and he dug his spurs in its flanks and as fast as the horse could gallop he went. Then the merchant went down to the marketplace and he saw me standing in the crowd and he came to me and said, "Why did you make a threatening gesture to my servant when you saw him this morning?" I said, "It was only a start of surprise. I WAS ASTONISHED TO SEE HIM IN BAGHDAD, FOR I HAD AN APPOINTMENT WITH HIM TO-NIGHT IN SAMARRA."

There is another parable told on the banks of the Nile that fits the psychology of JFK's groups of assassins:

The scorpion asks the frog if he can ride on the frog's back across the Nile, only to be rebuffed because, as the frog put it, "you'll sting me on the way over." The scorpion scoffs, "Why would I do that? We'd both drown." Persuaded, the frog tells the scorpion to "hop on". Halfway across, the scorpion stings the frog. As they descend to their deaths, the frog complains: "Now we'll both die. Why did you sting me?" Says the scorpion, "It's just my nature."

DEBUNKING THE OSWALD MYTH

During my years of research into the mystery of JFK's assassins, I fairly early ruled out the Lee Harvey Oswald fabrication as a classic frame-up. I focused sequentially on CIA Counter-intelligence Chief James Jesus Angleton, CIA Director Richard Helms, ex-CIA Director Allen Dulles and Paramilitary Spymaster Edward Geary Lansdale. None of them "gave the order", as far as anyone has discovered, although it is far-fetched to suppose that the assassination came as a surprise to any of them. Dulles was already out of the direct loop, busy promoting his memoir The Craft of Intelligence, which after its release in 1963 would climb to the top in the *New York Times* non-fiction lists. As for Helms, his loyal replacement, and Angleton, they were less than hostile to JFK. Nonetheless, none of them was happy with the president's threat after the Bay of Pigs fiasco to "shatter the CIA into a thousand pieces", particularly since much of the misplanning for the Cuban invasion could be laid at JFK's feet. Simultaneously, all three CIA stalwarts resented the presidentially endorsed intrusion by Robert F. Kennedy into the sepulchral halls at Langley, RFK after all being merely the attorney general, and not boss of all bosses. All or any one of them had the means, motive and opportunity to orchestrate the assassination; each in his own right was influential, powerful, in control of vast secret fountains of funds to pull it off. The author had a distinct admiration for the World War II and Cold War achievements of all four of these Central Intelligence Agency professionals while concluding that all four were at least tacit, elite endorsers, if not necessarily sponsors, of the assassination preparations.

The storied spy chief General Lansdale was not originally an assassination planner. He joined and became a catalyst in the already-shaped master conspiracy precisely three weeks before Dallas. Sharp on detail and prone to trickery, the tall, mustachioed, 55-year-old ex-advertising man had an enviable talent for planning and executing complicated guerilla attacks on foreign soil during his legendary career. Amidst the fictionalized ineptitude at American embassies throughout southeast Asia skewered in *The Ugly American*, the adulatory chapter on Col. Hillandale based on Lansdale was a lesson plan in foreign policy. He preached kindness by our soldiers, played a uke, did astrology charts out in the boondocks and championed American know-how through such simple engineering as improving water supply and sanitation. Recruited as a psych warfare expert when the U.S. Air Force first split off from the U.S. Army in 1947, Lansdale, wearing a gleaming silver shoulder star of a general, recruited and tutored Gen. Ramon Magsaysay as first president of the Philippine Islands, joining him to put down the fierce Huk rebellion. Lansdale was acclaimed a national hero. Magsaysay, who tragically died in a small plane crash in 1948, was still hailed years later by Hope, a Filipino physical therapist at offices of Dr. Michael Cooney in Rutherford, N.J., as "the best president we ever had." She added that his death was truly an accident since the plane crashed into a mountain that was a prominent topographic feature of his home island, which was also hers.

Why did Gen. Lansdale join the assassination plot?

On Nov. 2, 1963, he received a shocking telephone call from Saigon while working late in his office in the Pentagon. An American orchestrated coup against American backed President Ngo Dinh Diem had just gone horribly wrong.

Army tank commanders had surrounded and bombarded the three-story white presidential palace a few blocks from busy Tu Do Square in Saigon, now known as Ho Chi Minh City, which in the early '60s was justifiably lyricized as the 'Paris of the Orient'. Lansdale learned by telephone that the rebel generals had induced Diem and his brother, Air Force General Nhu, to surrender under a guarantee of safe conduct. While under siege, President Diem also talked to Ambassador Henry Cabot Lodge, who assured Diem that he and his brother would be flown out of the country. The two leaders were shot overnight, their bodies found in an open trailer in which they had been handcuffed while being transported by the Army of Vietnam (ARVN) coup teams led by Gen. Van Minh, a Buddhist whose command had been paid $41,000 in authorized U.S. funds to pull off a peaceful coup to end the eight year old rule of the Catholic mandarin Dinh dynasty.

The two heads of state, like Magsaysay, were protégés and personal friends of Lansdale. On holidays during monsoon season he had often joined the hardworking bachelor Diem and Diem's brother Nhu, together with Nhu's wife, the fiery Madame Nhu, unofficial palace hostess and an assemblywoman, for cooling breezes on bluffs overlooking the South China Sea at the family's jewel-studded White House. Lansdale in 1954 on the recommendation of famous Cardinal Spellman of NYC had recruited Diem out of exile from a monastery in Lakewood, N.J. to return home to Indochina to run for president of South Vietnam. The new country had been carved out of southern and eastern Indochina by U.S. and French negotiations with Ho Chi Minh at the Paris Conference of 1954.

Lansdale turned pale when his old sidekick Louis "Black Luigi" Conein called from Saigon. Over at the White House, President John F. Kennedy also got word from Saigon. The president was chatting with U.S. Army Gen. Maxwell Taylor when the phone rang. He turned ashen and raced to the rest room to throw up. Assassination had been listed tenth and last on a National Security memo outlining the coup plan, to which the president had reluctantly and weakly agreed at one of the rambling so-called action meetings during which everyone had a say and nothing seemingly was settled. Did JFK want the imperious ruling family out? Only because the native Buddhists were in open rebellion. Did he want Diem executed? Absolutely not.

Earlier, Kennedy had called Lansdale into his office to assign him the job of engineering the coup d'état. Lansdale told him it was a bad idea. Against all protocol, the general flatly refused to take part.

When Madame Nhu on speaking tour in California heard that Diem and her husband had been executed, she went ballistic. The always outspoken "dragon lady", as the young and irreverent American war correspondent colony in Saigon had named her after the character in a popular comic strip *Terry & The Pirates*, filled the airways with blasts at Kennedy and promised he would "rue the day". The toxic atmosphere of those early weeks of November has gone virtually ignored in reprises on the Kennedy assassination, yet at the time the Vietnam mess was the dominant international hard news story. Except for daily updates by news wire services, veteran war columnists and the New York Times, the chaos in southeast Asia was quickly swept under the rug as the American public was fed pap and poltroonery out of Washington about "the excitement" of JFK being accompanied by his wife on his opening reelection campaign swing through the southeastern United States.

There is no known record of what Madame Nhu said privately to old friend Ed Lansdale and sidekick Conein but it is certain the phone calls challenged the manhood, morals and maternity of the two hell-for-leather CIA big guns. What made it worse was the fact that Conein, as CIA station chief in a Saigon embassy absurdly headed by defeated Nixon running-mate Ambassador Henry Cabot Lodge, had followed orders from Washington to bribe three rebel coup generals for $41,000 in CIA funds to scramble American foreign policy in southeast Asia, which then went from bad to worse. Lodge was wrong for the post not only because he was not a true JFK loyalist, but because he despised the South Vietnam president as a "typical mandarin authoritarian", which many whether rightly or wrongly saw as the pot calling the kettle black.

As time would tell, a succession of Buddhist generals proved incapable of ruling the restless nation or quelling insurrection, forcing the United States into the Hobson's choice of "cutting and running", as the hawks liked to describe withdrawal, or getting sucked incrementally into the long, dragged-out, demoralizing Vietnam War that most chroniclers have in hindsight agreed was a waste of time and money, while leaving 53,000 American draftees and professional soldiers dead and many more wounded and disabled.

At the time, Conein had been patsied and was out for blood. From Miami came predictable curses about "another double-cross" from angry Cuba Libres still incensed about the Bay of Pigs calamity. Miami CIA honchos El Indio Morales, Eduardo Hunt, Station Chief Ted Shackley and Two-Gun Bill Harvey pulled out their "treason" bullhorns.

The bad blood between Attorney General Robert F. Kennedy and Harvey cannot be exaggerated. They flat-out hated one another. Supposedly exiled early in the year to Rome by RFK, Harvey was still seen periodically in Miami. Teamed with Lansdale who was handling things at the Pentagon, Harvey ran what amounted to a 'private army', paid for by the U.S. government. It was in the process of girding for beefed up attacks on Cuba, hostility to the Cuban Castro regime being its indispensable raison d'être. The anti-Castro guerilla army did not disband when the Kennedys' "hands off Cuba" deal with the Kremlin changed everything. Still in play was Florida's "biggest industry", the massive Operation Mongoose $50,000,000-a-year militia of 200 CIA agents and 2,000 paramilitaries run from a virtually abandoned storage hut in a remote section of the University of Miami campus.

Harvey never called RFK boss; he always referred to him as "that little mother f—ker". Bob Kennedy was unsparing in describing Harvey. He called Harvey an "alcoholic psycho."

Cecil B. DeMille of Paramount Studios famously billed his Hollywood epics as having a "cast of thousands."

He could have been talking about the JFK assassination epic. You needed a program to tell the players. The complexity might partially account for widespread capitulation to the Oswald 'Lone Assassin' cop-out. The always handy 'crazy mixed-up guy with gun' is a vaudeville stock character who did not go out with high-button shoes. He is found in all cases, it seems, particularly when discussing political assassination attempts. It may no longer have legs but it does have the virtue of simplicity.

It may be that *Vanity Fair* has given up on solving the case. The magazine in a slick piece in its November 2013 issue printed a wrap-up by writer James Wolcott titled '*Attack of the JFK Books*' in anticipation of a Niagara of 50th anniversary retrospectives on the Jack Kennedy slaying. Wolcott wobbled on the old Oswald crutch, a story unfortunately fouled by the original tripe of placing blame on the little guy who we all know by now was walking on the beach when the tsunami hit. The magazine can credibly claim it presents "both sides", but doesn't that balancing act undeservedly give the lie stature equal to the truth? For all of *Vanity Fair's* élan, its repetition of the Oswald canard is blaming the wallflower for being too noisy at the dance. The tank job by media giants is an unspoken national scandal that might have slipped by unnoticed if it did not trivialize valiant research by so many dragonslayers, if it did not ignore clear and bold disclosures in latter year memoirs, if it did not dissimulate in the face of mea culpas and deathbed confessions. *Someone Would Have Talked* writers Debbie Conway and Larry Hancock nicely raised a point nearly a decade ago, and indeed someone did talk, as did someone else, and someone else, ad serium. Were the powers in the towers listening?

Cable media star Bill O'Reilly was among television personalities to take the easy and golden path toward the JFK anniversary. He put his brand on a pricey coffee table book full of classy photographs of President Kennedy, his wife Jacqueline and the children from the Kennedy albums. It was coordinated production-wise with a book Killing Kennedy, a potboiler less concerned with historical value and accurate journalism than with its sale to be presented as another hackneyed Sunday night TV docudrama notable more for archival footage and photoflashes of Lee Oswald than for serious history. Outside his cable TV sphere, O'Reilly is a capable journalist who figures to make a ton of money from the Kennedy reprise, and God bless him for that. But please do not say that O'Reilly is in the "No Spin Zone", as he bills himself, or that he is "looking out for us". Heaven forbid. Not when spinning the Kennedy assassination.

Just for the record and with a cap doffed to legions of researchers, Dallas Police Chief Jesse Curry has stated forthrightly that the department could not connect Lee Harvey Oswald to the so-called sixth floor 'sniper's nest' in the Texas School Depository building or to the rifle fire that killed the president. Oswald was given a paraffin test that showed no sign on his hands that he had recently fired a firearm. He was quizzed at length by Chief of Detectives Will Fritz who never charged Oswald with homicide in the killing of Kennedy, one reason being that Oswald did not kill him. Despite his puzzled remark to a reporter that, "I have not been charged with killing the president", the suspect gathered that he was the designated "patsy," his word to describe his immediate plight. Oswald was eating a sandwich and drinking a Coke on the second floor of his workplace when Kennedy was ambushed outside the building, as at least two witnesses verified. As a floater manipulated by a cutout controller, "I Led Three Lives" Oswald knew something was up and had met to test rifles earlier in the week with gunman James Files from Chicago, but as his note to oil baron H.L. Hunt said, he needed to have his position clarified.

Oswald was not framed by top brass in the Dallas Police Department, as many erroneously assume to this day. Oswald was not supposed to be caught. He was framed as a convenient scapegoat by in-place conspirators after he "f—ked up", as airhop operator David Ferrie put it. He was silenced while in custody two days later by assassination insider Jack 'Sparky' Ruby, the Chicago Outfit's nightclub mob man in Dallas. Oswald had to die because as a dual infiltrator he had squirreled away enough information to put them all in hot water as he unfolded elements of the conspiracies. Suspect Oswald was confirmed as scapegoat on word from higher-ups in Washington who were only too happy to wash away a multitude of sins by focusing hatred on an apparently addled Marxist who could outshoot Wyatt Earp or Calamity Jane. For varied reasons and with shifting and shaded motives, the higher ups included the president's brother Attorney General Robert F. Kennedy, RFK's top aide Nicholas Katzenbach, Vice President Lyndon Johnson, FBI Director J. Edgar Hoover, Hoover's Counterintel Chief William Sullivan, CIA Director Richard Helms and the whole range of top CIA brass. Obviously their viewpoints ran a gamut from A to Z, but there was consensus that it should all be blamed on Oswald, in some cases because it would divert attention from their own complicity. They were more than capable of pinning the rap on Oswald, which they did with a flourish, feeding the press a fiction the public could easily understand. Thus, Oswald was convicted in the court of public opinion, but he was never convicted of or even formally charged with killing the president.

As a matter of history and good conscience, we should all make a 50th anniversary pledge to stop lying about and blaming

Lee Harvey Oswald for everything when facts fly in our face that gangs of killers swarmed into Dallas to do the deed.

At the Pentagon, General Lansdale no longer wanted to be JFK's fair-haired boy or, as the president called him, "America's James Bond".

Lansdale's autobiography years later had a strange, pointed ending.

After taking the long-distance secure phone call at his Pentagon desk from Saigon, he wrote, he wrapped up his work. He then and there filled out and filed his resignation papers. There, quite abruptly, the book ended. Where did he go and what did he do during the next three weeks?

A mysterious colonel was seen mixing with mobsters in Chicago, wrote Sam and Chuck Giancana in their book Crossfire, based on stories they were told by Sam 'Moony' Giancana, a top gun in 'The Outfit', a multi-ethnic Mafia-led syndicate that stretched from Chicago to Las Vegas to Los Angeles to Tampa to New Orleans to Kansas City to Dallas. Their source Sam Giancana was not head of the Chicago mob but he was the biggest gambling layoff bookie in the world, the best known and the most influential. The balding widower, then in his fifties and no Don Juan for looks, kept steady company with pretty young blonde Phyllis McGuire, lead singer for the very popular McGuire sisters. She seemed to really like him, not less so because of his ownership of two foreign gambling casinos, the take from which he refused to split with gumbas in Chicago, much to their annoyance. The mobster mix with whom Giancana saw the colonel — Lansdale was actually a colonel, his general's star a stage prop — included Chuck Nicoletti, the mob's top killer, who had the JFK contract, and John Roselli, who ran the mob's action in Las Vegas and Hollywood and who was teamed with the CIA's Bill Harvey in Miami in plots to kill Fidel Castro, the dictator of Cuba.

According to the Giancanas in Crossfire, the mysterious colonel was checking out some rifles and didn't stay long.

A tall stooped man in civvies photographed in Dealey Plaza on the day of the killing was Ed Lansdale, according to Col. E.

Fletcher Prouty, who had worked in Special Ops at the Pentagon as a liaison man for Lansdale. Lansdale was photographed from a rear side angle passing the famous three tramps next to a freight train boxcar and again from the rear. Prouty said he knew that slouch and swore it was Lansdale, out coordinating things.

Prouty was hired as a technical advisor by Oliver Stone for the movie JFK that portrayed Lansdale as a mysterious Pentagon general who wore a black eye patch, which apparently was a cinematic device since Lansdale had no eye patch.

Prouty was not too fond of Lansdale, who returned the favor. Lansdale outranked Prouty and to get him out from underfoot sent him in November on what Prouty described as a wild goose chase to Antarctica just to get rid of him. Prouty was in Christchurch, New Zealand when he learned that Kennedy had been shot.

Lansdale, Madame Nhu and Conein were part of the powerful Saigon clique that in the final weeks pumped up the flames that would engulf the president. They were joined by Kennedy-hating Harvey, who from his new posting in Rome found it convenient along with Madame Nhu to make sure the Corsican killers in Marseilles did not forget their mission. Madame Nhu pumped millions into the assassination kitty, according to six-five soldier-of-fortune Gerald Pat Hemming. The ex-Marine had known Lee Oswald at El Toro Marine Corps Base in California and at the CIA U-2 station in Atsuggi, Japan and rode from Miami to Dallas transporting rifles, ammo and scopes. So said two witnesses who rode in the two-car convoy.

By the time the Saigon backlash came into play, sniper nests were being scouted out by the mob in Chicago, the Corsican Brotherhood from Marseilles, the renegade Operation 40 Cuban guerilla gang from Miami and a Texas lynch mob of oligarchic oil barons and vengeful cowboys. Deathbed and third-party disclosures in books and memoirs demonstrated that the hunt for a single assassin was self-defeating because at least four separate and essentially unrelated plots were involved. Members knew there was a roundup going on, but they did not necessarily know the other assassins who were lying in wait. If one ambush were foiled, the perps could not finger any other assailants because they honestly had no idea who they were.

The plot fit a Sherlock Holmes script.

"There were so many assassination plots," retired CIA spymaster E. Howard Hunt admitted in the early 21st century, in a mea culpa shortly before he died.

In 1976, 13 years after Dallas, former *Washington Post* top executive editor James Truitt in an interview with the National Inquirer, followed by Associated Press and Washington Post interviews, broke the astonishing story of JFK's 18-month affair in the White House itself with a blonde divorcee from the Georgetown section of Washington D.C. We tracked her JFK blessed efforts to brainwash top government officials by use of LSD. For the first time, the Truitt exposé cast probable blame on JFK himself as a cause of his own killing, due to his wildly improper indiscretions in high office at a critical time in world history. The president's paramour was amateur artist Mary Pinchot, 43, the ex-wife of CIA Spymaster Cord Meyer, with whom she remained friendly since they were raising two sons together. Press notices made no mention that the slain woman's ex husband was a Mr. Big in the CIA. The cover-up merely described him as a "business executive".

Mary Pinchot Meyer was shot four times while exercise-walking along a backwater canal towpath in the Georgetown section in broad daylight Oct. 13, 1964, just a week or two after release of the Warren Commission Report which friends said she saw as a fraud. Newspapers said she'd been a friend of Jackie Kennedy, which was a stretch, but the press notices did not mention her long-term liaison at the White House with President Jack Kennedy. At the time, Washington Post senior editor Ben Bradlee was married to Mary Meyer's sister, Antoinette (Toni) Bradlee, 36. The trio had attended socials together at the White House, Bradlee was tight with Jack Kennedy, and the Post newsman was not such an ostrich hiding his head in the sand that he knew nothing about his sister-in-law's 33 trysts at the White House with his pal, the president.

Bradlee would in the 1970s win fame for helping to expose the White House cover-up leading to President Richard Nixon's resignation in 1974. It was what Truitt saw as Bradlee's hypocrisy vis a vis Nixon and Kennedy that prompted Truitt to spill the beans about the previously unreported affair between Jack Kennedy and Mary Pinchot Meyer. Truitt and his wife had been fast friends with Mary Meyer and Truitt revealed that he personally had supplied pot and other drugs to Mary for each of her trysts at the White House. A stray black vagabond was arrested for Mary's murder and acquitted at trial.

Two books authenticated that the FBI was investigating the LSD brainwashing conspiracy and other JFK sexpionage cases shortly before his death, although the FBI for whatever reason has never released or accounted for those known field investigations, which by force of law are in the public domain.

The books were Dr. Timothy Leary's *Flashbacks* published in 1983 and Nina Burleigh's 1999 *A Very Private Woman: The Unsolved Murder of Presidential Mistress Mary Meyer*. Leary's book is hard to find, yet without it the full explosive significance of Mary Meyer's long-running affair with President Kennedy is impossible to grasp since Dr. Leary, in diary form, unhurriedly documented the way this strange lady from Washington's inner circles contacted him to learn how to use LSD to brainwash people. She intended to work with wives of influential government officials in the Georgetown section of Washington D.C. to reprogram their respective husbands, and by that initiative foster world peace. The beauty of Leary's information was that it was in no way distended or overblown since he not only did not know that Mary's lover was the president of the United States, he obviously regarded the entire adventure with Mary as something of a personal fling subordinate to his own compelling life story.

While Mary's unorthodox mission might sound positive to some people, neither the CIA nor the FBI could or would tolerate her impudent heresies. As Mary had warned, the CIA would and did crack down once its precious obsession with secrecy was breached.

Leary said the CIA arranged for his imprisonment and drove him into exile in Iran and Tibet after his daring escape from a federal prison in California. Even more sensational was the stalking of Mary Meyer by the FBI during the fall into November of 1963 as she made a final desperate visit to Dr. Leary at Millbrook, N.Y. to reveal that a female member of her Utopiate brainwashing cell on the Potomac had "snitched" and that government investigators were closing in on her. Until that point she had never identified for Leary who the big official was with whom she was having an affair. Leary did not find out until he read about Jim Truitt's exposé of JFK and Mary Meyer in a San Francisco newspaper in 1976.

Introduced to Judy Campbell Exner in Las Vegas by crooner Frank Sinatra, a ladies' man and courier for mobsters, early in 1960, Jack Kennedy was then running for the job of president. He would not become president until a year later. In the meantime, FBI agents learned of her role as a courier between Giancana and Jack Kennedy, carrying cash back and forth, as time would tell. Within two months of his inauguration, JFK was contacted by Hoover who warned the new president of Miss Exner's dangerous liaisons, which did not come as any great surprise to Kennedy. Although Exner had fallen for JFK, by then she felt he was just using her. Kennedy had tired of the romance, so Hoover's warning gave JFK a perfect alibi to break it off, which he had wanted to do anyhow. Those who describe the Hoover warning as "blackmail" put a sinister twist on an everyday courtesy between a new president and his top security officer. Should Hoover have withheld the information and watched as the press got hold of the story and sensationalized it into a national scandal? He could then have been accused of fiddling while Rome burned. It was no secret that J Edgar might lean on a mark a bit to keep him in line by hinting of secret knowledge, implying possible exposure.

Hoover's habit of collecting news items was common for politicians, journalists and police and intelligence agencies at a time when there was no internet, no electronic retrieval, very little microfilming. Very few had the wherewithal to photostat or fax. It was an age of mechanical typewriters, ink-smudged carbon copies, primitive office reproducing machines, giant printing presses. Correspondents filed stories at storefront telex offices, AT&T registered and separately charged for all long distance calls, detailing toll calls on Baby Bell bills sent monthly to customers. If clipping newspaper items went with the job, it was less for purposes of blackmail than for everyday factual background and accuracy, undeserving of the opprobrium heaped on the FBI director by critics who did not like Hoover in the first place. In those days, everyone was clipping and filing newspaper pieces.

In fact, Hoover's seeming fanaticism was an outgrowth of old-fashioned Puritanical ways that were anything but uncommon in people of his generation, who had been born in the horse-and-buggy era of the 1890s. The world of the early 20th century was full of autocrats.

A top British counterintelligence professional from England described a meeting with Hoover at the Justice Department in Washington D.C. in the late 1950s as less of a meeting than "an ordeal". He said Hoover interrupted everyone and allocated talking time as if he were a cop directing traffic. Hoover abruptly cut off anyone who spoke too long.

"Do you get my meaning?" he said piercingly in the ear of the British spycatcher, as if he were the imperious Marine colonel talking down to people as played by actor Jack Nicholson in the movie "A Few Good Men."

Hoover referred to British traitors Burgess and McLean in an acid tone of voice while addressing the visiting Brit.

"That couldn't happen here, " he snarled.

The Justice Department visitor was Peter Wright, assistant director of MI5 of British Intelligence, who in his unauthorized autobiography in 1987 titled Spycatcher wrote of his meeting with Hoover, "But everyone knew Hoover suffered from God disease."

I found that Lyndon Baines Johnson and Hoover knew in advance that Kennedy would be assassinated the next day in Dallas. They did not interfere, and would become part of the coverup. Two multi-millionaire Texas oilmen would be identified as ringleaders of the Texas wing of the assassination.

The clearest exposition of its part in The Big Event, as E. Howard Hunt said the multiple ambush was known, came from a participant assigned to the job by The Outfit, the Mafia operation in Chicago. It was laid out many years later by one of the Dealey Plaza riflemen, James (Sutton) Files of Alabama, an ex-Special Forces guerilla who had switched from his career as a racing car driver to a job as chauffeur for ace Chicago mob hitman Chuck Nicoletti. Both fired shots that hit the president in Dealey Plaza. Nicoletti, who had 21 mob murders under his belt, was in his mid-fifties. Files was a 22-year-old Special Ops veteran of guerilla warfare in Laos who admired his soft-spoken boss Nicoletti and said he would do anything the killer asked. Hollywood John Roselli was supposed to take part but, like David 'El Indio' Morales, was told at the late stages to stand aside and let others do the actual shooting. Both Morales and Roselli were photographed looking on intently in the crowd on the building steps outside the Texas school depository building in Dealey Plaza, Morales wearing dark sunglasses. Files implied that the stand-down order came from Maurice Bishop, the nom de guerre of CIA case officer David Atlee Phillips, who was trying to divest the CIA of traceable direct involvement. Phillips became head of an association of retired intelligence officers in Washington D.C. later in life. In his celebrated hunt 15 years later for the elusive agent in Dallas known as Maurice Bishop, HSCA staffer Gaetano Fonzi once took Cuban exile leader Tony Vecciano to a face-to-face confrontation with Phillips, but Vecciano backed off, saying he couldn't be sure that Phillips was the man known as Bishop who was seen meeting the day before the assassination with Lee Oswald and Vecciano in the lobby floor of oil baron H.L. Hunt's Mercantile Exchange headquarters in Dallas,

CIA Agent Frank Terpil who had teamed with legendary CIA Agent Edwin P. Wilson in rogue oil well capers in Libya before Khadafy took over had no such uncertainty. He said it was no secret along Miami's waterfront that fellow CIA Officer David Atlee Phillips used the alias Maurice Bishop all the time.

The fourth hit team came out of the safe house in Miami of Dominican expatriate leader Orlando Bosch which was run by Frank Sturgis, a Cuban ex-cop, and a crew of Cuban Castro-haters, all directed by renegade CIA Black Ops expert David "El Indio" Morales and CIA paymaster E. Howard "Eduardo" Hunt.

Morales hated the Kennedys and never mentioned the president without calling him a traitor.

El Indio was rated the CIA's top Black Ops man in the southern hemisphere and had personally directed the trap in Colombia which led routinely to execution of Che Guevera by Morales' colleague, CIA paramilitary Felix Rodriguez. Rodriguez would win awards for valor and become known for his enduring friendship with George H.W. Bush. Rodriguez was apologetic to Che about having to shoot him. Some people think the elder Bush played some sort of sinister role in the JFK assassination because he was linked in some contractual form to the original Bay of Pigs initiative, and because he later was appointed CIA director by President Gerald Ford. His CIA connections certainly helped him become Reagan's vice president and didn't hurt when he received the nomination in 1988 to succeed Reagan as president. My research shows that he did have links to the CIA since his early Texas days, but seemingly in an above board way. Much is made of a photograph that probably was Bush in Dealey Plaza the day after the assassination and FBI Director Hoover's memo saying he briefed George Bush the next day, but even if true, as I found probable, neither proof implicated Bush directly to the whirlwind assassination preparations.

The Operation 40 crew was the original Bay of Pigs progenitor formed under then Vice President Richard Nixon early in 1960 by 40 anti-Castroites, its control relinquished to JFK early in 1961. Its role in the Dallas shootings was confirmed by Hunt, Morales, Sturgis and by Marita Lorenz, the 19-year old blonde daughter of a German cruise ship captain who had been seduced by Generalissimo Fidel Castro after he came aboard in Havana harbor flush with victory in January, 1959. She turned sour on Castro following an abortion she said was unwanted and which Castroites said she wanted. She took up with Havana cop Frank Fiorini, later to legally change his name to Frank Sturgis, and both fled to the United States where they fell in with forces in Miami devoting their lives to deposing Castro. Sturgis, who once owned and ran a bar in Navy country around Norfolk, VA, swore before a congressional committee that he was never a CIA agent.

Whether true or not, he was, based on hard information, a CIA payroller for most of his mature life, a major conspirator in the JFK assassination who took part in the Dealey Plaza "Big Event" and a secret Black Ops hit man.

I found that M.S. Lorenz revealed substantive elements of the Miami assassination operation to the FBI in New York in November, 1963, to the Warren Commission in 1964, to N.Y. News reporter Paul Meskill in a 1977 interview, to lawyer Mark Lane in a deposition for the Liberty Lobby libel trial vis a vis Hunt in 1985 and to the House Select Committee on Assassinations (HSCA) in 1977. Government interviewers branded her testimony unreliable, wrongly so. It was the inexperienced, lawyerly Committee probers who were unreliable for mistaking self-survival inconsistency from Lorenz as falsity.

Prior to his death in 2004, Hunt purged himself of all his lies and admitted in a virtual deathbed confession that Lorenz had been telling the truth. Hunt's video tube released by his son admitted that the senior Hunt and Frank Sturgis had taken part in the Dallas assassination as "bench warmers".

It confirmed a boast by Sturgis to her in 1964 when, she recalled repeatedly, he said, "You should have been there. We made history that day. That was the day we killed the president."

Sturgis stopped by a short time later to remind her to say nothing or she might wind up dead, she said. Sturgis was never pinned down for taking part in the assassination. He did take a hit, though, when he was arrested for burglarizing the Democratic National Committee headquarters in the Watergate Hotel in Washington D.C. in 1972 following which he was characterized as a member of the "White House plumbers" for whom E. Howard 'Eduardo' Hunt was imprisoned as the gang's paymaster.

The Watergate imprisonment of Sturgis temporarily sidetracked what shaped up as a booming new career as a professional government killer. President Richard Nixon, before his exit, had launched a war on drugs spearheaded by ex-CIA pro Louis 'Black Luigi' Conein, an honorary member of the Corsican Brotherhood. The crew set up headquarters in a special apartment in the nation's capital. The job was to roam the globe killing heroin dealers and drug smugglers.

One of the first people eliminated was Lucien Sarti, 42, Corsican, French Connection heroin dealer, who was a 32-year-old Marseilles international killer-for-hire on the day John F Kennedy was shot. Two fellow drug dealers held in prison would later say he was one of the riflemen in Dealey Plaza, possibly 'badge man' dimly photographed in a Polaroid shot by Dealey Plaza onlooker Mary Moorman. E. Howard Hunt would also mention the Corsican in his confession. Sarti died April 27, 1972 outside a disco in Mexico City in a hail of bullets during a shootout with Mexican police as his wife and several party girls ducked and screamed.

It was one of the early deaths adding to Texas author Jim Marrs' superb collection, which during the 1960s and 1970s would sweep like a giant vacuum cleaner to by murder, accident, prematurity or statistical improbability remove from the American scene anyone and everyone who might emerge as a direct witness to the events surrounding Kennedy's 1963 assassination.

JFK AND HIS LSD GAL PAL

Former President John F. Kennedy's plot with his mistress to brainwash fellow national leaders by use of LSD gave federal counterintelligence agencies no choice except to let him die.

"There were so many assassination plots..." CIA master spy E. Howard Hunt revealed in a deathbed confession while admitting that he helped organize the mutiny led by renegade CIA Latin American assassination expert David "El Indio" Morales. "Thank God one of them worked."

Morales was among hit men from Chicago, a Texas oil cartel, the Florida Keys and south France who swarmed into Dallas on November 22, 1963 for the "Big Event" allegedly funded by a $2,000,000 kitty raised by Texas oil barons and a cowboy posse – part of $10 million spread around to at least four separate teams of killers.

The massive pushback came from key targets of Attorney General Robert F. Kennedy's wars against the Mafia, Teamster boss James R. Hoffa, top-level CIA agents, FBI Director J. Edgar Hoover, the southern white power structure, oil barons, big steel, Madame Nhu of Vietnam and anti-Castro Cubans in the Sun Belt. They vied with one another to gain revenge for what they saw as doublecrosses and to by any means prevent a dynasty that aimed to put Bobby Kennedy in the White House after John F. Kennedy died or left office. The looming and not unexpected assassination ambush might have been headed off had such gatekeepers as Hoover, Pentagon overlords, CIA counterintel chief James Jesus Angleton and Vice President Lyndon Johnson not lost confidence in compulsive womanizer JFK's dangerous liaisons verging on espionage.

After a British ring of hookers had brought down the government of England and after British superspy Kim Philby in July had defected to the Soviet Union, the nation's hierarchy drew the line after John F. Kennedy recklessly arranged an assignation with an East European cocktail waitress who was linked to the Stasi and the call girl ring that had just ruined British War Minister John Profumo.

With that indigestible hot potato still in the pressure cooker, the lid blew off when criminal information and an inside witness were brought to the FBI's Division Five proving that JFK together with his mistress Mary Pinchot Meyer were engaged in a secret plot to "brainwash" high level government policymakers by use of LSD with a view to changing American foreign policy. The cell led by JFK's peacenik girlfriend and wives of officials had grown to at least 16 utopiateurs before one of the last recruited wives blew the whistle. JFK regularly used drugs during his trysts with the Meyer divorcee and had shared the hallucinogen LSD with her, authorities were reliably informed. White House logs pinpointed 15 of the chronicled 33 trysts between JFK and Mary Meyer, always when the president's wife was out of town.

By the time of JFK's assassination, Mary Meyer had become much more than his mistress. She was running a brainwashing drug mill and wielding pillow talk foreign policy. Her espionage had cornered her as FBI agents closed in.

TOYING WITH DRUGS

John F. Kennedy's yo-yoing in foreign affairs broke his presidency as surely as night follows day, but it was his jackrabbit sex life that undid him in the end.

Had it been sex peccadilloes alone JFK might have lived out his natural days. It was more – much more. Word had seeped out to the keepers of the kingdom that JFK and his paramour were toying with drugs. Even more dangerously, his lover was engaged in a mission to brainwash a clique of highly placed Washington officials by use of the dangerous hallucinogen LSD, including, with his assent, JFK himself. In the milieu of 1963, the first step in such a conspiracy would constitute espionage – if not treason.

The girl friend was Mary Pinchot Meyer, a Georgetown divorcee, aspiring artist, mother of three and ex-wife of Cord Meyer, a top-level CIA spymaster. Cord Meyer disliked Kennedy and Kennedy disliked Meyer. The ex-Marine disapproved of his ex-wife's affair with JFK and told her she was making a fool of herself, since the President was carrying on with all kinds of women – one of whom Cord Meyer himself happened to be dating.

Mary Meyer was a regular at White House socials. Both JFK and Mary came from money and elite private schools, he from Harvard and she from Vassar. Though both had dabbled in journalism, neither had ever been forced to earn a living. Gifted a ten million dollar trust fund, JFK had little grasp of economic need. He had never been broke. He was so clueless how the other half lived that during one of his campaigns he had naively inquired of an aide where people got their money.

Mary Meyer and JFK had a lot in common. They were by age and class compatible. They got along famously. She hung around the White House and was well known to staffers and Secret Service agents, some of whom were aware that when Jacqueline Kennedy, the president's wife, was away at Cape Cod or their Virginia retreat, JFK would dispatch a limo to fetch Mary to the White House for dinner and usually an overnight stay.

Journalists Seymour Hersh and Richard Reeves reviewed White House logs and revealed JFK's serious medical problems and dependence on "Dr. Feelgood's" speedball shots – Hersh in 1977 in *The Dark Side of Camelot*, and Reeves in 1993 in his fine biography *Kennedy: Portrait of Power* – well before startling disclosures and confessions relegated The Warren Commission Report to its intended purpose as a foil of history.

The Warren Commission facts were framed to fit preconceived theory, as JFK's successor Lyndon Baines Johnson and JFK loyalists Ken O'Donnell and David Powers later privately admitted. All three had fudged testimony before the Warren Commission. LBJ said he had lied to avoid a war with Cuba. O'Donnell and Powers told former House Speaker Tip O'Neill they lied because the Kennedy family wanted closure.

O'Neill revealed that during his chat with O'Donnell and Powers in a Boston steak house the two members of JFK's Irish Mafia had told him there were more shots than described by the Warren Commission and that they had never bought the story that Lee Harvey Oswald was a lone assassin. The conversation is related in O'Neill's autobiography, Man of the House. LBJ said it was more like an ambush. All three had been riding in the motorcade directly behind JFK's open Lincoln convertible when it was caught in a hail of bullets on Elm off Houston Street, Dallas, Texas in the early afternoon on a sunny Friday, Nov. 22, 1963.

THE ASSASSINATION and THE WARREN COMMISSION

THE ZAPRUDER FILM

Long before use of replay cameras in sports spotlighted the fallibility of sports refs and umpires, the Zapruder film exposed the biggest blown call of all time. The belatedly circulated "home movie" clearly showed a killer shot from the right front of the presidential limousine, a grassy knoll where uniformed Army G.I. Gordon Arnold stood watching. Fresh out of basic training with all of its rifle range richocheting, he would later swear that the fatal bullet whizzed right past his ear. Mary Moorman snapped a photo showing riflemen behind the wood picket fence on the knoll. Up in a 14-foot tower, railroad guard Lee Bowers had a clear view. He told investigators he saw two men milling around behind the wood picket fence atop the knoll and watched as they threw something in their car trunk before racing off. A reporter for the Dallas Morning News, Mary Woodruff, wrote an overnight story describing witness accounts of shooting from behind the fence on the knoll. The hot story went unprinted, edited out by a deskman caught up in the bigger news that "they've already caught the guy."

The guy they caught, Lee Harvey Oswald, was a self-described "patsy", who within two days would be rubbed out gangland style while in Dallas police custody. FBI field offices would almost instantly get word from bosses J. Edgar Hoover and FBI Counter-Intel chief William Sullivan to drop their investigations since the culprit had already been nailed. In what could never be described as the FBI's finest hour, accounts would later emerge about witness statements being twisted or flatly falsified by interviewing or deposing federal agents. There would be no way that the Special Agents In Charge (SAC) or FBI field agents would in concert want to defeat the ends of justice, but orders from the top were another thing, it being widely understood that there was no future in bucking Hoover. Besides, Sullivan ran the counterintelligence side and Oswald's past floating around in Minsk, USSR and apparent renunciation of American citizenship at some point smacked of national security interests too ticklish to tackle.

At epicenters of the drama, FBI field offices in Dallas, New Orleans, Miami, Chicago and New York City dropped the case like so many hot potatoes. As a result, there has never been a true federal investigation into the assassination of John F. Kennedy, whose brother Robert Kennedy was attorney general of the U.S. at the time of the murder. Beyond dispute, RFK wanted "closure" and so stated to Asst. Attorney General Nicholas Katzenbach, for the sake of the family. Katzenbach on behalf of the late president's brother promptly told Hoover and wrote a memo to new President Lyndon Johnson saying it would be best all around if there were general agreement that Oswald had acted alone.

"My God, I've killed my brother," said Attorney General Robert F. Kennedy after he was informed by J. Edgar Hoover of the murder. Blaming himself for his revered older brother's assassination – while as time would tell was an accurate assessment – remains a puzzle because Bob Kennedy never said exactly what he had in mind.

WARREN COMMISSION

In 1964, a shrewd ex-teacher from modest origins in Texas named Lyndon Baines Johnson was running for president of the United

States. His predecessor JFK's death a year earlier had given him an easy path. He wanted everything just right so he could crush his likely foe, conservative Sen. Barry Goldwater, R-Arizona, a mall owner and Air Force Reserves general.

There was a form of historical precedent in the tale of fake villages built by Russian minister Grigory Potemkin to impress Catherine the Great on her tour of the Crimea and Ukraine. The military leader wanted to hide the squalor and shabbiness that actually existed, and by most accounts it worked as designed. A Potemkin village is a deception, an elaborate charade.

After JFK's assassination and Johnson's ascension to the presidency, Johnson moved swiftly to mop up lingering murder conspiracy rumors. Using every skill learned in his quarter century in Congress from longtime House Speaker Sam Rayburn, LBJ went on a charm offensive.

Johnson would resort to the old Potomac two-step, a dance he knew well. Give the nation a choir of angels, a blue ribbon panel of experts to orchestrate an exhaustive inquiry into Jack Kennedy's assassination. Leaving no stone unturned while marshaling every expert under the sun, the commission would report that a loner tainted by Marxism had used a mail-order foreign rifle to slay the president as the motorcade drove past the book warehouse where the miscreant worked. This sick and depraved act would be explained as Lee Harvey Oswald's maniacal tour de force to find fame, it being of little consequence that the scapegoat had told people that he liked President Kennedy. A week prior to the assassination, acting on instructions from his CIA control agent Maurice Bishop, cover name for David Atlee Phillips, Oswald told his summertime girl friend from Florida, "If something happens to Kennedy they're going to blame it on me."

The fingering of Oswald had a nice ring to it. As a low level ex-ONI contract floater Oswald was "put together" by master manipulators who exploited his post-Marine Corps mission to Russia as part of what former top-level CIA insider Victor Marchetti described as an American Intelligence "fake defector" spy project. Oswald was first "painted pink" and then at an opportune time labeled "red". He was "so confused he didn't know who he was working for" probers learned during the Washington D.C. congressional probes of the late 1970s.

OLIVER STONE'S "JFK" INTRODUCES VITAL EVIDENCE, BUT MUFFS MOTIVE

The disclosures echoed findings aired in the late 1960s by author Jim Marrs in his book *Crossfire* and by New Orleans District Attorney James Garrison, author of *On The Trail of the Assassins*, whose investigation became grist for the mill for Oliver Stone's 1989 movie "JFK". The flick gave viewers a look at the Zapruder film for the first time, an eye opener that for millions of people around the world cast the Kennedy assassination in a new light. No one had told them there were multiple shooters. No one had told them there was an exploding round fired from behind a fence on the knoll to the right front of the motorcade. It was 16 years down the line and no one had told the public why so-called "experts" were unable to escape their little prisons of carefully crafted disinformation.

The Oliver Stone movie about D.A. Garrison's 1967 investigation was a masterpiece of verisimilitude, jigsawed around a flawed prosecution bereft of incriminating evidence. The theatrics uncovered fascinating interpersonal connections, riveting characterizations and intriguing possibilities. The denouement of the flimsy case against Clay Bertram Shaw, executive director of the New Orleans Trade Mart, was a jury summation by Kevin Costner depicting the real life D.A. Garrison. The final plea to jurors made a good case that a conspiracy was certainly involved in the killing of the president. The Costner character then launched a paranoid lament that the late president was killed because he was trying to end a war in Vietnam that greedy munitions-makers desperately wanted. This was propounded as the motive for assassination. The jury immediately found the accused not guilty, understandably so.

Garrison and Stone took the position that the people had lost a champion, we had lost our innocence and the world would never be the same. All three cloying claims rang false.

The movie missed the target on motive.

As research would show, a toxic brew created by the president himself had forged a bond between overworld and underworld that sprang from double crossing and crossing too many outraged people, too many countries, too many power elites.

The Kennedys were playing dangerous foreign policy and nuclear games, flouting espionage laws, assuming dictatorial powers, trashing conventional rules of good order and giving nepotism no more redemption than could be found in the worst banana republic. The president was using the White House as a seraglio and scrambling to screw every attractive woman in range, something JFK not only admitted but openly advertised. He was on speed and steroids every day – dangerous combinations whether for health reasons or not. His kid brother ranted when he didn't get his way, abusing tried and true public servants many of whom were men who took nothing from no one and who would like to have thrashed him on the spot. In 1963 the addition of U.S. Senator Ted Kennedy, barely of Constitutional age, pyramided the monopolistic power wielded by John F. and Robert F. Kennedy over the White House, Justice Department and Central Intelligence Agency. The so-called New Frontier was assuming earmarks of dictatorships that Americans and their allies had lifted heaven and hell to repudiate less than a generation earlier during World War II. The nation was at swords' points even now, facing two vicious totalitarian powers, the Soviet Union and China, whose ambition was to turn the United States into a doormat servile to Marxist screeds and its people into a howling dictatorship of the proletariat.

We should not fault actor Kevin Costner for the comic book caricature of a summation in the motion picture JFK, but hadn't anyone ever told Oliver Stone what was going on in the halls of power inside Washington D.C.? His slant was spoon fed to D.A. Jim Garrison by a supposed "anonymous insider," at the

Washington D.C. mall, played by actor Donald Sutherland. His rant ventriloquized from the mouth of Pentagon aide Col. J. Fletcher Prouty, a personal rival of celebrated Cold War Southeast Asia superspy General Edward G. Lansdale. There was a reason Prouty's obsessions were so prominent; he was a "technical advisor" on the movie set. His Leninist claptrap about munitions-makers drooling with greed while drumbeating for war was so old it had whiskers. We knew this villain: Daddy Warbucks in the 'Little Orphan Annie' comic strips of the 1930s.

John F. Kennedy was not on a noble quest to end the Vietnam War. He as much as anyone escalated the war, having famously staged a memorable photo op in which he saluted U.S. Army Special Forces as "my green berets." The stirring photo was front-paged across the nation. He "augmented" troops in South Vietnam from 685 in 1961, to 16,732 in 1963. JFK chauvinists like to portray Kennedy's misgivings about the war as if private maunderings have stature equal to action, a juxtaposition that would allow a leader the luxury of firmly straddling every issue. We hear a great deal about Lyndon Johnson's reversal of a confidential JFK memorandum calling for withdrawal of 1,000 troops before Christmas of 1963. The proposed withdrawal was a gesture to make it seem like we were winning the war, projected for the benefit of voters in the approaching presidential election. It was part of a numbers game designed early in 1963 when some 4000 troops – far more than needed – were dispatched, according to George McTurnin Kahin in his landmark study *Intervention: How America Became Involved in Vietnam, 1945-1966*. Vietnam was Kennedy's war before it became McNamara's war.

Here is how one Pentagon insider viewed the idea that JFK planned to pull the U.S. out of Vietnam: "I think not. He was a Gung Ho Cold Warrior. He was a fan and big supporter of unconventional warfare."

With more than 16,000 armed Army advisors training Army of Vietnam (ARVN) troops, Huey helicopters ferrying combat squads to the Central Highlands, and a green felt MAC-V inside the war room in Saigon, the U.S. was up to its eyeballs in actual warfare. Green Berets shared helicopters with and commanded ARVN troops. It may not have been a war the United States wanted; it was forced by Ho Chi Minh's assignment of thousands of Viet Cong infiltrators into South Vietnam in 1959.

GENTLEMEN, TAKE YOUR SEATS

Immediately following the events in Dallas, LBJ sketchily ran the Oswald Straw Man scenario past his pal and neighbor J. Edgar Hoover. Then he gave former CIA Director Allen Dulles a call. It sounded reasonable all around. Dulles agreed to be a panelist while sidestepping the chairmanship, since a question of objectivity might arise. Some might insinuate bias since JFK had bounced Dulles from leadership of the Central Intelligence Agency in November of 1961, an implicit scapegoating for the disastrous Bay of Pigs fiasco seven months earlier.

In April, 1961, as the covert invasion by 1400 CIA-trained Cuban exile guerrillas had unfolded, CIA Director Dulles had been poised on a U.S. aircraft carrier loaded with jet fighter planes in the Caribbean waiting for word to send them into battle. On that lazy Sunday morning, three months after he had taken office, President Kennedy had received an urgent telephone call at the Virginia estate he rented for his wife, little girl and himself. It came from Charles Cabell, deputy director of the CIA. Dulles wanted a green light to unleash the jets, which could have shot down Castro's four-plane air force in a New York minute. The air assault would have turned the tide by springing free anti-Castro commandos who were trapped and dying on the beach as Castro's backyard air force strafed them. Kennedy balked, leading to a fiasco that would haunt his presidency and contribute to his eventual assassination. He would later privately tell CIA liaison Cord Meyer that in a parliamentary government the nation's leader would have been ousted from office but since the U.S. has an elected representative government, "your boss has to go", meaning Dulles.

Kennedy was devastated by the setback. His brother Bobby said he'd never seen his brother so close to tears.

"This is the worst job in the world," President Kennedy said. "Lyndon can have it."

"Those bearded bastards can't do this to you." Bobby Kennedy said of the Castro Cubans. "We've got to save this man," added Dean Rusk, secretary of state.

Dulles and two other top echelon CIA careerists, Richard Bissell and Charles Cabell, were pink slipped. They departed graciously late in 1961. Who screwed up the Bay of Pigs? Kennedy publicly took the blame. In a sit-down with old adversary Richard Nixon during the next few days, however, as recalled in Nixon's Memoirs in 1978, JFK told him: "I was assured by every sonofabitch I checked with – all the military experts and the CIA – that the plan would succeed."

As we shall see, two CIA veterans who lost friends among the 156 who were killed on the beach never forgave JFK for not releasing air power to save the brigade. Both would later figure prominently in JFK's assassination: David El Indio Morales, who forever after openly labeled JFK a traitor; and E. Howard Hunt, whose 1973 documentary novelette Give Us This Day described and emotionally mourned the failed effort by Cuban exiles to recapture their homeland.

After being cashiered by JFK late in 1961, Dulles was not heard from until he resurfaced as a member of the Warren Commission, where one of his functions was to exclude or gloss over any potential suggestion of CIA involvement in the subject under examination. He kept the agency's secrets superbly, there being no public disclosure of the Kennedy/CIA/Mafia plots to kill Castro until U.S. Senator Frank Church's Committee exposed them in 1975.

EARL WARREN

Already wrapped in the robes of justice, Earl Warren, chief justice of the U.S. Supreme Court, would be a perfect front for the commission. It would be known as the Warren Commission. Understandably, Warren, a former California governor, was reluctant to take on the job but with the persuasive Johnson gripping his arm and pleading that it was for the good of his country, how could Warren turn him down?

Warren was told he would have a free hand and, naturally, no expense would be spared to uncover the facts. Commission spots would become a springboard to stardom for two key players, House Minority Leader Gerald Ford, a Republican, and Arlen Specter, chief counsel. In time, Ford would become Richard Nixon's vice president and move up to the White House. Specter would move up to U.S. Attorney in Philadelphia and then win election as a Republican senator from Pennsylvania, for a third of a century.

Of the seven Warren Commission members, three sharply disputed the findings, a fact unknown to the public. They cited the forensic impossibility of the "magic bullet theory," cornerstone of the commission's unanimous conclusion that Lee Harvey Oswald had acted alone. "We were not told the truth about Oswald," protested Sen. Richard Russell, D-Georgia. A longtime LBJ ally, Russell voiced astonishment when he found that notes showing dissent among the members had been destroyed after release of the 26-volume report.

Joining Senator Russell in dissent were Sen. John Sherman Cooper, R-KY and Rep. Thomas Hale Boggs, D-LA.

BOGGS FED BUILDING COMES UP ACES

Boggs had none of the good fortune that smiled on Ford and Specter. He ascended to the second highest post in the lower house of Congress, Democratic Majority Leader, where in 1971 he took the floor to denounce FBI Director J. Edgar Hoover for "lying through his teeth" in his presentations to the Warren Commission six years earlier. Boggs also targeted wiretapping of several congressmen by the FBI, concluding: "Gentlemen, 1984 is closer than we thought."

The widely respected congressman, whose widow Lindy Boggs would later be elected to Congress, died in a mysterious private plane crash five months later en route between Anchorage and Juneau, Alaska. The crash also claimed the lives of Rep. Nick Begich of Alaska, Begich's aide and the pilot of the Cessna 310. A generation later his son, Dr. Nick Begich Jr., produced FBI telexes derived from old top secret NASA signals intelligence, which he said contradicted the FBI claim that they never found the missing plane. Dr. Begich's documents proved, he said, that the FBI had found the plane and abandoned the two survivors who had been photographed from space milling around. He said the FBI did not want to disclose what was then top-secret NASA technology to Coast Guard rescue teams who were denied enough information to save the survivors. Dr. Begich said the top-secret technology went on line in the 1980s. He said it enables users to read the print on a dime from outer space.

CHIEF JUDGE: "I DON'T HAVE JURISDICTION"

There is evidence that a serious inquiry was desired by Chief Justice Earl Warren, a former California governor whose liberal Supreme Court was detested by reactionaries calling for his impeachment, He proactively visited Dallas where he interviewed Jack Ruby in his Texas prison cell in an attempt to learn from Oswald's murderer details of JFK'S assassination. Ruby feared reprisals. He pleaded with Warren twelve different times to be transferred to a safer prison environment in or around Washington D.C. There he would be able to talk with a sense of ease. Warren tried every rhetorical approach, hoping to glean insight usable for guidance.

The man who held the U.S.Constitution's Article III federal judicial power in his right hand was hamstrung. Ruby was imprisoned for a state crime, murder. Half the country thought Justice Warren could wave a magic wand enabling him to take Ruby wherever he pleased.

"I can't do it," Chief Justice Warren told the gunman. "I don't have jurisdiction." Ruby in short order was convicted of murdering Oswald and – conveniently some say – died in a Texas prison of a supposed cancer within two years. There is a body of belief that Ruby was injected with the cancer, particularly since such a fatal antibody was being medically researched by Judith Vary Baker, a summer fling of Lee Harvey Oswald when both worked – as proven by their W-2 forms – at the Reily Coffee Co. in New Orleans.

Winner at her Bradenton, FL high school of a National Science Foundation award, Baker had been given a summer job to research cancer cures with a brilliant woman researcher, Dr. Mary Sherman, employed at the famous New Orleans cancer hospital called the Oschner Clinic. The woman would later turn up dead and Judith Baker fled to Europe where she was regularly assailed by a blogger whose excess of zeal disputed her disclosure that she had been Lee Oswald's lover in New Orleans during the summer of 1963. The bad news for Baker's critics is that Oswald and Baker were photographed together outside the Oschner Clinic, clear, smiling and innocent.

HOME MOVIE SHOWS ALL

Like Tip O'Neill, many had uncomfortably accepted the Warren Commission until a long chain of startling disclosures rocked its foundations. The investigation by James Garrison in 1967–68 – four years after the killing – unearthed the vital Zapruder film, which clearly shows a fatal shot to JFK's head by a bullet fired from the grassy knoll on Elm Street to the right front of the motorcade. The film had been quietly purchased for $30,000 from Abe Zapruder by Dallas oilman H.L. Hunt's aide Paul Rothermel Jr. and iced in a vault at the Time-Life building in New York City by C.D. Jackson, a senior *Time Magazine* staffer and CIA liaison for the publishing empire of Henry Luce and his wife, Congresswoman Clare Booth Luce. Although Garrison succeeded in subpoenaing the 8-mm Bell & Howell film and showing it in court as evidence, it went unseen by the vast general public until vividly screened and dramatized in the popular Oliver Stone movie of 1992 titled JFK — nearly 30 years after the assassination.

The fake forensics spoon fed to the public over a span of fifty years persistently dispute the obvious. There was denial of eyewitness proof of a sniper perch behind the picket fence atop the grassy knoll on Elm Street. Although fifty to eighty witnesses who were in Dealey Plaza that day pinpointed the grassy knoll as the source of the fatal head shot, the eyewitnesses were brushed aside by powers obsessed with scapegoating Lee Harvey Oswald as a lone kooky assassin. If there were two or more sniper nests, the theory of a solitary gunman would go up in smoke. In the long-buried Zapruder film, we see Mrs. Jacqueline Kennedy scrambling on hands and knees rearwards, toward the Texas School Depository sniper windows, to recover her husband's brain. To this day, with the noteworthy exception of Cyril Wecht of Pittsburgh, forensics "experts" have failed to explain by what trick of suspended laws of physics the "boomerang bullet" propelled matter back in the direction from which the bullet had come. Dr. Wecht saw the fatal shot as an exploding bullet fired from the grassy knoll.

The spin woven by the Washington D.C. overworld and lords of the media in the aftermath of the assassination persisted despite wave after wave of fresh evidence that, when evaluated by rational standards, deconstructed the conclusion that the suspect had committed the crime all by his lonesome.

Was there a public outcry objecting to the capture and framing of a kooky Marxist, as loner Lee Harvey Oswald was portrayed? Not at all. Given the Cold War climate of the day, that simple "solution" was acceptable to a passive public that had no reason to dispute the conclusions, nor any means of contesting them even were skeptics so inclined.

In 1963–64, the leading shaper of weekly news was *Time Magazine* and its sister photojournalistic weekly *Life*, with *Newsweek* a weak second. Together *Time* and *Life* pretty much framed American and free world opinion on public affairs, especially for people too busy to wade through the *New York Times* or some alternative urban newspaper. Radio had seen its best days as a news source. Television had yet to refine its role as an overnight news medium.

Would the mighty *Time-Life* empire assign a team of reporters to dig out the truth? One would expect no less. Instead, within weeks *Life* would print on its cover a snapshot purporting to be a grinning Lee Harvey Oswald posing in his Texas back yard as a rifle brandishing guerilla. So amateurish was the photograph that any team of high school yearbook staffers could spot it as a graphic arts hybrid, a fake, a gluepot and exacto-knife special in which Oswald's head had been superimposed on the photo's body. The forgery trick is one that propagandist E. Howard Hunt would later be caught at when, in his zeal to reinforce JFK's tie to the Diem assassinations, Hunt took his gluepot and exacto-knife in hand to plant a fake memo in national security files with intent to discredit the late president. It was taking coals to Newcastle since JFK was already on record as having given at least tacit approval to the coup against Diem. By whatever means *Life* came into possession of the tampered Oswald snapshot, it did not pass ordinary visual inspection and should never have gotten past the keen photojournalistic eyes of sophisticated desk men at *Life* magazine. This was the bright, bold photo magazine that had covered itself with glory presenting unforgettable action shots during World War II and Korea. It did not befit such a cherished and trusted national treasure to become a shill in a scam to blame a patsy for a crime anyone with a grain of sense could see he could not have committed alone.

Time found itself in an awkward position. So embroiled in anti-Castroism were the Luces who owned the magazines that Henry Luce had abandoned all pretext of objectivity vis a vis Cuba. Overriding American foreign policy restraints, Luce had editorialized openly and loudly for the United States to get rid of Castro. There was family involvement. Luce's son-in-law, a wealthy adventurer named William Pawley Jr., had given his life for the cause. He had joined the anti-Castro guerrillas in Miami and sent a party of gunmen across the straits, where all were killed. A U.S. Navy gunboat had destroyed the war party. In utter despair, Pawley shot himself. Claire Booth Luce, Republican congresswoman, patrician grand lady, and spirited journalist, co-owner of *Time* and *Life*, was not only a foe of Castro, she was using private money to sponsor an attack boat run by the irregulars out of the Florida Keys. After Kennedy was shot, it took the Luces no time to learn that a rogue anti-Castro gang from Miami and the Keys was involved in the Kennedy assassination. It was not known whether they shared glimmerings that the event was foreshadowed.

Over the years there has been uncommon resistance from the *New York Times* against what it calls "conspiracy theorists" who do research and write books and blogs seeking to make sense of a major event in American life. The books number in the hundreds if not thousands. Much of the research is brilliant, some of it disjointed. Beyond doubt it is a cottage industry. With all its prestige, excellence and resources, the Times should have been in the forefront of the story rather than a laggard either ignoring it or sniping at those who sought to unravel the mysterious mass of misinformation. The *Times* conferred its blessings on the Warren Commission Report, front end and back. Famed *Times* columnist James Reston was among the first and most prominent to call for a blue-ribbon panel to investigate the assassination, while prize-winning reporter Anthony Lewis worked with Chief Justice Earl Warren as the commission study unfolded while arranging to print and publish under the *New York Times* imprimatur an authoritative précis of the voluminous report. So far so good. However, the Warren Commission Report came under almost immediate attack. Leading the charge was New York lawyer Mark Lane who disputed the commission's incomplete investigation, its omissions, factual selectivity and skewed analysis. Lane's assertion that a squad of riflemen as part of a cabal assassinated Kennedy challenged not only the commission report but also the entire assassination story.

Over the years, the *New York Times'* Anthony Lewis stoutly defended the Warren Report, using his featured back page column to skewer critics. He ridiculed "grassy knoll nuts", referring to researchers and writers who since release of the Zapruder film had proof that the fatal head shot came not from the School Depository but from behind a picket fence atop a grassy knoll to the right front of the motorcade route. The fact that firing had come, of course, from opposite directions proved there was more than one sniper, ipso facto a conspiracy, overriding the obsession with a single rifleman as the Warren Commission by a split 4–3 vote had concluded. Chairman Warren wanted and announced a united front, said panel member Sen. Richard Russell. In fact, Russell and two others disputed the findings and voted no, the veteran southern lawmaker revealed.

The longstanding *New York Times* bias about the event came to a head in the early 1990s when its back news section ran photos of four authors of books touting contradictory conspiracy theories and ideas. The *Times* story ridiculed the four books and authors, obviously to boost "Case Closed", whose author went on a commercial book tour of Barnes and Noble stores. The four targeted authors were infuriated by the gratuitous press lashing and sued for libel. The court eventually dismissed the suit based on, among other things, the Sullivan v NY Times precedent.

The Random House book was unoriginal and relatively uninteresting, merely abstracting and recycling material from an earlier book called *Marina and Lee* by Sovietologist Priscilla Johnson McMillan. Johnson had culled information for her book during her curious year long "babysitting" job immediately following the assassination. Johnson had surfaced inexplicably in Dallas in the last week of November 1963 to move in with Lee Oswald's widow Marina. A secret angel had bought Marina a house and was giving her money, changing her overnight so that she abruptly cut off her mother-in-law, Oswald's mother testified before the Warren Commission. Oswald's mother said it was no surprise that Soviet citizen Marina preferred getting a free house and money to possibly being prosecuted, deported or worse.

Priscilla Johnson speaks and writes Russian which partially accounts for her presence at the American embassy in Russia where Lee Harvey Oswald, in an earlier incarnation, surprisingly popped up to proclaim that he was renouncing his American citizenship. As a correspondent for the North American Newspaper Alliance (NANA) Johnson wrote the story about ex-Marine Oswald's supposed defection. While in Minsk for two years, Oswald met and married Marina, who thought Oswald was Russian since he spoke the language so well. No one has yet explained how Oswald learned to speak Russian. The best guess is that while stationed at El Toro Marine Corps base in California he was detached to attend the Army Language School at the Presidium in Monterey, Cal., where Marines were sometimes accepted as visiting students. As a future Office of Naval Intelligence (ONI) agent seeking to enter the Army Language School, Oswald would have needed a top secret security clearance, a record of which should exist in unrecovered military files. The ALS web site does not show his name these many years later, a fact which neither affirms nor refutes, since files can be and often are erased. Another view aired by fellow Marines is that Oswald was keeping company at the time with a Russian speaking Japanese girl who was a whiz with languages, and that he was mixing business with pleasure, learning Russian while he romanced her. If so, he was a fast learner. A woman friend who had been laboriously studying Russian for many months as part of a year long language program remarked that within the span of a few months Oswald's linguistic progress simply amazed her because he was already speaking the language far better than she could.

There is a chain of links between Oswald and American government intelligence that does not appear to be tied to the covert arm of the Central Intelligence Agency. Oswald's gestalt was ONI. Calling in to a West Coast radio talk show, an ex-Marine who said he had been in the same platoon recalled that in weeks prior to his early "hardship" discharge in the late '50s, Oswald was being groomed for some sort of secret mission. The caller said Oswald was summoned repeatedly to the CID headquarters for special training and briefings before being mustered out a few months early, supposedly because his mother needed his financial support.

Oswald visited his home area around Fort Worth for only a few days before flying to Scandinavia en route to his destination in Belarus in the USSR.

By the time of the Kennedy assassination, the CIA was overgrown. It had spawned too many directorships, each walled off internally from the others. By design, one hand did not know what the other was doing. The "Company," as it was called, was suffering the curse of bigness. Across the Potomac River in Langley, Virginia, the government behind lifetime OSS/CIA mother hen Allen Dulles was christening a gleaming new 1.4 million foot pre-cast concrete castle to function as the CIA's worldwide headquarters. Knowing Kennedy was dumping him, an understandably resentful Dulles swallowed his pride. It was November 1961. With flashbulbs popping, Dulles took President Kennedy on a grand tour of the new headquarters, like a real estate agent showing a mansion built for a king. There was such a thing as carrying good sportsmanship too far. Not that they were being pink-slipped to the unemployment line, but the CIA's Big Three, namely Dulles himself, his deputy director Charles Cabell and six-foot-six Richard Bissell — under whose leadership the nation's spy satellites and U2 reconnaissance had been lifted into the skies — were about to become history.

Kennedy had little reason to celebrate since his father and guiding star, former Ambassador to England Joseph P. Kennedy, suffered a severe disabling stroke from which he would never recover. The self-made founder of the Kennedy dynasty was robbed of speech and reason until his death eight years later, lucid enough only to rarely mutter "no, no". It was as if he were reliving a lifetime of family tragedies: the anguish of losing a daughter to mental illness, his first son Joseph in a World War II plane explosion, a daughter in a plane crash over France and his politically successful sons Jack and Robert to assassins' bullets. Only one son lived out his life, his youngest son Senator Ted Kennedy, who survived a 1961 plane crash, a 1969 car crash in Chappaquiddick MA, and his peripheral involvement in a drunken evening in West Palm Beach, FL. Ted persevered to beat back a challenge to his Senate seat in 1988, overcoming a 24-point poll deficit to outrun Mitt Romney, setting the stage for a final 22-year run of liberal Senate leadership that must forever rank him among Washington's most influential and finest voices ever in the U.S. Senate.

Still unresolved is why so many of American society's brightest and otherwise well informed people still believe or act as if they believe the fiction that President John F. Kennedy was shot by a lone assassin, for no reason whatsoever. The weight of evidence now shows that he was done in by a posse of snipers assembled to stop the impending Kennedy dynasty and to remove President Kennedy from office because there was no other way short of violence to do it. Nonetheless, from a historical perspective, the phony original rollout is still in play in many formal venues where the attitude seems to be "please don't bother us with the truth".

The mega spin is a page from Lewis Carroll's *Alice In Wonderland*: "The truth is not what it is, it's what I say it is." Let's see about that.

CHERCHEZ LA FEMME

Definition: "Look for the woman" – a French phrase implying that a woman is at the bottom of the matter under discussion.
– *Webster's New International, Second Edition, 1934*

A GEORGETOWN DIVORCEE UTOPIATES WITH JFK

Flashbacks, the 1983 autobiography of Dr. Timothy Leary, the Harvard pharmapsychologist who emerged in the 1960s as guru of an LSD subculture, tells of Mary Meyer's series of visits to his Harvard center to learn the techniques for conducting LSD sessions. She told him she was having an affair with an important man. She wanted to induce her lover and other Washington influentials to use LSD as "utopiates", as she enjoyed calling them," to "brainwash" them and promote "world peace", her presumption being that the Soviet empire might reciprocate by laying down arms, allowing the world to live in peace. Neither of them seemed to be aware of the folly of unilateral disarmament.

MARY PINCHOT MEYER AND TIM LEARY: THE LSD PEACENIK PLOT

At this juncture we must point out that Dr. Leary's public reputation in 1962–63 was that of a dangerous crackpot. Middle

America still hated narcotics in any and all forms. Leary's clarion call aired widely and mockingly by tabloids was to "turn on, tune in, drop out". He was pictured grinning like a fool, his features baked by apparent excess drug use. Idolized by druggies, he was perceived as an enemy of society, degenerate and depraved, an unwitting Soviet tool. He menaced our youth and decent folks everywhere.

A fair reading of Dr. Leary's autobiography tells a different story. Here we see an academician of vast knowledge, an enterprising spirit at frontiers of inner consciousness, a robust advocate of entry through the portals of "magic mushrooms" and LSD under a controlled environment into a nirvana of peaceful bliss, light and harmony. (Editor's note: the author has never used drugs, narcotics or hallucinogens and discourages their use.) While the Harvard pied piper was hobnobbing and drugging with Beat Generation writers such as Allen Ginsburg and Jack Kerouac, we learn that the widespread perception of him as a pariah was anything but universal as he describes tripping with such talented and prominent people as Henry and Clare Booth Luce, Aldous Huxley, Cary Grant, Jack Nicholson, Stanley Kubrick, James Coburn, and Ken Kesey. Ethel Kennedy, wife of Attorney General Robert Kennedy, was reported to have used hallucinogens in a medical treatment. As if to prove that he was a serious man of impressive intellectual stature, Dr. Leary was teaming with Aldous Huxley in translating *The Tibetan Book of the Dead* as Huxley faded from cancer. Huxley died during a planned final LSD trip on November 22, 1963 – coincidentally the same day on which President Kennedy was assassinated. Author of the futuristic *Brave New World*, Huxley was among the foremost seminal thinkers of the 20th Century. His passing went almost unnoticed, pushed off the front pages by the news from Dallas.

Dr. Leary in his 1983 autobiography (*Flashbacks*, J.F. Tarcher Inc., Los Angeles, 1983, Pages 128-150) wrote:

"While sitting at my desk (Ed: at Harvard) I looked up to see a woman leaning against the door post, hip tilted provocatively, studying me with a bold stare. She appeared to be in her late thirties. Good-looking. Flamboyant eyebrows, piercing green-blue eyes, fine-boned face. Amused, arrogant, aristocratic. 'Dr. Leary,' she said coolly. 'I've got to talk to you…. I'm Mary Pinchot. I've come from Washington to discuss something very important. I want to learn how to run an LSD session."

It was the spring of 1962, May or June. Dr. Leary's visitor was 41, not late 30s as Leary had guessed. She was a freelance artist who experimented with riotous colors. She had two sons after losing one, a young boy, who had been tragically killed by a motorist on a sharp curve outside her home in 1956 in Washington D.C. The trauma had led to her divorce in 1958 from Cord Meyer, the father of the three boys, a U.S. Marine Corps veteran of the South Pacific who had lost an eye when a grenade exploded in his foxhole. His luck was running bad. A month later, his brother who was also a Marine, was killed in combat on Okinawa.

Unknown to Dr. Leary, her ex-husband was a high level executive in the Central Intelligence Agency's covert action directorate responsible for secretly funding and infiltrating liberal groups such as college students, labor organizations, veterans and dissidents of various descriptions. Meyer handled millions of dollars for "The Company". His best friend was James Jesus Angleton, the CIA counterintelligence chief.

Mary Pinchot Meyer continued: "I have this friend who's a very important man. He's impressed by what I've told him about my own LSD EXPERIENCES AND WHAT OTHER PEOPLE HAVE TOLD HIM. HE WANTS TO TRY IT HIMSELF. SO I'M HERE TO LEARN HOW TO DO IT. I MEAN, I DON'T WANT TO GOOF UP OR SOMETHING."

He offered her wine but she made a cute face and took him out to a cocktail lounge instead for champagne. They returned to the Newton Center where they joined Leary's girl friend Malaca, a New York Muslim model, and a friend Michael Hollingshead. They dined, drank and "took a low dose of mushrooms and sat around the fire". Hollingshead regaled them with tipsy recollections of LSD trips and tips about inner navigation until

Mary Pinchot suddenly tensed up. 'You poor things', she said, according to Leary.

'You don't really understand what's happening in Washington with drugs, do you?"

"It's time you learned more. The guys who run things – I mean the guys who really run things in Washington – are very interested in psychology, and drugs in particular. These people play hardball, Timothy. They want to use drugs for warfare, for espionage, for brainwashing, for control.'

She said she wanted to see drugs used to promote peace. At one point earlier in the conversation she said she'd heard the poet Allen Ginsberg on radio say if Kennedy and Khrushchev would take LSD together they'd end world conflict. 'Isn't that the idea – to get powerful men to turn on?'

Dr. Leary knew Ginsberg very well and had done drugs with him, but recalled that he had told Pinchot he thought otherwise.

'Allen says that, but I've never agreed. Premier Khrushchev should turn on with his wife in the comfort and security of his Kremlin bedroom. Same for Kennedy.'

'Nothing that involves brain-change is certain,' Dr. Leary continued, adding that with nuclear bombs proliferating, more countries being run by dictators, no political creativity, "It's time to try something, anything new and promising.'

Despite feeling the pleasant conspiratorial glow of those sharing a psychedelic session, Dr. Leary said he felt uneasy.

'There was something calculated about Mary,' he recalled. 'That tough hit you get from people who live in the hard political world.

"I asked once again, who are these friends of yours who want to use drugs for peace?' Laughing, she said, 'Washington, like every other capital city in the world, is run by men. These men conspiring for power can only be changed by women. And you're going to help us.'

Leary drove her to the airport the next day where he loaded her with books and research papers. He told her he thought she was not quite ready to start running LSD sessions. She agreed, promised to return for more practice and ended by saying, 'Don't forget, the only hope for the world is intelligent women.'

One woman had already jumped ship. Malaca was subdued after the session. She told Leary she had seen the other three of them 'as aliens very distant from her culture.' 'These drugs make you see too much,' she lamented. She flew to Puerto Rico on a modeling assignment. Aside from a few late night phone calls when she admitted missing the 'mushroom world', Leary said he and Malaca never got together again.

MUSHROOMS CLOUD THE HORIZON

The summer of 1962 passed amid exploding atomic bomb tests from the far Pacific and Siberia as the United States and the Soviet Union engaged in a mano y mano attempt to impress one another with the ferocity of their nuclear arsenals.

It was a fall afternoon, according to Dr. Leary's diary. Just ahead waited the Cuban missile crisis that would commence on October 13 – just a few weeks away. The Soviet Union without knowledge of the rest of the world already had begun secretly shipping unassembled intermediate continental ballistics missiles (ICBMs) tipped with nuclear warheads into Cuba. Premier Khrushchev had not taken his LSD and was out to make trouble. Big trouble.

That fall afternoon Dr. Leary received a phone call from Mary Pinchot Meyer in Room 717 of the Ritz Hotel where she waited with a bottle of Dom Perignon iced in a silver bucket.

'I'm here to celebrate.'

'Your hush hush love affair is going well?'

PINCHOT: 'Oh yes. Everything is going beautifully. On all fronts in fact. I can't give details, of course. But top people in Washington are turning on. You'd be amazed at the sophistication of some of our leaders. And their wives. We're getting a little group together, people who are interested in learning how to turn on.'

LEARY: Really. I thought politicians were too power-oriented.

Pinchot said there are a lot of very smart people in Washington, especially with the Kennedy administration. She said power is important to them and drugs do give a certain power, freeing the mind. She turned to a new tack.

She told Leary that dissident organizations in academia are controlled. The CIA creates the radical journals and student organizations and runs them with deep-cover agents.'

"Oh come now. Mary, that sounds pretty paranoid to me,' Leary said.

She said it no doubt would surprise him to learn that a liberal group to which Leary once belonged called the American Veterans' Committee was started by the CIA, just like the American Legion had been started by Teddy Roosevelt after World War I. She then revealed inside details, naming names, as to CIA manipulation of several people whom Dr. Leary had idolized as liberal heroes.

LEARY: 'How do you know all this?'

PINCHOT: 'I knocked you with those facts to get your attention. It's a standard intelligence trick, I could tell you hundreds of little stories like that.'

Leary said his head was spinning as they refilled their champagne glasses and drained them. She asked rhetorically what these guys are most interested in now and O'Leary guessed it was drugs.

PINCHOT: 'You got it. A few years ago they became absolutely obsessed with the notion that the Soviets and the Chinese were persuading our POWs in Korea to defect by brainwashing them with LSD and mescaline.'

Dr. Leary said it was certainly possible since with minimal information about a subject's personal life and two or three LSD sessions 'you could get the most conventional person to do outrageous things.'

If a person wanted to be brainwashed and to change himself?

DR. LEARY: "Easier yet.' He said changing a mind-set to develop a 'new reality fix' was a simple and straightforward proposition, but the real problem was to change the outside world to conform to the new vision.

He struggled for a word and came up with 'Utopiates'.

Pinchot clapped her hands, delighted with the new word 'Utopiates'.

Like a teacher instructing a child, Mary advised Dr. Leary that since drug research was vital to the intelligence agencies he could continue his experiments as long as he kept quiet and didn't allow the work to get 'out of hand'. She said he was doing exploratory work the CIA had tried to do in the 1950s.

She did not mention that CIA Director Allen Dulles had once bought the entire supply of LSD produced by the proprietary inventor and producer of LSD, Sandoz Labs of Switzerland, for $250,000 to control its use and to keep it out of general circulation. Dr. Sidney Gottleib of New York City had been enrusted to experiment with it under the XK Ultra project with some successes but too many misfires. The program was halted after a CIA agent named Frank Olson either jumped or was pushed out of a 12th story window in New York City, a CIA bungle that once Olsen's family found out and sued many years later cost the agency $750,000 in a negligence settlement. Dr. Gottleib had allowed questionable use of the hallucinogen including slipping it in drinks of unsuspecting GIs, use in hypnosis experiments and overdoses that caused bad trips as he searched for a formula that would fill the bill of a Manchurian Candidate, as Richard Condon named the Pavlovian in his 1958 book.

Dr. Leary asked Mary Pinchot what she meant by 'out of hand'.

PINCHOT: 'Timothy, think. You're involved in the Big Game here. Mind-change is the key to power. They'll deal with you about the same way the Soviets would handle a nuclear physicist with liberal, libertarian ideals. They'll indulge your utopian fantasies. They know that creative scientists tend to be free thinkers. They'll run you with a loose silken cord as long as you don't stir up the masses.'

He agreed to refrain from stirring the masses and elicited once more from Mary Pinchot what she wanted.

PINCHOT: 'I told you the first time we met. I want to learn how to brainwash.' She continued, 'If I can teach the use of utopiates to the wives and mistresses of important people in our government, then we can... well shit, Timothy, don't you see what we can do?'

'What?'

PINCHOT: 'Use these drugs to free people. For peace, not war. We can turn on the Cabinet. Turn on the Senate. The Supreme Court. Do I have to explain further?'

Dr. Leary reflected that here he was, a 42-year old man, 'being lured into a feminist plot to turn on the leaders of the United States government to the idea of world peace.' He thought of it as scary, he said.

LEARY: 'Okay, what do you want from me. The drugs?'

She replied 'Just a little bit to get started.' She said with their connections they'd soon be able to get all they wanted. Mainly what she wanted was direction on how to run LSD sessions and how to deal with any problems that might arise.

Leary said he spent the next four hours giving her a cram course on psychedelic sessions including 'set and setting' and 'centering' as room service brought them more champagne and dinner before he drove her to Logan Airport in Boston for her night flight back to Washington D.C.

MARY: "I GOT EXPOSED PUBLICLY"

Mary was tense and joyless when she next met Dr. Leary. She called and arranged to meet him at the Ritz. It was late spring of 1963, a few days before Dr. Leary's departure for a beachside summer in Mexico where he would establish a retreat for LSD and drug experiments.

"I had to see you," Mary said. "Things are getting more complicated. I got exposed publicly."

They hadn't seen one another for several weeks. This time there were no happy smiles, no bubbly champagne.

"The drug experiments?" Leary asked, rattled by her talk of being exposed.

"No – everything there is going fine. It's my love affair."

"Tell me what happened," Leary prompted.

Mary replied: "There's a tremendous power struggle going on in Washington. A friend of mine was losing the battle, a really bloody one. He got drunk and told a room full of reporters about me and my boyfriend,"

LEARY: "Your boyfriend's married, I gather."

MEYER: "To say the least." She managed a hollow laugh.

LEARY: "Was there much publicity? I didn't read anything about a big Washington scandal."

"No, here's the scary part. Not a word printed about it," Mary said.

"That's scary," Leary agreed.

"It's really scary. You wouldn't believe how well-connected some of these people are, and nobody picked it up."

Mary continued, telling Leary it was really nothing new because she'd seen it in media politics a hundred times: news manipulation, cover-ups, misinformation, dirty tricks.

She said because of drugs she could now see things clearly.

"America doesn't have to be run by these Cold War guys. They're crazy, they really are. They don't listen, they don't learn. They're completely caught up in planning World War III. They can't enjoy anything except power and control."

Leary interrupted to remind her that this is where she came in, to loosen them up.

Mary stopped pacing, thanking Leary for reminding her.

"You restore my hope," she said.

Leary said if she would accompany him to Mexico she'd get training enough to become "the best brainwasher since Cleopatra."

Mary said she was too exposed already, urging Leary to be careful too. "Things are getting edgy in Washington," she warned. "As we start loosening things up, there's bound to be a reaction."

Urging him to "keep things low key," Meyer warned that if Leary stirred things up, "they'll shut you down."

"Or worse," she added for effect.

Mary said she did not trust the phones or mail, and that rather than he contact her, she would get in touch.

His program in Mexico was a magnet for publicity.

Life sent a reporter and photographer in July. The major networks, CBS and NBC, planned feature stories. From England the BBC wanted an appointment date.

It was something new. Everyone wanted a share.

There was no sign of Mary Meyer making a visit. She did send him an unsigned short cryptic note:

"Program going very well here. Extremely well. However, I won't be joining you. Too much publicity. Your summer camp is in serious jeopardy. I'll contact you after you return to USA."

A PSYCHEDELIC CELL ON THE POTOMAC

The federal police in Mexico had closed down and evicted Tim Leary's over-publicized beach paradise by proclaiming it a public embarrassment. In late June, a week after Leary's return to the Newton Center at Harvard, Mary Meyer telephoned from Logan Airport in Boston. She was anxious to see Dr. Leary. She had only the afternoon available so they met hurriedly at a downtown seafood restaurant.

"Oh you reckless Irishman,' she said, "You got yourself in trouble again. It's magnificent, these headlong cavalry charges of yours. Mais ce n'est pas la guerre."

When Dr. Leary asked what he'd done wrong, she lectured that she'd warned him to avoid publicity at risk of being shut down by the CIA.

The Agency would have gladly infiltrated every chapter of Leary's IFIF to avail itself of his training expertise, but not if it meant public exposure of its interest in the subject, The CIA refused to tolerate publicity, Mary indicated.

"They're not going to let CBS film you drugging people on a lovely Mexican beach. You could destroy both capitalism and socialism in one month with that sort of thing."

In his autobiography, *Flashbacks*, Dr. Leary at this point soliloquized, venting frustration about having his Mexican Valhalla expelled from that country due to intervention by Mexican federales and unseen CIA censors. Mary seemed to be getting on his nerves.

"I was struck again by the brittleness this aristocratic woman had picked up from those stern-eyed business-suited WASPS who shuttle from home to office in limousines – the information brokers, editors, board members, executive branch officials – youngish men with oldish eyes (faces you used to see around Harvard Square or in the Yale Quad), initiated early into the Calvinist conspiracy, sworn to be forever reliable, working for Wild Bill Donovan in Zurich, for Allen Dulles in Washington, for Henry Luce as bureau chiefs and then shuffling from Newsweek to the Post, manipulators of secret documents, facts, rumors, estimates, arms inventories, stock margins, voting blocs, industrial secrets, gossip about the sexual and drug preferences of every member of Congress, trained to grab and maintain what they can, all loyal to the Protestant belief that the Planet Earth sucks."

This jeremiad—a style not unlike Phil Wylie's misanthropic *Opus 21* or the harangues once heard from soapbox Marxists and Fascists in NYC's Union Square, could not have been spoken to Mary since the single sentence was 136 words long, wearying enough for Dr. Leary to fall into his fish fries before it was over.

"Never mind all that," said Mary. She told him she'd been working hard while he'd been goofing off.

"My friends and I have been turning on some of the most important people in Washington," she told Leary. "It's about time we had our own psychedelic cell on the Potomac, don't you think?"

Replied Leary: "So you need more drugs. That's going to be a problem. My plans for chemical plants in Mexico got wiped out."

"Oh that's no problem," Mary scoffed. I can give you a contact in England. And if things go the way I hope, we'll be seeing lots of good drugs produced here at home." Leary said he pressed her for details but she declined to elaborate.

"A WIFE SNITCHED ON US"

Mary Meyer kept looking in the rearview mirror.

She was on the lam. Stalked. Hunted.

It was late in the afternoon on a glorious day in November 1963. She could not be seen at Millbrook. She had rented a green Ford at LaGuardia Airport in Queens, NY, driven two hours to upstate. She called Tim Leary to leave the estate, her voice walking the tightrope of hysteria, as he put it.

Once outside the gate, Leary spotted the green Ford tailing him. He slowed, she pulled up behind him. She climbed in, motioned to Dr. Leary to drive on.

Leary said the autumn scene was unforgettable, trees turning technicolor, golden fields grazed by black cattle – with the bluest girl in the world seated beside him.

"It was all going so well," Mary told him. "We had eight intelligent women turning on the most powerful men in Washington. And then we got found out."

She began to sob, then burst into tears.

"I was such a fool. I made a mistake in recruitment. A wife snitched on us. I'm scared."

Leary consoled her, stroked her hair. He asked whether she'd had a bad drug experience. Not at all, she clarified. "That's all been perfect."

"I may be in real trouble," she blurted out. "I really shouldn't be here."

"Are you on drugs right now?" Leary asked.

It's not me, it's the situation that's fucked up. You must be very careful now, Timothy. Don't make any waves. No publicity. I'm afraid for you. I'm afraid for all of us."

Leary suggested they go back to the big house in Millbrook, relax, drink some wine, maybe take a hot bath. Then figure what Mary should do.

"I know what you're thinking but this is not paranoia," she persisted. "I've gotten mixed up in some dangerous matters. It's real. You've got to believe me."

She glared at him, demanding to know if he believed her. He told her he did, her alarm being totally convincing.

Mary asked for a future favor. "Look, if I ever showed up here suddenly, could you hide me out for awhile?" "Sure", Leary said.

She handed him a pill bottle from her purse. "This is supposed to be the best LSD in the world. It's from the National Institute of Mental Health. Isn't it funny that I end up giving it to you?"

Time was closing in. Leary said a telephone call came that night from Laura Huxley. She said Aldous was dying and that he wanted to see Leary about the manual they were adapting from the *Tibetan Book of the Dead*. Leary flew to Los Angeles the next day where he saw his friend Aldous Huxley for the last time. During their hospital chat they arranged for Laura to guide her husband through a psychedelic version of the *Book of the Dead*, an acid trip contributing to the serenity of the terminal patient as she read him instructions for reaching the White Light.

Leary's diary style was to record entries by season rather than by date. Consequently, the precise date of his final visit to Huxley's deathbed is unrecorded. His book *Flashbacks* serially compressed the three events, as if they were timed one, two, three: Mary's visit, Huxley's deathbed, JFK's assassination. Mary's visit coincided with Indian summer, well into November 1963. Leary's visit to see Huxley in Los Angeles occurred one day after Mary last visited to tell him she'd been found out and feared for her life. The date is important because it reveals the tremendous pressure being applied in Washington on the president's mistress at a time when JFK — facing FBI investigative pressure himself for his part in Mary's brainwashing conspiracy — was dodging assassination attempts in Miami and Tampa on Nov.17–18, before going on to Texas at week's end to keep his date with destiny.

Wrote Leary, back now from Los Angeles: "Everyone remembers exactly where they were on November 22, 1963, when the dreadful news hit. That evening a friend at the Associated Press in New York called with an item he had just pulled off the wire. Aldous Huxley was dead. In the grief for Kennedy no one noticed. We held a long candlelight vigil for both our departed guides."

MARY MEYER MURDERED A YEAR AFTER JFK

Around the time the Warren Commission Report was released in 1964, the press reported the daylight murder of a pretty divorcee named Mary Meyer, age 43, while strolling on a towpath in Washington D.C. She had been shot to death. News reports described her as an aspiring artist and former wife of a corporate executive, never mentioning that the executive was top echelon CIA disinformation boss Cord Meyer. They had raised three children together before splitting five years earlier following the tragic death of one of their sons.

The story noted her aristocratic background as a Pinchot of Eastern Pennsylvania related to a former Pennsylvania governor and to the Teddy Roosevelt Interior Secretary who pioneered the national wildlife and park preservation program.

She was described almost in passing as a friend of Mrs. Jacqueline Kennedy, with whom she would occasionally walk. As time would tell, she was no more than a casual acquaintance of Jackie Kennedy, who knew of her intimate relationship with JFK during his last two years while either being indifferent to it or ignoring it for the sake of surface harmony.

Was Mary Meyer's death connected to her intimacy with the late president? For those who do not stretch the boundaries of coincidence, there is little doubt. She knew a great deal as an insider about Kennedy and about the CIA. Her brother-in-law, Ben Bradlee, was editor of the influential Washington Post and she had remained friends with her former husband, Cord Meyer, after sharing secrets as his pillow mate for a dozen years. Mary Meyer kept a diary. No sooner did the CIA's counterintelligence chief James Jesus Angleton get a heads-up from a mutual friend about the diary than he was caught in surprise by Bradlee as he rummaged through the late Mary Meyer's effects. He found the diary and walked off with it, following standard CIA practice when confronted with the "ex-wife problem".

It was not the only time the CIA counterintelligence chief would go diary hunting. Shortly after the death two years later of CIA station chief Winston Scott in Mexico City, while the Lee-Oswald-in-Mexico mystery was still being sorted out, Angleton jetted to Mexico City where he confiscated the manuscript of a book the late station chief had been writing, making sure it never saw the light of day.

Angleton knew where all the bodies were buried and it is not too far afield to suspect that he had Kennedy assassinated. It is certain that he got wind of the "Big Event" that veteran spymaster E. Howard Hunt would admit to in a videotaped deathbed confession in March of 2007. Hunt said he had helped to plan and carry it out. Yet for all of Angleton's cunning and conniving, for all his wiretapping and bugging of the White House and JFK's trysts, for all his claims of keeping Mary's diary while threatening to expose the "real Jack Kennedy", Angleton seemed content to virtually ignore the Kennedy assassination while playing cat-and-mouse with Soviet defectors in his ultimately futile crusade to ferret out a CIA mole who may or may not have existed. A steady Martini drinker and borderline alcoholic, the orchid-cultivating Angleton was not exactly a Kennedy-hater as were many of his brethren. His wife was a fast friend and had been a college classmate of Mary Pinchot. The Angletons and other couples formed a social circle called the 'Georgetown Set' of top echelon CIA, government and journalism movers-and-shakers whose barbecues and pool parties involved heavy drinking and frolicking.

When pinned down late in life by a reporter as to what he knew about the plot to kill Kennedy, Angleton revealed a great deal while resorting to his customary doubletalk. He replied with an allusion misquoted from the scriptures whereby the Lord speaks of His house having many mansions, in this case referring to the compartmentalization of the CIA with all of its cutouts, false legends, paperwork blind alleys, front groups, hidden funding, plausible deniability, doppleganging, scapegoating, need-to-know isolation, disinformation and secret tradecraft. Angleton said the agency had many mansions. He then issued a standard dissimulation: "I was not privy to who killed John."

KILLED BY THE "SAME BASTARDS"

It was not until 1998 that a true behind-the-scenes lowdown on Georgetown society in the early 1960s emerged with publication of Nina Burleigh's *A Very Private Woman, The Life And Unsolved Murder Of Presidential Mistress Mary Meyer*.

The author is gentle, tolerant and apologetic, yet leaves no stone unturned in dishing the truth as she knows it. Aside from the oxymoronic title and some surprising moral ambivalence, we see both Mary Meyer and her circle of movers and shakers under the microscope of an observant biographer. Her book is indispensable toward shattering stereotypes and bringing into sharp focus the daily rhythms of a Georgetown elite whose maunderings and drumbeats were not so different than our own.

Her generally sympathetic portrayal of Mary Meyer as a restless divorcee well thought of by those in her social circle does not shrink from citing a few critics. With men, says a woman friend without condemnation, "Mary was bad", a reference to her serial affairs and liaisons. She was casual about lounging nude on her remote lawn before selling the house and moving into a townhouse. One male acquaintance found her flitting about annoying, leading him to characterize her as a "starf____er". The author relates a gossipy exchange during which Meyer mentioned to a group of Georgetown women that she thought scuttlebutt about the president's womanizing was exaggerated, setting off a round of titters since the president apparently had proven otherwise to some of the ladies in the group.

Burleigh dutifully reports on the arrest of a hapless black straggler picked up near the scene of the murder and his trial leading to acquittal for lack of evidence.

Shortly before he died from cancer at a ripe old age, Cord Meyer was asked by a journalist if he knew who had killed his former wife Mary Meyer? The old CIA veteran replied: "The same bastards who killed John F. Kennedy".

PAVLOV, POWS AND LSD

There was no doubt that LSD could bend the mind, permanently altering the subject's mental state. Dr. Timothy Leary, openly testing it at his ISIS lab at Harvard University's Newman Center and at his sprawling upstate New York mansion called Millbrook, had amassed enough clinical research data to scientifically validate the premise. LSD –lysergic acid diethzlamide – was an effective brainwasher.

Operating secretly over a ten-year span, so had the Central Intelligence Agency. It was not puzzling as to why the CIA was obsessed with "brainwashing", as mind bending was spectacularly known throughout the 1950s.

Pavlovian psychologists who had tortured and brainwashed American POWs (prisoners of war) were producing films showing POWS robotically denouncing American aggression in the Far East. The pitiful POWS acted out scripts like trained monkeys. American journalists just as robotically televised the Chinese Communist propaganda.

The decade had begun with three years of war in the Far East known as the Korean War that broke out in June 1950 when North Korean troops invaded South Korea across the 38th Parallel. The unexpected naked aggression violated the boundary set by the United Nations to separate the Communist dictatorship in the north from Syngman Rhee's American-backed pseudo-Republic in the south.

The North Korean troops overran the entire peninsula during the summer months until being defeated at the last-ditch Pusan Perimeter, which reversed the tide of the war. As the counterattack reversed the field by pushing back the North Koreans, General Douglas MacArthur, in his finest achievement in a long military career, essayed a surprise amphibious landing in mid-peninsula at Inchon near the capital city of Soul, choking off the already floundering and retreating North Korean armies encapsulated to the south. UN troops spearheaded by American soldiers and a reinvigorated Republic of Korea (ROK) army swept northward to the Yalu River, Korea's border with Manchuria in China.

At that point, with newly arriving F-86 Saberjets more than a match against Russian MIG fighter planes that had dominated early months of the war, General MacArthur thrilled the American public back home by speculating that some of the troops would be 'home by Christmas if they move fast enough". The bridges across the Yalu River were bombed out, but there was a surprise. An estimated 150,000 to 240,000 battle-hardened Chinese troops had already slipped across the border and were hidden in the mountains. They pounced on the overconfident turkey-stuffed Eighth Army and Korean corps on November 25, 1950, driving them on a 125-mile retreat back to the 38th Parallel. During "the longest retreat in American military history", the Chicoms rounded up hundreds of prisoners and shipped them off to bleak Manchurian POW camps where they were brutalized, starved and "reeducated". As if that were not enough, it was the coldest Korean winter in 100 years, with temperatures that dipped as low as 30 degrees below zero. Frostbite was as big an enemy as mortar rounds and bullets.

A LITTLE MISCALCULATION

The CIA was convinced that the 'confessing' POWS had been brainwashed by use of drugs. It was against this background that CIA Director Allen Dulles in 1951 received from the American military attaché in Switzerland a report that the Russians had purchased from Sandoz Pharmaceuticals in Basel, Switzerland "50 million doses" of Sandoz LSD-25. A follow-up memo said an added purchase of 10 more kilos increased the buy "100 million doses". Dulles in a talk given to the Princeton National Alumni Conference said the Russians and Chinese were engaging in "brain perversion techniques." An internal CIA memo dated 1953 estimated that a smidgen of LSD could destroy sanity for a considerable time while 100 million doses was enough to sabotage "a whole nation's mental equilibrium".

Dulles moved to deny the enemy LSD by cornering the market. LSD had been first synthesized in 1943 in a Sandoz laboratory by Dr. Albert Hofmann. The CIA contacted Sandoz and insisted on buying its entire supply, posting $240,000. The only problem was that the corporation had very little in stock. Never prone to pass up a profit, the firm agreed to meet the supply order over a ten-year span. To ensure a lockout of all hostile purchasers, the CIA went for the deal. Sandoz cranked up production of LSD to fill the order. Later, Eli Lilly in Indianapolis, Ind. came up with the LSD formula. Pointing to the Sandoz deal, the American pharmaceutical manufacturer insisted on the same terms to guarantee an exclusive. The American Central Intelligence Agency had become by far the biggest LSD customer in the world.

That there was a fly in the ointment did not become obvious until the CIA itself in a 1975 document acknowledged a monstrous metric miscalculation by the Embassy attaché, who didn't know the difference between a milligram (1/1000th of a gram) and a kilogram (1000 grams), according to ex-CIA operative Ira 'Ike' Felton in an interview he gave to Richard Stratton for a 1987 *Spin* Magazine article. The source for CIA Director Dulles' panicky market-cornering moves to buy up all the LSD in sight had miscalculated the Soviet purchases. At a gram a dose, the Russians had bought 150 doses --- not 150 million doses. No one had double-checked the arithmetic or the metric conversion tables. It turned out to be a big boon for Sandoz and hallucinogen makers everywhere.

Having cornered the LSD market due to overestimating the opposition, the CIA possessed vast quantities of the hallucinogen that it went to work testing. It had none of the expertise that Dr. Leary in future years would acquire.

The testing job was given to Dr. Sidney Gottleib, head of the CIA's Technical Services Staff (TSS), a small club-footed inventor of tricky devices such as exploding cigars, poison pens and toxic scuba diving gear intended to eliminate Fidel Castro. The MK-

Ultra Program, as it was named, involved slipping trace amounts of LSD into the drinks or coffee of young servicemen, CIA workers, agency employees, doctors, prostitutes, mental patients, prisoners and members of the general public. The unwitting experimental subjects were observed for reaction.

One of the tests backfired badly. During an informal conference of CIA agents and technicians in a rustic lodge, Dr, Gottlieb spiked LSD into fellow worker Frank Olson's Cointreau, laughing as he did so. Olson, a chemist at Fort Dietrich, Md., had a bad trip. Reeling and incoherent, he called the high-spirited group a bunch of clowns. In ensuing days, he became morose and withdrawn and decided to leave the agency. Several days later Olsen met with Dr. Gottleib and another CIA man at the Statler Hotel in New York City and either jumped or was pushed out of a 10th story window to his death. Many years later it would cost the CIA $750,000 to settle a wrongful death suit brought by Olson's family survivors.

Feldman told the *Spin* writer that he posed as a heroin dealer pimping for a stable of prostitutes in San Francisco in the 1950s while working for Bureau of Narcotics legend George Hunter White, who went by the name Morgan Hall at 81 Bedford Street in Greenwich Village. The gin-drinking, blue-eyed White worked on the MK-Ultra project using LSD that he nicknamed 'Stormy'. Testing LSD on his prostitutes in San Francisco, Feldman said, his project was labeled 'Operation Midnight Climax'.

"The LSD, that was just the tip of the iceberg." Ex-con Feldman told writer Stratton. "Espionage. Assassinations. The study of prostitutes for clandestine use. That's what I was doing when I worked for the CIA."

He said that White, who died of liver failure in 1975, was what he called a "minor missionary" in the quest for a 'truth serum' which would simplify the process of interrogation and figured that cannabis indica was helpful.

The psychedelic effects of LSD were said to produce a riot of colors and dreamlike sequences not unlike the sometime exalted sensations experienced from use of mescaline and certain mushrooms by southwestern Indians during tribal rites. Unknown except for use medically by psychiatrists and licensed psychologists until 1962, LSD was initially classified as an experimental drug by the U.S. Food and Drug Administration. It was introduced into the counterculture as protest movements grew. The more it attracted condemnation, the faster it spread. The psychedelic drug was widely touted by Dr. Tim Leary, Aldous Huxley and beat poet Alan Ginsburg for recreational and spiritual release. Leary described LSD as potent, so much so that once it was used, a person would never be the same. By 1966, too many bad acid trips, too much adulterated bootleg LSD and too much bad publicity routed the swamis, pied pipers and gurus. Dr. Leary was hounded, hunted, arrested and imprisoned until he ingeniously escaped from a California penitentiary and fled overseas. State legislatures one after another acted to ban possession and use, imposing stiff prison sentences for violations. By 1971, Sandoz and other pharmaceutical houses discontinued marketing LSD. It faded away entirely, perhaps used sub rosa in a few ashrams here and there, but otherwise out of sight and out of mind. Only recently were there reports that experiments have resumed without fanfare.

Given the pall of silence now about LSD, it is difficult two generations later to believe that a presidency ended in bloodshed due to the leader's sexpionage indulgences culminating in dalliance with an LSD-pushing mistress on a mission to brainwash him and his power structure.

That John F. Kennedy had forfeited trust is given little weight by those who philosophize that Kennedy was a martyr to the cause of ending war and seeking world peace. More to the point is that JFK was so erratic and inconsistent in his conduct of foreign policy and so duplicitous in political statecraft as to justify a reputation as a double crosser whose dynastic pretensions forced the hands of his assassins.

If John F. Kennedy had presided without his kid brother as underboss and if he had avoided sexpionage and adultery with spying honey trappers, he would have made a grand president.

JFK on his own was exceptional. With all the baggage, he was an accident waiting to happen.

THE MARILYN MONROE MESS

In the summer of 1962 one day after blonde bombshell Marilyn Monroe OD'd in Hollywood under strange and suspicious circumstances, President John F. Kennedy consoled himself by trysting in the White House with Mary Meyer.

On that very same day presidential secretary Evelyn Lincoln logged and fended off two incoming calls to the White House from Judith Exner Campbell, a Las Vegas goodtime girl who when not liaisoning sexually with JFK was palling around with Mafia overlord Sam Giancana. Few could forget the voluptuous Miss Monroe's heavy breathing "Happy Birthday Mr. President" performance at the nationally televised birthday tribute only a few months earlier on JFK's 45th birthday.

That shameless exhibition had so burned up JFK's wife Jacqueline that she browbeat her husband into dropping the blonde movie star cold turkey, no ands, ifs or buts. The president had spent one overnight with Ms. Monroe on Saturday, March 24, 1962 at a cottage on the grounds of Bing Crosby's home in Palm Springs. She told her masseur the hasty encounter had been less than satisfactory since the president's chronic back problem had acted up, causing her to telephone the masseur on JFK's behalf from the cottage.

After being read the riot act by his wife, JFK cut off Miss Monroe cold, seeing her just once more to explain and ease the end of what appeared to be little more than a casual flirtation and one-date encounter. It was more than a flirtation to Ms. Monroe, a promiscuous yet choosy thrice-married 36-year old who was turned on by power celebrities and who chose as mates top guns in their fields: first, baseball great Joe DiMaggio and second, prominent playwright Arthur Miller. By all accounts, she was dazzled by the charming John F. Kennedy, who she fancied she might someday add to her string of winners as his bride in the White House.

Initially bent on extricating his older brother from the troublesome swoon of Miss Monroe, Attorney General Robert Kennedy interceded as emissary, clearly developing a crush on the actress. She in turn liked Bobby Kennedy, who danced and did some handholding with her, but she told confidantes she liked him only as a friend and not a lover. Nonetheless, in June prior to her August 5 death, she checked into a facility for a medical procedure said to be a D & C, an intervention used often at that time as a euphemism for abortion.

RFK'S HOUSE SEARCH FOR MISS MONROE'S RED DIARY

The denouement of the spring frolics with the Kennedy brothers came with Miss Monroe being disinvited from a White House reception she had eagerly planned to attend. The cold shoulder caused her to go ballistic. She threatened to hold a press conference to expose her affairs with the Kennedy brothers, leading to panicky efforts by RFK and his brother-in-law, Miss Monroe's Hollywood friend Peter Lawford, to calm her down. During the late afternoon of the day Miss Monroe died, Bobby Kennedy, Lawford, her pill-doctor and two household employees rummaged through her home searching for the diary. He feared the diary contained compromising details that she might reveal if she followed through on her threat to call a press conference two days later to reveal things she knew about the Kennedy brothers.

During West Coast parties at the Lawfords' manor she had been seen studiously jotting notes in her little red book while JFK confided secrets that could be interpreted as breaches of security. Witnesses said Bobby Kennedy used this as a pretext to angrily stomp about, cursing and threatening Miss Monroe.

Bobby Kennedy and Lawford departed within two hours of their arrival, empty handed. The red diary disappeared with Miss

Monroe's death, which was not reported to police until 4 a.m., seven hours after she had expired.

The death was noted by the coroner as "probable suicide," a ruling that the assistant coroner who also signed off said was pressured upon him by his boss. In a perhaps too tardy retraction, he claimed in January 2013 that Miss Monroe was murdered, adding to numerous books alleging the same thing.

Adding spice to the tale was the sordid episode of a boozy and drugged Miss Monroe being gangbanged less than two weeks before her death by Mafia big shots John Roselli, Skinny D'Amato and Sam Giancana, at Frank Sinatra's Cal-Neva Lodge in Lake Tahoe. She had been invited by her good friend Sinatra to the resort to talk over a movie project that Sinatra told her his newly organized production company would put together. As the story goes, Miss Monroe arrived around noon to play bingo, swigging mixed drinks that soon had her woozy and staggering around. She was led inside, where late arriving Sinatra and Peter Lawford were aghast to find the lady crawling around leashed like a pet dog as assembled hound dogs and prostitutes – both male and female – sexually preyed on her and took Polaroid snapshots, nine in all. Giancana, widower boyfriend of Dorothy Maguire of the Maguire Sisters singing group, was helping Monroe to her feet by the time Sinatra and Lawford arrived to scoop up the photos, which were destroyed with one exception. As Sinatra and Lawford tried to sober Miss Monroe by forcing her to drink hot coffee, someone scooped up the undestroyed photo and mailed it to *New York Journal* columnist Dorothy Kilgallen, well known at the time as a panelist on the TV show What's My Line?

Untraumatized by the seedy sexploitation, Miss Monroe in the following week went about her business, apparently none the worse for wear. Dorothy Kilgallen did nothing with the photo of Monroe at the time, gathering information instead. Like almost everyone else, she lacked the muscle to tackle the Warren Commission Report, until the Garrison investigation out of New Orleans started raising new questions. Although three years had elapsed, Kilgallen told close friends she planned to blow the lid off the whole sordid Kennedy/Mafia background of the assassination. She went home from the TV show where as a panelist she had cleverly identified the occupations of three contestants, to die in her sleep while her husband and child sat watching television in the next room. Her blood alcohol level was .13, drunk by today's road sobriety tests, but not so tipsy in the free-drinking mid-sixties.

Her death in 1966 was ruled a heart attack. It left many people wondering, just as the premature death of ABC-TV newscaster Lisa Howard in New York from some kind of supposed pill overdose raised major suspicions in 1963. Howard had been spearheading a homemade campaign to defuse the U.S.-Cuba standoff. She had hosted the Cuban ambassador in her New York apartment together with Ambassador William Attwood, who, as luck would have it, was olive-branching at noon in Havana with Cuban President Fidel Castro on the very day that Kennedy was shot in Dallas.

What shrouds Marilyn Monroe's death in mystery is the fact that her house in Brentwood had been wiretapped by at least two private detectives. Hoping to get incriminating information on the Kennedys, Teamster boss Jimmy Hoffa had hired former Los Angeles police detective Fred Otash to wiretap the house. So had J. Edgar Hoover, who saw Attorney General Robert Kennedy's liaison with Monroe as a national security threat due to her marriage to leftist Miller and her open consorting in Mexico City with a flamboyant and well known Communist from New York City. This made her a national security threat under FBI counter-intelligence guidelines subject to intense scrutiny from 1962. The surveillance included a wiretap of her home.

There was also evidence that Marilyn Monroe herself had installed a wiretap in her own home, presumably to get information on the Kennedys in case she might need it someday.

JFK ARM-WRESTLES KHRUSHCHEV WITH A-BOMB TESTS

Fast-forward two months. We now find JFK at the White House amidst the Cuban Missile Crisis, Oct. 13 to 23, 1962, caused by the Kremlin arming Cuban dictator Fidel Castro with nuclear-tipped ICBMs capable of wiping out 80 million people with the simple push of a button.

It had now dawned on JFK that his administration's public boasting about American nuclear superiority and deliberate initiation of nuclear tests in the Pacific – 40 tests in all – had disturbed a delicate equilibrium known since 1958 as Mutually Assured Destruction (MAD). The tests cast a garish glow that could be seen as far away as Hawaii in photos taken by Life Magazine. Tit for tat, Khrushchev retaliated with thermonuclear tests in remote Siberian wastelands throughout the summer and fall until and during the October missile crisis. Some claimed he had acted first by setting off a huge A-bomb test underground in Siberia, though underground tests were supposedly not easily detected. People were scared to death. The world teetered on the brink of Apocalypse.

Scrambling for solid footing, JFK opened secret communication with Khrushchev, who was coping with a similar catalog of catastrophic options. That a deal was made on the brink of doom was slim solace to a world already in a state of neurotic anxiety over the prospect of fiery explosions, mushroom clouds and nuclear extinction. Such widely read nuclear horror books as Philip Wylie's *The Disappearance* and Neville Shute's *On The Beach*, the latter made into a movie in which Ava Gardner and Gregory Peck wait in Australia as the killer radiation closes in, dramatized the hopelessness of atomic warfare.

Ever since Hiroshima and Nagasaki had been devastated by atom bombs 18 years earlier, World War II had morphed from a debilitating hot war into an insidious Cold War pitting the surviving titans, the United States and the Soviet Union, in a struggle for domination. Border wars erupted in Korea and

Indochina and Berlin, while enduring espionage battles spawned a worldwide spy culture built upon the reality that the Soviet NKVD (later KGB) apparatus had stolen not only atomic but even more dangerous nuclear secrets from missile testing and fabricating facilities in New Mexico, Tennessee, Manhattan, N.Y., Chicago, London, Washington D.C. By 1950, the United States had built and tested hydrogen bombs whose capacity and range dwarfed that of the atom bombs dropped on the two Japanese cities. The H-bomb if dropped on Times Square in NYC would obliterate not only the five boroughs of New York City but northern New Jersey and southern Connecticut as well. By 1951 the USSR had stolen the H-bomb secrets and replicated a 20-megaton bomb that it detonated in Siberia, allowing American scientists to track the seismic tremors.

As president of the United States, Kennedy was forced to cope with the fierce ideological and practical problems the Cold War spawned. He had to balance foreign policy within parameters of a chaotic realpolitik and to deal delicately with the intricate spy culture in which the nation's future had become entwined. He had inherited a nuclear nightmare, complicated by a military-industrial complex in the United States whose power and influence outgoing President Dwight D. Eisenhower had somberly warned against in his swansong speech. Coming from former five-star General Eisenhower, an architect of the victory over Hitler's World War II juggernaut thanks to the men and materiel and sheer ingenuity of that selfsame military-industrial complex, it was like the ace mechanic throwing a monkey wrench into the gearshift.

FBI DIRECTOR HOOVER FEARS ANOTHER "PROFUMO AFFAIR"

Researchers into the JFK assassination have long disregarded the role of the femme fatale in undermining empires.

It was never ignored by J. Edgar Hoover, who in 1963 reigned as the grisse eminence of the finest and one of the most lawful federal police forces the world has ever known. The Federal Bureau of Investigation was Hoover's baby, a bureaucratic creature into which he breathed life from the day in the early 1920s when he assumed command –with assurances it would be above politics – until his conflicted final days and his death in May of 1973.

As the years have gone by and especially since Hoover's death, it has become something of a parlor game to poke fun at the FBI. In Nazi Germany, the national police force called the Gestapo routinely tortured, dispossessed, robbed and killed many of its own citizens, particularly minorities such as homosexuals, gypsies, Jews and foreigners. In the Soviet Union, Hoover's counterpart, Lavrenty Beria, was a serial sexual predator whose goons collared Moscow women off the streets, allowing Beria to rape or failing there murder them.

The half-century span from just before World War I until 1963 was an era of autocrats — bossy leaders who ruled over personal fiefdoms. Hoover fit the mold, even typifying it. A businesslike bureaucrat who was devoted to his moralistic mother until her death around the time he reached age forty, Hoover never married and stayed free of female attachments through the years. He has been portrayed by critics since his death in 1972 as probably a closet gay. The characterization may well be a form of what the late *New York Times* columnist William Safire called "presentism", a word he coined to mean judging the past by inapplicable present day standards. Hoover was not known as gay in his time. His agents regarded him with awe and respect.

Whether for fear of his power as a career buster or not, they did not speak against him. He was a bachelor who buddied around with FBI colleagues, particularly Clyde Tolson, his top aide. They lunched together almost daily at the Mayflower Hotel in Washington. Hoover courted actress Ginger Rogers' mother and, seemingly out of character, enjoyed a brief romance with sultry Latin singer and actress Dorothy Lamour.

When asked whether she and Hoover had been lovers, Lamour replied, "I can't deny it." That aside, he seemed to be too much in love with the FBI and America to spend a lot of time chasing women, with whom he was courtly, deferential and a tad awkward. He liked to gamble and, like most Americans in those days, could think of no better outing than a trip to a racetrack to watch the thoroughbreds run. Almost every summer, he and his chief deputy Clyde Tolson packed up and vacationed in southern California where Texas oilman Clint Murchison hosted them at a hotel he owned near his Del Mar Racetrack. Hoover had met Murchison in the post-war years and Murchison was only too happy to let it be known he was in tight with the FBI director, if for no other reason than to discourage kidnappers and shakedown artists. Two generations of Americans who looked up to Hoover saw or cared little about his bachelor lifestyle.

So interwoven into the fabric of public life was Hoover that he was the first public person the late Ambassador Joseph P. Kennedy thought about the night in November 1960 that late returns pointed to the election as president of his son, John Fitzgerald Kennedy. The family patriarch immediately advised his son to announce that he would keep Hoover as FBI director, and that he would retain Allen Dulles as CIA director, according to Theodore White's Making Of The President 1960. JFK made the announcement the next morning. They were the first acts of his presidency and were regarded by most of the new president's constituents as reassuring.

JFK'S INDISCRETIONS BECOME A MATTER OF STATE

By mid-1963, the president's indiscretions alarmed J. Edgar Hoover.

Across the Atlantic, London was reeling from the Profumo scandal that would, before it was over, take down the Conservative government of Harold MacMillan, mostly because of sensational photos and headlines there and in the United States. Tabloids went wild once it was discovered that John Profumo, British Secretary of State for War, was sharing with a Soviet spy the sexual favors of a goodtime girl named Christine Keeler.

Adding international intrigue, a British MI5 agent while interviewing the not very well informed Miss Keeler stiffened with alarm when she casually tossed off the term "nuclear payload", which he said was a term not in common usage at the time but one which would certainly interest Miss Keeler's Soviet consort, Yevgeny Ivanov, a senior naval attaché at the Soviet embassy in London. It was the height of the Cold War, only a few months after the Cuban Missile crisis between the Soviet Union and the United States that had frazzled everyone's nerves to a raw edge the previous October.

After initially denying the affair in March before the House of Commons and promising to sue for slander, Profumo less than three months later confessed to the affair and resigned his high cabinet post in disgrace.

An official government report on September 25, 1963 excoriating the dangerous liaison set the stage for Prime Minister Harold MacMillan's resignation in October. The Conservatives never recovered and MacMillen's replacement lost the election to Harold Wilson's Labour Party a year later.

Is the Profumo scandal forgotten? Hardly. A new play titled "Stephen Ward" was set to be produced in London in 2013. Ward was the osteopath pimp for Keeler who was so distraught by being put on trial that he hung himself in his jail cell the night before the verdict was to be returned.

LONDON SEX SCANDAL SCARES DC BIGWIGS

Even before satirists such as Peter Sellers and Joan Collins together with Anthony Newly started producing comedy sketches and recordings such as *"Fool Britannia"* that year, official Washington and London were coping with another espionage scandal, the defection of English superspy Kim Philby from his posting at the British Embassy in Washington. Recalled to London, Philby remained in London only long enough to pack his cold weather gear before permanently defecting to the Kremlin, for whom he had been spying since he and his gay mates Guy Burgess and Donald McLean graduated from their young communist cell at Cambridge in the 1930s. The *New York Times* described Philby's treason as the biggest case of double agentry in the history of espionage. It all seemed to be a weird taint on spy craft, since CIA superspy James Jesus Angleton, chief of counterintelligence, had lunched with Philby in Washington D.C.'s toney Georgetown section seemingly every Monday, gurgling martinis and swapping sea stories despite warnings by Angleton's colleague Bill Harvey that Philby was "nothing but a fucking Commie spy".

CIA and EL INDIO

EL INDIO'S REVENGE

"So it was in him, then – an inherited fighting instinct, a driving intensity to kill." – Zane Grey, *Lone Star Ranger*

The best snipers didn't fuss around. Dressed in wrinkled khaki pants and a T-shirt, padding lightly in gym shoes, he wore a lightweight jacket with plenty of pockets jammed with cartridge clips, a Swiss knife, a pack of Luckies, some gumdrops and a two-way miniature radio. The hiking pack slung over a shoulder was big and bulky enough to conceal his rifle.

Assigned to the boxed-in Sixth Floor window by the boss, Dave Morales, the sniper would have preferred using a Garand M-1 for range and accuracy, but the rifle that won World War II and Korea was too long to hide.

A lot of people in Dealey Plaza in Dallas, Texas that Friday in 1963 saw the three men pull up next to the old brick Texas School Book Depository building in their light blue Rambler station wagon. No one paid them the slightest attention. The crowds jockeyed around for position on the sidewalks near the corner of Houston and Elm Streets waiting for the presidential motorcade that would slow to a crawl right at this corner to make more than a right angle cutback into Elm Street. It was lunchtime. People camped out on the park lawns and grassy knoll, carrying cameras, shading their eyes, adjusting their sunglasses. Women preened and gawked, thrilled at the prospect of seeing the Kennedys who, politics aside, certainly were a nice looking couple. JFK was launching his reelection campaign. The atmosphere was festive as a bright holiday.

The sniper and his crew ambled casually through the back entrance. They climbed interior warehouse stairs as far as the sixth level, where reconnaissance had found there would be no one around at noon hour and probably no one there period. The entire floor was used only to store crates of books. It was devoid of activity except for a few hours a week when a couple of guys lazily did some tile flooring replacement.

At one end of the book storage warehouse was an open window. The leader craned a look and would later be described by a few people who had noticed him looking out from the window as a dark-complexioned, swarthy-looking man with dark hair wearing sunglasses. No, not a Negro, but dark skinned, like a Mexican or Latin type. A big man, sort of hefty.

They would be right. David Sanchez Morales, 37, a native of Arizona of Mexican and Yaqui Indian blood nicknamed El Indio, was supervising the Dealey Plaza posse of the Big Event. A crack shot himself, El Indio had foresworn his desire to be a shooter himself in favor of watching over the ambush. He'd put the pieces in place before returning to street level to position himself behind the crowd near the critical corner of Houston Street turning into Elm Street. He watched the assassination from there before rejoining his team to hop in the Rambler and depart through back streets.

Where did Morales gain entry into the national government? He had been raised as a virtual foster son of friends. He grew strong and silent, respected by all, elected his high school president. He loved justice, living by a code of courage and fair play. He could handle his fists, a classmate recalling how he had collared and tossed around three bullies who were picking on a smaller kid.

Growing up, El Indio was a cowboy, a horseman, a farmer and a macho drinker who hated to see a day go by without tossing down a few tequilas, Cuba Libres, Mexican beers or straight whiskeys. He thrived on chili, jalapeno peppers and rare sirloin steak. His idea of Paradise was to own a farm where he would grow chickpeas. He could bareback ride a barely trained stallion and liked to ride like the wind in the painted hills around Tucson. He had left Arizona State in Tempe and Southern California University in 1946 to enlist as World War II vets came tramping home, falling all over themselves to get out of the military.

Not so with El Indio, as he was known at Fort Bragg, North Carolina, home of the storied 82nd Airborne All American Division, and later in "The Company", the Central Intelligence Agency (CIA). The paratroopers were known for their famed jump cry, "Geronimo", named after the fabled Apache Indian chief.

El Indio was a Gung Ho warrior in an American frontier war tradition that was to span a generation stretching from Korea to Vietnam and beyond, built on heroic World War II tales from Normandy and Sicily to the South Pacific and Burma. Less visible were the almost unnoticed and silent Latin American struggles to rid the hemisphere of Soviet and Communist influence, the Monroe doctrine of the 20th Century. In 1947 Morales shipped to Germany with the occupation army where he was recruited into the Army C.I.C. (Counter Intelligence Corps). He was doubled to the payroll of the CIA in 1951 by two rough-and-tumble career agents who headed the pivotal West Berlin Station, William King Harvey of Chicago and his backup, Ted Shackley Jr.

Morales had become an Army Intelligence operative well before the CIA was much more than a gleam in the eye of Allen Dulles. The big Mexican had been recruited into Army Intelligence based on his fluency in Spanish and Indian tongues, his courage, his crafty ways and his physical superiority. While Army intelligence had held the fort for a generation, the newcomer CIA's ace in the hole was money. Its rainmakers in Washington D.C. knew how to line up massive legislative funding.

There were post-war geopolitical miscalculations, which in hindsight could be seen to mushroom into incredible blunders, Indochina being foremost. Here in 1945 a rebel in a conical hat who had led guerillas alongside allied armies to defeat the Japanese occupation joined in a festive celebration with bands playing to commemorate their joint victory.

U.S. Army Col. Philip Gallagher embraced and mutually saluted the Vietnamese liberation insurgency leader, Ho Chi Minh, who had sent a joyous telegram to U.S. President Harry S. Truman expecting protocols leading toward Vietnamese independence. Truman did not often make mistakes, but he did in handling this one. Perhaps as mere oversight or perhaps in deference to the lingering colonialist plans of French allies, Truman did not respond to Uncle Ho's telegram. The rest is history.

Gallagher, mystified by Washington's insensitivity to geopolitical reality and the sweep of emerging nationhood, returned to the United States where he would by the 1950s become Brig. General Gallagher, commander of the U.S. Army Counter Intelligence Corps Worldwide, the Pentagon's G-2, in charge of coping with Ho Chi Minh's emerging latest-in-a-lifetime of Indochinese insurrections.

Over General Gallagher's desk at the CIC Center in Baltimore was an engraved sign which read, "If you work for a man speak well of him, or the first big wind that comes along may blow you away, and probably you will never even know why."

Loyalty was a virtue to which David "El Indio" subscribed. Up to a point.

COLD WAR REHEATS IN KOREA

The increasingly frigid Cold War was defined by what former British prime minister Winston Churchill would describe in a Missouri speech as The Iron Curtain, a term referring to the split between East and West Europe. The title would catch on and define reality until collapse of the Soviet empire 45 years later. In the immediate postwar years, OSS Ivy Leaguers and old World War II Burma hands would stanch the bleeding in the Philippines and salvage the lower half of the Indochina peninsula called South Vietnam due mainly to the inspired leadership of psych warfare expert Col. Edward G. Lansdale. Lansdale had left an advertising job in Detroit to enter the newly independent U.S. Air Force after its 1947 split-off from its former status as a branch of the Army. Lansdale would swiftly be commissioned a major, soar higher to wear the wings of a colonel and in almost no time don the star of brigadier general, a fake intelligence rank that he never actually achieved. Five years after the glories of VE Day in Europe and VJ Day in Asia, United Nations forces led by a new generation of U.S. Army draftees would be forced to repel an invasion by North Korea, rebound from a sub-peninsular trap called the Pusan perimeter and recapture the mid-peninsula capital city of Seoul. From there it would seem to be a victory lap as a formidable U.S. Marine division advanced from the historic dividing line at the 38th Parallel northward to Manchuria itself, at the Chinese border. It would mean extinguishing quarrelsome North Korea entirely, which most countries in the United Nations regarded as fit punishment for North Korea's naked aggression against a sister state.

With the war seemingly won inside of a year, advance Marine units were surprised and overrun when tens of thousands of Chinese troops unexpectedly entered the war to swarm across the frozen Chosen Reservoir. They surprised, outnumbered and routed the Marines, forcing the toughest retreat in a proud U.S. Marine Corps history which had burnished its glory so recently in the WWII campaign built around such missions as Guadalcanal, Tarawa, Okinawa – names burned into the American consciousness alongside Valley Forge, the Alamo, the Marne.

Repulsing North Korea was one thing, war with massive and menacing China a horse of a different color. Suddenly there loomed the dark prospect of many more years of war against an enemy whose leaders dispatched its soldiers like so many ants to swarm over an enemy, regardless how many of them had to die. In the closing months of the Okinawa campaign and on American aircraft carriers in the Pacific, American soldiers, sailors and marines had tasted and feared a repetition of the kamikaze suicide attacks by Japanese foes that swelled the numbers of combatants killed and wounded. Hundreds of thousands had been killed and wounded in vain merely to preserve the tarnished honor of an aged emperor.

The Americans had won, but only at a cost that no soldiers or sailors should be forced to pay, on either side, simply to enshrine leaders in bloodstained glory.

General Douglas MacArthur had once again overplayed his hand, as he had at Corregidor in the Philippine Islands at the outset of World War II. He had described the island bastion as impregnable. When it fell a few weeks later, he made the grandiose prediction, "I shall return." He did indeed a few years later, but by that time his soldiers had suffered the terrible Bataan Death March.

Now in Korea, either MacArthur's negligent Air Force and Army intelligence or uncharacteristic carelessness had caused an inexcusable letdown. Still aglow from his successful backdoor amphibian landing at Inchon only weeks earlier, MacArthur was caught completely off guard by the Chinese entry into the war. He now had F-86 Saberjets capable for the first time of outflying dominant Soviet Migs once American pilots learned to masterfully fly them. His Inchon landing had recaptured Seoul. Crack U.S. Marines under his theater command were swarming toward the Manchurian border. The tide of a war begun by North Korean aggression in June had been decisively turned by the United States and United Nations in a few short months, and would be over by Christmas.

Could MacArthur not have sensed a problem with the massive Chinese buildup of troops at the border? Even if he regarded Chinese invasion as unthinkable, would not ordinary caution have been militarily prudent? Why would he underrate the wily and resourceful Mao who had made a living outwitting stronger armies?

Caught off guard and beset by retreating Marines, MacArthur called for air power and blunt reprisal. He proposed dropping atom bombs on Manchurian emplacements and troop concentrations north of the Yalu River. It was a possible tactical resource but a strategic excess that the United Nations had opted to avoid at all costs, a paralyzing factor that Mao with his chess master insight probably had foreseen. Wars were not always won on the battlefield, Mao had long since learned from Sun Yat Sen's centuries old primer on the art of war. MacArthur, a former commandant at West Point and professor at the Army War College, could strategize with the best of them but years of serving as acting emperor of post-war Japan had taken its toll in hubris.

     Fed up with MacArthur's single-minded obsession with determining American policy from his Far Eastern war room, President Harry Truman had recalled MacArthur and replaced him with no-nonsense Gen. Matthew Ridgway, whose troops would outmuscle and outfox Mao's armies over the next two years until General Dwight Eisenhower took over as president. No one may ever know by what combination of backdoor maneuvering or veiled back-channel threats Ike intimidated the Chinese warlords, but within five months of entering the White House he had engineered a welcome ceasefire. Character, stature and calm intelligence in a leader fortified by still another American army of underpaid and under-appreciated draftees had ended the Korean War. Americans would in the future disregard only at their own peril that so soon after World War II's 1,078,245 casualties including 405,399 dead, Korea had killed off another 36,516 American soldiers and left 92,134 more wounded, many never to walk again on their own two feet.

CIA IS LATEST BIG KID ON THE BLOCK

Until its celebrated psych warfare coup in Guatemala in 1954 to fend off what it described as preventing a Communist foothold in Latin America, the CIA was a phantom among firmly established American Intelligence circles such as the Army CIC, the Navy ONI, the Air Force OSI, the Civil Service Commission, the FBI's Division Five, the Atomic Energy Commission (AEC), the National Security Agency (NSA) and other agencies primarily concerned with collecting intelligence on American shores. Those services fielded highly trained agents who day in and day out conducted field investigations before granting top-secret security clearances for jobs in sensitive government, atomic energy, Pentagon, military, language and technical facilities. The networks sought to identify threats to the nation and to prevent espionage, sabotage and infiltration by spies and hostile foreign powers.

The U.S. Army Counter Intelligence Corps (CIC), which until 1947 encompassed the Air Corps as well as the Army, was firmly entrenched as the largest, best established and most comprehensive of all the agencies worldwide. Its Far East intelligence network run by General MacArthur's G-2, General Charles Willoughby, was considered to be one of the world's best. It meshed well with a South Korean CIC that specialized during the Korean War in tactical intelligence, mainly interrogating line crossers and weeding out spies, a function increasingly replicated in West Europe especially in such four-power occupied cities as Berlin and Trieste. The far less widespread ONI, covering the Navy and Marine Corps, boasted advanced technical reconnaissance. It had far fewer field agents than the Army, which in fact trained some of them, including Marines, as inter-agency enrollees at the top secret U.S. Army CIC agents and administrators school then located at Fort Holabird, Maryland. The school has long since relocated to the southwest, replaced by a rinky dink industrial park.

The nationwide investigative apparatus into the 1960s, before granting an individual secret clearance, crosschecked between agencies to screen for information that might bear on an applicant. Called a National Agency Check, it involved, for example, an applicant for a routine civilian job at a defense industry being screened through a network of agency files such as the CSC, the ONI, and the FBI. Around 1953 a new agency surfaced on the checklist. It was designated as CIA which inquiry revealed to be an acronym for Central Intelligence Agency. Intelligence veterans found the listing amusing because the CIA inquiries without exception came back marked negative.

FBI'S HOOVER SEES EARLY CIA AS "WIERDOS"

There was an old OSS Yugoslavia hand, a legend in the emerging CIA named Frank Wisner, who was a father figure for many younger CIA men. FBI Director J. Edgar Hoover had a sarcastic pet name for CIA spies. Privately, he called them "Wisner's Wierdos".

Tensions between the FBI and CIA mushroomed over the years as the CIA beefed up its ranks by hiring a fairly large number of ex-FBI agents. Often among those seeking more adventure or better career opportunity were malcontents or castoffs. One of them was a roustabout who became an agency legend, William King Harvey. While serving as SAC (Special Agent in Charge) at the Chicago Field Office in his seventh year in the FBI, hard-drinking Harvey, then 32, crashed his car in 1947 into a ditch where he was found dead drunk. He was banished to the Indianapolis Field Office but refused to go, jumping ship to the CIA instead.

It did not sweeten the atmosphere between Hoover and the CIA when "Two Gun Bill Harvey" proved to be so good at his trade that he soared to the upper echelon of the CIA covert service including the then secret assignment of trying to assassinate Cuban President Fidel Castro.

What no one was saying as the CIA muscled ahead in the early '50s was that the CIA was just getting started. You had to be a Washington D.C. insider to know that the agency's clout was making a giant leap forward propelled mainly by funding put in the pipeline by old OSS veteran Allen Dulles and OSS flag-bearer Wild Bill Donovan, a New York City lawyer. New CIA Director Allen Dulles was the brother of President Eisenhower's secretary of state, John Foster Dulles. He, too, had been a New York City lawyer in civilian life. The brothers together with President Eisenhower formed a team that would dominate American foreign policy for eight years until JFK took over the White House early in 1961.

Over the years, the new Washington-based CIA bureaucracy had spun a web of spidery elusive gangs whose careerist case officers ran unrelated projects, paying off army and military pros and hiring contract agents by time and money. The contract hires could and did run into the low thousands, depending on the mission. For example a case officer could visit Fort Bragg, NC and outright hire a talented paratrooper, allow him to keep his Army stripes, clear it with the brass and double the soldier's monthly pay working him under CIA cover. One of the agency's most effective field operators, David Sanchez Morales, a career hit man in Latin America, held 82nd Airborne rank as a sergeant first class that he still continued to retain even after he retired on the pay of a one-star general. His Arizona gravestone ID, marked after his death of a supposed heart attack at age 53 in 1978, carries the etching Army SFC, Korea War. At Langley, he had a preferred parking space listed as brigadier general, CIA.

Contract employees worked as temps, signed up for six months or a year at specified pay for a set job or mission. Career case officers, the project bosses, were given the job of figuring out how much contract agents should get, which was a lot more than they could make bartending, digging ditches or shuffling paperwork in civilian life.

Case officers were sometimes compared to circus masters who coordinate their dogs' tricks. They report to higher authority such as head of the western hemisphere, head of the Far East desk, and assistant deputy director for plans. The unwieldy last named was the chief of the covert spy service.

FEASTING IN A BANANA REPUBLIC

The agency's stature grew overnight after it turned the tables in Guatemala. The Company, as it was already being called, swung into action a year after the Korean War had ended. The newly elected president, Jacobo Arbenz, had seized massive acreage from hacendatos, or large landholders, and redistributed the land to approximately 100,000 farmers, proposing payment of less than twenty cents on the dollar of ownership's appraised values. Included were vast land holdings of New York based United Fruit whose imports filled popular United States open air markets with bananas and lush Central American fruit. Agricultural reform was seen then as vanguard of Communist expansion. When the taking edicts issued in April, 1954 were followed by a shipment of arms from Soviet-bloc Czechoslovakia in May, red flags went up in Washington and especially at the CIA then scattered in pre-Langley walkups around the nation's capitol. It would for the first time seriously test the still emerging successor to the World War II Office of Strategic Services (OSS).

When case officer David Atlee Philips asked Washington desk man Tracy Barnes whether it was right to go after the duly elected president, Philips recalled, Barnes convinced him by emphasizing that the Communists could not be allowed to gain a foothold in Central America.

The company recruited and paid a fortune to a mercenary army in nearby Nicaragua, airlifted 100,000 leaflets with threats to bomb the capital, warned of a Communist takeover and set up a Radio Free Guatemala which among other things aired fake newscasts telling of fictional armed military columns advancing on the main city. The mounting threats pressured Arbenz to resign his office for fear of a revolutionary coup that might leave him dead or in chains. It was a turning point that launched the long and violent career of David El Indio Morales and burnished the career of the imaginative writer from Hamburg, NY, E. Howard Hunt, Mexico City station chief. The Guatemala campaign spawned a mythology within the agency, a cult of belief in invincibility. The victorious participants would fight over the next decade and beyond to keep Latin America free from what it considered Communists and dangerous leftists until Castro, fending off assassination attempts and invasions, finally outlasted his foes in Langley and in the White House.

El Indio had found a home in the Army. A Sergeant First Class, Airborne, U.S. Army on paper, he was doubled to the CIA, one of their best since the Guatemala campaign. David Morales was a linguist, a loner, a patriot and a killer. His CIA pay more than doubled his miserable salary as an Army sergeant. He soon became the agency's foremost Black Ops agent in Latin America, assigned to the hush-hush Executive Action project, operating under State Department cover from the U.S. Embassy in Caracas, Venezuela from 1955 through 1958.

Big, brusque and menacing, El Indio was never one to shrink from danger.

"I do it myself," he would say. He'd stalk off and next thing, it would be done.

He had gone into Havana with Batista's security in 1958 just before the regime collapsed like a marshmallow. Morales could scarcely believe that Batista's blowhards turned it all over to blowhard Fidel, the phony medico caudillo. He would like to strangle Castro with his bare hands, and at 6'3" with furious power, colleagues would bet he could manhandle the athletic Castro who fancied himself a great baseball pitcher. The State Department's Wayne Smith recalls an occasion in a Havana bar in 1960 when Morales became very indiscreet after heavy drinking. He rambled about frogmen operating secretly from Guantanamo Bay.

"He was a roughneck," CIA Agent Robert N. Wall told HSCA investigator Gaetano Fonzi in 1978, after Morales' death from a heart condition at age 53, three years after his so-called retirement. "He was a bully, a hard drinker and big enough to get away with a lot of stuff other people couldn't get away with."

Known throughout the agency as the CIA's top assassin in Latin America, Morales was annoyed when the Company kept calling him back to Washington for one reason or another, until he died from a heart attack in D.C. in 1978 while the HSCA was probing the CIA'S Executive Action history. El Indio had confided to friends that he was installing the best security system in the world at his Arizona ranch. When asked why since the banditos from the Mexican border were a safe distance away, Morales told his friend, "It's not the bandits I'm worried about, it's my own people." His funeral in Arizona was one of the best attended in agency history, including some mourners who knew that if you lived by the sword you might die by the sword just as well.

From CIA perspective, Morales was among its most effective agents ever. From diplomatic cover in Venezuela he would help overthrow the government in Chile. He would take part in overthrowing the Arbenz regime in Guatemala. He would fight the Stasi in Berlin, work the Phoenix program with Meo tribesmen in the Central Highlands of Indochina and hunt down and see to the execution of Che Guevara in the jungles of Colombia. He was not the type to sit idly by while JFK tried to make good his promise to shred the CIA into a thousand pieces.

The barefoot Mexican-Indian boy from the old southwest had one perk that only the sons of cattle rustlers and big ranchers could match. The company had issued him a small black "magic card" which friends said opened doors everywhere and provided seeming endless credit. They did not describe it as a credit card, such as the elitist big-spender cards American Express had begun to merchandise in the early 1960s, but it took him everywhere and allowed him to spend whatever he needed.

El Indio's personally selected expert rifleman knelt behind the Sixth Floor crates waiting. Standing behind the crowd at the foot of the Dal-Tex building, a few folks away from fellow plotter John Roselli, Morales peered through narrow black sunglasses at the passing motorcade with stony satisfaction. What El Indio remembered most was that President Kennedy had double-crossed Brigade 2506, men with whom Morales had broken bread and whom he had trained month after month. The paralysis at the White House precisely when a few waiting nearby jets could have turned the tide had left many of El Indio's friends to flounder and die at the Bay of Pigs in Cuba. More than 1100 commandos were forced to rot in Cuba's prisons before they were finally ransomed out.

Six stories above in the improvised sniper's nest, El Indio's sniper drew in and exhaled a breath, aimed, softly squeezed and fired a bullet that hit the president almost simultaneously with an even more lethal exploding bullet fired from behind a fenced rise to the right front of the convoy, later known as the grassy knoll shot. The two shots were fired split seconds after the first muted bark of a gunshot from the Dal-Tex Building which had hit the president in the upper back, causing him to stiffen and lurch upward. It was fired by Chicago hit man Chuck Nicoletti. That first shot was muffled, sounding like a firecracker or auto backfire. It caused the president to grasp with two hands toward his throat. The sound sequence was "bang... bang bang". There were several other shots – some counted six in all — one of which missed the target and wounded Texas Governor John Connelly who was seated in a jump seat right in front of President Kennedy.

Besides the shots fired in Dealey Plaza, other rifle tag teams waited to act if needed at the Trade Mart where JFK was to speak and at Love Field, the Dallas airport from which he was to fly back to Washington D.C. The Chicago Outfit's hit men and the Operation 40 guerrillas and Cuban exiles from Gator Ridge in the Florida everglades handled the plaza stakeout, while teams of Corsicans, cowboys and redneck killers had taken up perches along the freeway and at other vantage points in case they were needed for what had been code named The Big Event.

Morales had been among the handful of ringleaders in the Miami hotel room when Frank Sturgis got E. Howard " Eduardo" Hunt on board together with the main cog, "Two Gun" Bill Harvey. Harvey was infuriated at being dumped and exiled to Rome by Bobby Kennedy. Harvey had been Morales' 'big brother' in West Germany, the man who recruited and brought him along. Not only need the Kennedys be stopped, it was payback.

The Miami crew had driven from Orlando Bosch's safe house in the Florida Keys to Dallas in a convoy carrying rifles and ammo. Bosch was getting even with the Kennedys. After the assassination in the Dominican Republic of 30-year strongman Raphael Trujillo in 1961 while JFK and his wife were in Paris, Bosch had campaigned on a reform ticket and legitimately won election as president. With a nod from the Kennedy White House and CIA, he was then within less than a year thrown to the wolves in another coup sanctioned by the Kennedys because the military caudillos did not like it that Bosch was cutting their overtime and curtailing the influence of the police and the military.

MARITA BUGS OUT, TELLS ALL

Sturgis had brought his favorite contract agent Marita Lorenz along but she had gotten chicken and bugged out, hopping a flight back to Florida en route to New York City.

In years to come, both Sturgis and Morales would privately confirm their participation in the Big Event. So did E. Howard "Eduardo" Hunt. All three were part of the Miami contingent, referred to in unattributed press references as "part of a rogue CIA element". The presidential hit was not an authorized CIA mission. On the other hand, almost nothing ever was so who could tell.

"You should have been there," Sturgis would tell Marita Lorenz once he caught up with her in New York. Then a young blonde, Lorenz had been romanced as a 19-year old daughter of a German cruise ship captain in Havana harbor by Cuban rebel leader Fidel Castro in 1959, before having an unwanted abortion. Speaking of JFK and warning her to clam up if she valued her life, Cuban soldier-of-fortune Sturgis waxed nostalgic:

"That was the day we killed the president," future Watergate plumber Frank Sturgis told Lorenz, the woman swore under oath.

Morales did not talk about his role as a rifleman, unless he was deep in recollection and drinking heavily.

Years later in Arizona, after a long night of very heavy drinking at his home with his lifelong boyhood friend Ruben Carbajal and a trusted business partner, Bob Walton, Morales flew into a rage when Walton reminisced about having worked as a volunteer for JFK during an early political campaign in Massachusetts. Morales stomped around the room, cursing the Kennedys while recalling the men lost at the Bay of Pigs because they were, as Morales described it, betrayed by the president. Then he abruptly cut off the tirade, calming down before muttering:

"Well we took care of that sonofabitch in Dallas, didn't we?" HSCI investigator Gaetano Fonzi affirmed that both Walton and Carbajal agreed Morales had confessed his complicity in that manner.

After the shooting of JFK on November 22, Morales' sniper had staged a deception intended to suggest that the crime was the work of a religious fanatic. Morales had left a religious leaflet that suggested 'Jesus Saves.'

There was a big bounty of $10,000.000, a kitty to be split among the four hit teams, $2,000,000 each to cover expenses, hiring of mercenaries, payoffs to managers and fixers. Lawyer Bob Walton said Morales had come into a big chunk of the fund and had told him to quietly buy up real estate in the southwest. The ten million number was referred to as well by a member of the Texas law firm who claimed the firm's senior partner had divided up $2,000,000 to the posse put together by Texas oil multi-millionaires H.L. Hunt and Clint Murchison. Sunbelt Mafia leaders Santo Trafficante and Carlos Marcello had offered bounties. Sam Giancana kicked in. According to an ex-Marine associated with the Miami gang, Madame Nhu contributed a healthy sum through her Rome connections with the Corsican brotherhood. The full fundraising story of greased wheels remains fragmentary and unknown, since no one would go around saying, "I hired riflemen to gun down the president."

CHICAGO HIT SQUAD

When Alabaman James E. Files confessed that he and the Chicago mob had shot President Kennedy in Dallas, Files had to straighten out the questioner as to who was really in charge of the Chicago Outfit.

No, it was not Sam Giancana or Files' boss, hit man Charles "Chuck" Nicoletti. It was Tony Accardo, nicknamed "Joe Batters," even though Accardo had ostensibly removed himself from the front lines of The Outfit. He preferred to take the title of consigliere while leaving day-to-day operations to nominal boss Joey "Doves" Aiuppa, supported by gambling czar Sam Momo Giancana and ace hit man Nicoletti. It was compartmentalized, Files explained. Giancana had been the best known not only because he was dating attractive songbird Phyllis McGuire, but even more so because he was running two casinos in Europe and building a palatial new night club in suburban Illinois. Ever since he had been identified but not rounded up by New York state troopers at the national underworld convention held in upstate Apalachin, NY on November 14, 1957, Giancana by 1958 had become the number one target of FBI Director J. Edgar Hoover's newly formed "Top Hoodlum Program", a historical fact which refutes the canard that Hoover always pretended the Mafia did not exist. With the publicity splash from Apalachin, Hoover put aside his traditional reluctance to use wiretaps by authorizing his Chicago FBI office to install three wiretaps at Giancana's three favorite offices and hangouts in Chicago, according to FBI Agent Bill Roemer.

NEW YORK TROOPERS BARE NATIONAL CRIME SYNDICATE

This immediately followed nationally publicized disclosures that Joseph Barbara, a lieutenant of Buffalo Mafia boss Stefano Maggadino, had hosted a huge autumn shindig at his rustic spread in upstate Apalachin, New York attended by 116 crime bosses from across the country, 60 of them blood relatives, to settle the overlord struggle mounted by Vito Genovese against his old compari Frank (Castiglione} Costello, boss of the popular moneymaking Broadway Mob.

Two New York State Troopers who had gotten wind of the meeting interrupted the conclave. They later said they were curious as to why so many big black luxury cars bearing license plates from Illinois, Michigan, New Jersey, Rhode Island, Florida and other "foreign" states were assembled there, but in fact Troopers Edgar Croswell and Vincent Vasisko had overheard Barbara's son making a hotel reservation. Aware of Barbara's standing in the mob and having ticketed New York City Gambino underboss Carmine "Lilo" Galante a few weeks earlier, Croswell halted an exiting car before waving him on. In the next car came Vito Genovese, recognized that afternoon as head of the largest mafia family, making him chairman of the Commission, or what the press and organized crime investigators liked to erroneously call the "capo di tutti capi" (boss of bosses). This time State Trooper Croswell detained the car and attempted to question Genovese. Genovese stonewalled him, asserting that he didn't have to answer any questions. By then, a line of cars had formed due to the expectation by the departing guests that they would be allowed to drive off as the first car had done. A panic erupted, persuading many of the men who remained in the house to flee into the woods. Among those who escaped arrest was Sam Giancana of Chicago. At least half of the Apalachin delegates were identified and immediately released, since attending a barbecue is not a recognizable crime. Frank Costello was not an Apalachin guest.

Costello, a comparatively modern godfather known as "the prime minister", and the prickly Genovese, had been underbosses during the 1930s for Syndicate founder Charles "Lucky" Luciano. Luciano was sent to Sing Sing prison in 1936 on a white slavery rap until he won release and deportation to his native Italy in 1946 for using his influence to help Naval Intelligence secure the New York City docks against sabotage. That left a vacuum to be filled by Costello and Genovese. Genovese in 1949 was convicted of smuggling heroin and did an eight-year stretch in Atlanta Federal Penitentiary during which the major New York crime family under Frank Costello reigned rich, fat and happy, with violence held to a minimum. The release of Genovese from prison changed everything.

The sensational 1957 Apalachin revelations of a federated national Mafia crime network came as almost as much of a surprise to Hoover as it did to the rest of the nation. The "Mafia", then a widely unused term, had been thought of as an old country bunch that ran rackets in their own neighborhoods, even though the Mafia had always been a presence along the Hudson River piers.

Leading the syndicate's heyday during and after World War II until the late 1950s, Costello would breakfast daily at his personal booth in the Waldorf Astoria Hotel in New York City, hobnobbing with celebrities, judges and politicians as well as his two top lieutenants, Willie (Moore) Moretti and Joey (Adonis) Doto, both suburban Jerseyites transplanted from Brooklyn, N.Y. Costello was so little identified with the Mafia that half the truckmen and everyday people in New York City thought he was Irish. Returning from a long stretch at the federal pen in Atlanta, where he antagonized Joseph (Cosa Nostra) Valachi, Genovese hired a young ex-pug named Vincent Gigante to kill Costello in his hotel lobby. Costello survived a glancing bullet shot and, after pretending at Gigante's trial that he had not recognized the shooter, retired to his comfortable estate on Long Island to live out his days in peace. Meanwhile, a Genovese hood murdered Costello ally Albert Anastasia, an underboss in control of a Brooklyn clique of mainly Jewish gangsters led by Louis Lepke Buchalter called Murder Inc. The hit was made in a barber chair at the fashionable Park Sheraton Hotel in New York City.

It is a fallacy of conventional wisdom that Hoover ignored the Mafia. We hear this often from Kennedy partisans who wish to dramatize the late Attorney General Robert Kennedy's indisputable initiatives in seeking prosecution of major underworld criminals, particularly Mafioso. Federal statutes at the time did not provide the legal arsenal that is available today to mount federal prosecutions for murder and extortion. They were local crimes, beyond the jurisdiction of federal agencies until the conspiracy statutes were tightened. The widespread wiretaps of organized crime figures during the 1960s that supplied volumes of information were more significant as intelligence rather than prosecutable crime. While pressing hard for more and more wiretaps, Attorney General Robert Kennedy, in an informal aside to an aide, once remarked, "All illegal". Not until enactment of the federal Racketeering Influenced and Corrupt Organizations (RICO) Act in 1970 was added to Title 18 did federal agencies have a weapon to use against organized crime, and that weapon was not a gun but a cannon the civil liberties aspect of which is still being chewed over by lawyers and judges.

BOB KENNEDY PLAYS SUPERCOP

Robert Kennedy, age 35, who had never tried a case in court, had a personality clash and generational gap with J. Edgar Hoover, the 66-year old founder of the FBI. To develop some familiarity with his new job, Kennedy had gone to New York City to learn the ropes from the weakly staffed Federal Bureau of Narcotics and from the New York City Police Department's Intelligence Bureau. The

NYPD Intelligence Bureau at the time was the best American Mafia tracking organization in the world. Run by Irish city cops, it had direct and fresh information on members of the five New York Mafia family members. The detectives could tell you where the mobsters ate lunch, with whom and where they were cheating on their wives, who they hung out with and where they made racket stops and why. The cops followed the mob guys around all day and sometimes at night. Bobby Kennedy loved mixing with the big city pros. He soon acquired a cop mentality, getting a kick out of riding shotgun. He quickly amassed a Justice Department staff of loyal and able lawyers who even if they might lack evidence to go to trial could at least question people and go before grand juries to get indictments. Attempting to circumvent Hoover by using the IRS and narcs for investigations, Kennedy soon found out why the FBI played such a big part in American law enforcement. Gathering evidence was the name of the game, and only disciplined FBI agents who could take depositions, line up witnesses and analyze evidence, knew how to play. The agents in those days were college grads; recruits in the mid-fifties had to be lawyers or advanced accountants or they were not hired. The agents operated out of Hoover's 800 field offices, methodically collecting information, transferring leads from city to city, making the rounds of schools, police stations, and personnel offices. They fanned through neighborhoods picking up information which folks generally were pleased to share. The goal was to spot national security hazards, to find fugitives, to make cases that would stand up in court.

Contrary to public opinion, the life of an FBI agent was neither dangerous nor glamorous; it was mostly hard work.

Hoover had been building his army for 37 years, fashioning it to cope with threats to the nation from anarchists, terrorists, Nazis, Ku Klux Klanners, Communists, white slavers and kidnappers. Murderers, loan sharks and bookies were not subject to federal jurisdiction and were left to state, county and local police and to sheriffs.

BUGGING THE UNDERWORLD

Unable to crash through Hoover's bureaucratic wall or to get use of FBI agents in the network except through the FBI boss, Bobby Kennedy tried alternate agencies such as the Federal Bureau of Narcotics, the US Postal Service, the US Labor Department, the Alcohol, Tobacco and Firearms (ATF) Division of the Treasury Department and the Internal Revenue Service (IRS). None of them had the muscle of the FBI so Bobby Kennedy again put pressure on J. Edgar Hoover to go after the Mafia kingpins, chafing and mumbling about pushing Hoover out of office once JFK would win a second term.

Hoover swung into action with a vengeance.

His agents soon had planted electronic eavesdropping devices known as "bugs" in the plumbing supply office of "Sam the Plumber" DeCavalcante in Kenilworth, N.J. FBI eavesdroppers learned details of an immense upheaval among the five big New York families through overheard conversations between DeCavalcante and his close friend Joseph Ziccarelli aka Joe Bayonne. The "Commission" wanted to talk to Sicilian godfather Joe Bonanno. Bonanno wouldn't go despite the mandatory summons since he didn't have that much respect for the "Commission". With things at loggerheads and pressure building, Bonanno arranged to disappear.

The DeCavalcante Tapes involved hundreds of hours of work by stenos and typists and FBI agents who needed to patiently review and transcribe the wireless recordings, which were taped from electronic transmissions. The electronic "bugs" were planted by "blackbag" agents who make illegal surreptitious entry. The devices were usually hidden in light and wall fixtures or in plants.

Besides tons of eavesdrops from the Chicago Outfit and Giancana, the FBI is estimated to have deployed nearly 800 "bugs" in the years 1961–64. Some were quickly detected and thrown away. Others produced nothing worth transcribing or didn't work. Hundreds were laboriously transcribed into thick, green-paper covered volumes a great many of which, at the behest of defense attorneys demanding Brady discovery material, were thrown into the courthouse hoppers of US District Court clerks across the nation. Given access to protected public information, newspaper reporters dug out the juiciest passages and splashed stories that did something the Justice Department alone could not do. The newspapers destroyed the syndicate.

From 1958 on, FBI Agent Bill Roemer's job was to bug Giancana, including such close surveillance as bumping into him by accident on purpose. The burly former Notre Dame agent's wiretappers heard a lot of gloating after JFK was killed. There was no tipoff before or after that the wiretap subjects knew anything about the event in Dallas. It suggested that the targets knew wiretaps were everywhere. Numbed to the possibility that investigators were listening and yet unwilling to forfeit everyday life, the word on the street was, "Don't talk on your home phone. Use a pay phone." As a result, eavesdroppers heard endless chatter about cooking up some sausages and peppers, was the pasta maybe not drained yet, personal talk that the agents listening in were supposed to switch off.

Any word about an upcoming presidential assassination, or any murder for that sake, would be far too sensitive to whisper a word.

As boss, Accardo would have had to be consulted and either approve or disapprove anything so important as a murder, implying that Accardo would have known, as Files laid it out. Accardo supposedly did not condone aimless murders and had a policy against them.

CHUCK NICOLETTI GETS THE CONTRACT

Nicoletti was the Outfit's best hit man, favored for important assignments. It was no big deal – a hit like any other. A job was a job, nothing personal. He handled contract killings, working for the Accardo/Aiuppa Outfit, often tight with Giancana. Born of Sicilian American parents, Nicoletti's life of violence began at age 12 when he shot and killed his father as the old man in a drunken rage attacked him with a knife. An eighth-grade dropout, he hooked up with the Forty-Two gang, Giancana's clubhouse. Nicoletti handled an estimated 20 contract killings in his time, not counting the Kennedy assassination.

Files worked as Nicoletti's driver and gofer. Every week Nicoletti would take out a wad of bills and peel off ten Andy Jacksons. Two hundred a week was good money in 1963. He'd fork over an extra C-note or two as bonus pay, more for 'special projects.' Files said he got 15 grand for the JFK hit.

"I would do anything Mr. Nicoletti told me to do," he said of the soft-spoken mobster, who had seen him driving racing cars and hired him as his own wheelman and bodyguard. Files, 21 when he teamed with older underworld higher ups Nicoletti and Johnny Roselli of Los Angeles for the assassination job, spoke of Nicoletti with awe and respect.

He said an earlier plan to assassinate Kennedy in Chicago was scrubbed because a lot of people didn't like the idea of doing it in their own city. This was after Nicoletti asked him if he wanted to join him in making a hit, which Files mistook to be against a local hood who he didn't think deserved it since the guy hadn't done anything so bad as to be rubbed out.

"No, the big guy."

"What big guy?"

"The president,"

"Oh, yeah, if you say so, I have no problem." Files had trained Cuban guerillas at Gator Ridge in Florida in small arms and explosives for the Bay of Pigs fiasco. He made no secret of his anger at Kennedy for not bailing out the trapped landing parties.

Files was already a U.S. Army 82nd Airborne veteran who had done special forces work in Laos giving guerilla training to Hmong tribesmen. It had involved a lot of violence and killing, he indicated, so more of the same was something that did not bother him.

He said his boss next mentioned that he wanted to bring John Roselli in on the hit and wondered how Files felt about that. Files said he had talked to Roselli a couple of times in the Everglades training camp in Florida and liked Roselli okay.

On Nicoletti's orders a week before the assassination, Files asserts he took their new Chevrolet and a stack of weapons and ammo and drove to Dallas where he kept a meeting with Lee Oswald at the Lamplighter motel in Mesquite, Texas. He went with Oswald to a field where he fired rifles, adjusted the sights and calibrated the scopes. He provided researcher Pamela J. Ray with a snapshot he says Oswald took of him and details on the weapon he had chosen to use which was a specially designed Remington XP-100 "Fireball", the best you can get, which looked like a big pistol with a curved stock and a two-foot barrel.

Files said he never talked to Oswald about the nature of the operation or who was to be targeted. He returned to Chicago and then drove again to Dallas on November 22 where he rendezvoused with Nicoletti in mid-morning. Files said Nicoletti sounded out his opinion on the best place to perch for a good shot and Files told Nicoletti the Dal-Tech second floor looked ideal. The older man agreed. Files said his own role was supposed to be that of a helper but he found a spot behind the fence atop the grassy knoll just in case. They were told to make a head shot and to make sure they did not hit the first lady. Files said he thought he might help out if Nicoletti and Roselli missed their mark.

When the Lincoln limousine convertible rolled into his front he took a safe angle so as to avoid enfilade risk to Mrs. Kennedy. He fired one round which skulled the president. It was a hollow-point bullet laced with mercury that made the shot explosive, Files said.

He left his mark by biting on the shell casing as he was used to doing in Laos because he liked the smell of gunpowder, Files claimed. He left the shell casing on the fence, he said. It went unfound until 24 years later when a man and his child while panning for precious metals on the knoll found it buried in the dirt three inches beneath the surface. The shell casing had teeth marks in it, an orthodontist confirmed. There was an inability to confirm that the tooth mark belonged to Files because by then his teeth were gone.

The former Special Forces guerrilla wore a reversible jacket that he then flipped to the plaid side. Railroad tower man Lee Bowers would later describe a young gunman in a plaid jacket. Files tucked the fireball gun under his jacket and drove off, the assassin said. He was paid an extra $15,000 for the job which would be a value ten times that amount in 2013 dollars, part of a $30,000 outlay counting expenses which Files mentioned at another point in the interviews.

According to Files, Roselli was Nicoletti's spotter but did not take part because in the pre-assassination late stages Roselli had been told to withdraw by his CIA contact, who was not further identified. Roselli stood watching the motorcade from the foot of the Dal-Tex building, a few yards away from David Morales. Files and Oswald had been dealing with David Atlee Phillips, a case officer who used the nom de guerre Maurice Bishop, according to ex-CIA renegade agent Frank Terpil, who had no part in the assassination.

In the 1960s FBI Agent Bill Roemer, as described in his book Man Against The Mob, tried to turn Nicoletti. The mob hit man pleasantly turned over documentation showing the car dealerships for which he worked, and that was the end of it, Roemer said.

Throughout the 1960s neither Roselli nor Nicoletti were mentioned in connection with the Kennedy assassination. Both were murdered in the 1970s as they were on the verge of being formally quizzed by Congressional investigating committees.

Files as of early 2013 remained a prisoner at Stateville Correctional Center in Crest Hill, Illinois, near the old Joliet State Pen where he has been incarcerated since May of 1991. He was sentenced to a prison term of 55 years after being convicted of attempted murder of two policemen. He says the policemen drove an unmarked car and were hired to kill him, the third attempt on his life by people who wanted him silenced. He did not fire a shot and his associate, driver of the car, shot one of the assailants in the rump in self defense because the unidentified duo were trying to murder them, Files claims.

After the first attempted rubout of Files in 1988 or 1989, the ex-Special Forces gunman went into downtown Chicago to see if the mob was targeting him. He believed their denials. The attempted rubouts between 1988 and 1991 were designed to eliminate him as one who knew too much about the JFK assassination, Files says. It could not have come from Giancana or Nicoletti since by then they were both long dead. Giancana had been shot four times in the head by someone he knew and for whom he was cooking sausages in his basement in 1975. He was under subpoena to testify within weeks before the Senate's Church Committee probe into the CIA Executive Action program to remove hostile foreign leaders and inquiry into CIA-Mafia murder plots. Giancana's murder on June 19, 1975 in Chicago occurred six weeks prior to the disappearance and presumed murder in Detroit of Teamsters ex-boss James R. Hoffa on July 30, 1975. Hoffa was also under subpoena to testify before the U.S. Senate's Church Committee.

Nicoletti's bullet-riddled body was found floating in a bay off the Florida coast in 1977, a short time after he had testified before the House Special Committee on Assassinations (HSCA) and shortly before he was to appear again to be quizzed about the Kennedy assassination.

Giancana in the mid-1960s did a year in prison for refusing to talk to an Illinois state investigating committee despite being given a grant of immunity. Regarded as too flamboyant while drawing heat to the Outfit, he relocated to Mexico where he lived in a plush villa for nearly seven years until he was kidnapped by Mexican police and shipped back to the states. He had taken to buddying with James Cain, an ambitious and cocky made man who had once worked as an investigator for the Cook County Sheriff's office and as a southwestern United States gunrunner and operator inside and outside the law.

By the early 1970s there was talk that Giancana and Cain might be considering a stab at taking over The Outfit. There was said to be long simmering resentment among fellow Outfit mobsters over Giancana's refusal to spread around some of the huge rakeoffs from his gambling casinos in Iran and Central America. Giancana was said to be in protective custody, possibly talking to law enforcement authorities. Some said police had placed security around his house, although it had been withdrawn the night Giancana was murdered, June 19, 1975, four days past his 67th birthday. The killer shot him once in the back, then turned him over to rim his mouth with bullets as if to say he was talking too much.

It suggested he was silenced as insurance against his opening up about the CIA/Mafia plots of the early '60s to assassinate Fidel Castro. Hoffa and Giancana were both victims of what remain to this day unsolved murders in the summer of 1975. Both knew a lot about the JFK assassination. The Kennedys, Jack and especially Attorney General Robert Kennedy, were enemies of both Hoffa and Giancana. Hoffa was on federal trial in Memphis for jury tampering on the day JFK was assassinated. He was found not guilty by a federal trial jury almost immediately after word reached the courthouse from Dallas.

Mafia boss Sam Giancana is cited as the source for the book Double Cross published in 1993 under authorship of Sam's kid brother, Chuck, and his nephew, also named Sam Giancana. Chuck Giancana, who was kept out of the mob by Chicago Sam, claims that his big brother in 1968, after putting in a year in jail in Chicago for defying legal immunity ordering him to answer questions, told him the story of the JFK assassination. The author said this occurred just before Chicago Sam took off for Mexico where he would live in exile for the next seven years. The yarn describes a far-reaching conspiracy involving the mob, the CIA, fat cat businessmen and the Bay of Pigs. Although the first impulse is to doubt that an old pro like Mooney Giancana would talk so freely to a mob outsider, even a younger brother, the gist of the story remains plausible despite the passage of 45 years since Chuck Giancana says he first heard it. Chuck Giancana could have heard the story elsewhere, from James Files, Chuck Nicoletti, John Roselli or second hand storytellers, attributing it to his long deceased brother to give it a 'Chicago Sam' first-person aura, family name identification and protection of the true source if it is not who they claim. Whatever the case, the book holds up to longtime scrutiny and must be regarded as authoritative. It is not necessarily accurate in all particulars.

FILES SUPPORT FILES

Although suspected by some of being a jailhouse storyteller, Files, from the time of his first interview in March 1993 with Robert G. Vernon, provided realistic details that have a ring of authenticity. For example, he names the motel where he stayed, not in Dallas as everyone might suppose but in the town of Mesquite, Texas. He said that prior to making his trip a week before the assassination to Dallas, he had picked up weapons and ammunition from a storeroom in the old Bally warehouse, insider information that only a bona fide mobster would know. A retired FBI man in Texas told the video producer that he could find a man in a prison cell at Joliet who knew a lot about the Kennedy assassination. Files only reluctantly told his story and required persuading before finally doing so. His story of being a paratrooper with the 82nd Airborne Division at Fort Bragg, NC, who had worked with Special Forces in Laos as an expert in small arms and explosives checked out as did his story of recruitment by CIA case officer David Atlee Philips at a military prison in Maryland prior to joining anti-Castro Cuban guerillas at Gator Ridge in the Florida everglades.

Perhaps most telling was that he did not passively agree when asked a leading question assuming that the Chicago mob in 1963 was headed by Sam Giancana and Charles Nicoletti, as even most Justice Department insiders across the country thought. Files politely contradicted the questioner, informing him that the universally known Giancana and Nicoletti merely headed divisions of the Chicago Outfit, Giancana for gambling and Nicoletti for hits and enforcement, and that the real boss was quiet background figure Anthony Accardo. A lot of people thought Accardo had long since retired to his suburban estate. As a mob insider driving for

Nicoletti every day, Files knew otherwise. The ex-special forces sniper was also handier with a rifle than anyone.

SATYRIASIS OR JUST HORNY?

JFK's track record for womanizing staggers the imagination when one considers the risks of exposure and susceptibility to blackmail.

Kennedy was a jackrabbit, ready to jump any good-looking girl, anytime, anyplace. There were rare exceptions.

The predatory president's drive not only extended to nubile young White House interns, it also reached offshore into the untouchable quarry of foreign spies.

In an age when bosomy calendar girls leaped from the pages of Playboy, an era when Sean Connery as James Bond of his majesty's service could mix espionage and minxy women, shaken not stirred, were there any limits?

Not for Jack Kennedy, top stud in the barn, the skinny teenager having sand kicked into his face magically transformed into the Charles Atlas of Saville Row.

He would tell almost anyone who would listen how he craved nooky. For his health of course.

To wit, lounging in Bermuda in May of 1961 with Prime Minister Harold MacMillen, a boyish confidence: "I wonder how it is with you, Harold? If I don't have a woman for three days, I get terrible headaches."

Would you care for an aspirin, sir? Or would a woman do as well?

Kennedy's unabashed candor showered everywhere.

He told regal lady Rep. Claire Booth Luce of the *Time-Life* Luces that if he didn't "get laid everyday" he got headaches. With Dick Nixon he confessed that he had to get laid every day or you know what.

Shortly after he took office, he called in LBJ's veteran wheeler-dealing legislative aide Bobby Baker to put the South Carolina charm boy into the hunt. Baker said the new president didn't want to talk about legislation. He wanted to talk about finding willing young women, the prettier the better.

"If I don't get a fresh piece of ass at least every three days, I get these terrible headaches, " Baker recalled the president telling him.

JFK's technique couldn't have been all bad, since for years no one blew a whistle or called a cop. As Mel Brooks said, "It's good to be king."

Kennedy scored left and right. In the White House he had two mini-skirted secretaries from Baltimore known to staff as Fiddle and Faddle who provided JFK sex on demand. Their names were Priscilla Weir and Jill Cowan. Yes they could type.

"Men are so very very visual," one told the other as they vied for attention. "High heels, a clinging dress, a short skirt – it's all over."

Pam Tunure," a Jackie Kennedy lookalike who had been JFK's Senate aide in the late 1960s, had bridged the gap between the Senate and the White House once her boss became president. She wound up as Jackie Kennedy's press secretary and was said to remain close to the president, although no longer necessarily intimate. Mary Meyer once put her up for a brief time in Meyer's townhouse because, as Turnure told Meyer, she had been evicted from her own lodgings because she was seeing a married man. As the office girls matured and found boyfriends, JFK was often forced to look elsewhere.

One such happy camper during summertime was a virginal college girl from Red Bank, N.J., a campaign contributor's 19-year old daughter, Mimi Alford. Miss Alford found her summer internship to be just what the doctor ordered for Kennedy — an apple a day. Her book written in her 70s tells us JFK never kissed her, just cold turkey. Water relieved the president's chronic back pains, so he would get in the pool with her and play with some toy yellow boats he had on hand for their amusement, she wrote.

No one should fault Kennedy's tubbing toy boats around because as we shall see, small sailboats were his lifetime obsession, a passion other than women learned in his adolescence.

A president's dalliances invite information overload.

HOLLYWOOD HONEYS

Kennedy had an actor agent in Hollywood named Peter Lawford, husband of JFK's sister Patricia Lawford. To be a member of the insider's club, the sophisticated British-born actor saw his side job as lining up starstruck women for JFK's plunking around. One such was gorgeous Marilyn Monroe who went to bed with the president once, just once, in a back cottage at Bing Crosby's spread in Palm Springs, Cal. Maybe it was a prestige thing, since crooner Crosby in an earlier incarnation had hosted Dwight D. Eisenhower, without the Monroe dressing, or shall we say undressing. The sex may not have been that great because Monroe, so one biographer says, from the cottage telephoned her personal masseur to solicit tips on how the president's back pain might be eased. This brought out the nurse in Miss Monroe because she developed a crush on JFK that would prove an embarrassment. A month or so later in response to JFK's invitation she showed up at JFK's birthday party fundraiser in Madison Square Garden barely wearing a shimmering form-fitting white party dress to sing seductively, "Happy birthday, Mr. President". The display made everyone's skin crawl, including the president if his refusal to ever see her again was any indication. The president's wife Jacqueline cancelled Miss Monroe's invitation to a White House reception. This left Miss Monroe bewitched, bothered and bewildered to the point that she threatened to "tell all about the Kennedy boys". That was not long before she got so bollixed coping with Frank Sinatra's gangbanging Mafia pals at his Cal-Neva Lodge on the California/Nevada border and Attorney General Robert Kennedy's frantic search for her red diary that she supposedly overdosed and died from two clashing types of barbiturates prescribed by her psychiatrist and physician on the same night. The doctors all kept their licenses, though no one can figure out why. A coroner who certified her death as accidental recanted and now says she was murdered.

STAGGERING LIST

Lawford held parties at his fancy California home attended by featured, fabulous and often beautiful Hollywood motion picture queens. Although JFK in post-World War II and early congressional years was so skinny and frail that he looked like a candidate for hospitalization and a rehab center, biographers chart a staggering list of affairs and intimacies supposedly enjoyed by JFK that would turn girlophyllic *Playboy Magazine* publisher Hugh Hefner green with envy. It is easy to say that the future president, for most of those years no more than a diamond in the rough, enjoyed the advantages of easy free time, wealth and a prestigious and powerful family back east. Would that have been enough to persuade starlets and movie queens to immediately jump into bed with him? Was Peter Lawford touting JFK as a genie that would make you a star, or if you were already a star, guarantee continued and future success?

The 1940s and 1950s in America were overpopulated with athletic, sculpted, dashing, aggressive, suave, witty, charming, attentive, debonair young men, many in uniform or newly returned from battle, who left little doubt that they would gladly fling down a coat to assist a lady across a rushing rivulet. The last thing these young women wanted was a roguish fiend cornering them to without ceremony begin ripping away at their clothes. Not on a first date.

An often run ad in that era had a bodybuilding system known as Charles Atlas featuring a scrawny- looking guy on the beach getting sand kicked in his face. He was powerless to confront the offending ruffian who enjoyed the attention of the sunbathing beach beauty. Until... he took the Charles Atlas dynamic bodybuilding course, returned to the beach buff and brave, and, pow, dispatched the bully to the delight of the admiring beach bunny. Was this false advertising? Was it best to be undernourished and sickly?

Those who found women and girls unimpressed in those days by skin and bones and frailty read today with shock and awe the reported ease with which the early Jack Kennedy ran around Hollywood scoring at will.

"Guys like that," they used to say on the ball fields, in the locker rooms, at the dance halls, "couldn't make out in a two-bit whorehouse with a fist full of quarters."

Au contraire. Kennedy had a boyish charm, a light in his eye, and the single-minded mission of, as he so often bluntly put it, getting laid. He did not yet have the bulk that came with a late physical maturity and with the ministrations of Dr. Max Jacobson's amphetamine cocktails and the cortisone shots that would become staples of his medical regimen. He was both a romantic and a makeout artist, his name associated with these Hollywood women: Gene Tierney, Audrey Hepburn, Jayne Mansfield, Kim Novak, Marlene Dietrich, Marilyn Monroe, Janet Leigh, Rhonda Fleming, Mrs. David Hjordis Niven, Angie Dickinson. And those were only the names we knew.

We know that Novak, Leigh and Fleming attended one of his inauguration parties early in 1961, but we can find no verification that this meant they must automatically be counted as notches on JFK's gun belt. He did gambol with someone that night, but no one seems to know who. Novak was consorting with rat packer Sammy Davis Jr. at the time but she told interviewer Larry King it was only a friendship, not a romance, even though Davis did love her. Who wouldn't fall for the queen of the Labor Day celebrations in the movie Picnic? As to Janet Leigh? Forget it. Too much class to run around doing quickies. She flipped when she heard people were saying she and JFK made out at the Inaugural party. "Are you crazy? I was with my husband." Her husband was handsome actor Tony Curtis, who also happened to be a notorious ladies man. Beautiful flaming redhead Rhonda Flemming was likely just soaking up the excitement of the presidential ball. The same might be said for the vixenish former ballet dancer Audrey Hepburn, who played Holly Golightly in *Breakfast at Tiffany's*. She sang a sanitized Happy Birthday song at JFK's 46th and last in 1943, but did that make them an item?

"MOST EXCITING 20 SECONDS…"

Mrs. Niven was a storied neurotic from whom Niven wished he could somehow be rid. The strange and comely Scandinavian from the far north did reportedly accommodate the president with lightning speed in an outside shed while the Nivens were visiting Camp David for some skeet shooting. It could happen to anyone when the little woman takes her turn with a pellet gun.

One does not doubt that Kennedy hooked up several times with the bountiful and bubbly blonde Jayne Mansfield before she met, married and doted on Hungarian beefcake Mickey Hargitay, the two of them a living advertisement for the body beautiful. She died young in a car crash down south, leaving a daughter Mariska Hargitay whose fine acting skills are seen weekly on the Law and Order television series.

Kennedy was said to have consorted with burlesque queen Tempest Storm. His rumored affair with country beauty Blaze Starr was a false alarm. She was the live-in mate of Sen. Russell Long, D-Louisiana, a widower. Her name was linked to JFK when during the 1960 campaign Johnson mischievously pushed the duo into a hatcheck booth at a New Orleans nightclub. Starr said nothing happened. She added that Kennedy was not her type.

There was a verified brief White House date with Marlene Dietrich who said she had only a half hour to spare because she had a 7 p.m. appointment "to receive a plaque from 200 Jews." The sultry German bisexual siren, twenty years older than the president, said he was very sweet to her before she rushed off to accept her award. He asked her if as rumored she had once had an affair with his father Joseph Kennedy, to which she replied no.

The saltiest and most sarcastic comment came from actress Angie Dickinson who had been ushered to a White House lunch by actor Peter Lawford. After consorting with Kennedy, Dickinson was asked how it went. Her tongue-in-cheek reply: "The most exciting 20 seconds of my life".

There may have been a stream of Hollywood bimbos around all the time, but Kennedy had his serious moments.

SOMEBODY STOLE MY GAL

He returned from the South Pacific late in 1944 expecting to resume wooing textile heiress Frances Cannon, a debutante with whom he was in love when he shipped out. At the time, Kennedy was hospitalized in Massachusetts when his father arranged for him to be interviewed by John Hersey, the tall and talented Yale prodigy who was one year older than JFK. Hersey wrote a lengthy story about Kennedy and PT109, a harrowing 17-day odyssey of grueling rafting and flopping around in the Japanese-occupied Soloman Islands in August 1943 before miraculously finding natives who could send them rescuers. As skipper of the PT boat, Kennedy at 2 a.m. cruising on one of its three engines, made a turn and was crashed mid-ship by a Japanese destroyer, splitting the 78-foot U.S. Navy speedboat in two. Two members of the 13-man crew died and Kennedy was slammed around, aggravating his chronically bad back.

Hersey's account was so good that *The New Yorker* printed it in its entirety, displacing a number of features in the usually dry, sophisticated and sardonic periodical. The Kennedy story won admiration, Hersey's writing won acclaim and Kennedy was on his way politically, starting with election to Congress in 1947. The campaign went easily after JFK's father purchased and distributed 150,000 copies of the New Yorker story to voters in the Kennedy district.

But it was Hersey who won the coveted prize, the hand of Miss Cannon. "I got the glory, he got the girl," Kennedy complained bitterly. Hersey would go on to write two celebrated WWII books, *A Bell for Adano*, the story of the Sicily campaign, and *Hiroshima*, a series of interviews with survivors of the atom bomb dropped from the Enola Gay super-fortress on that luckless city.

JFK's ROMANCE WITH GENE TIERNEY

The most beautiful girl of the 20th century was being filmed in the darkly brooding atmosphere of Dragonwyck Manor supposedly in New York State when she slowly turned to stare into the eyes of a handsome blue-eyed naval officer standing by at the Hollywood set. It was 1945. Photos from the time show a droopy, sick-looking sailor who, let's be honest, looked like a Sad Sack refugee from Beetle Bailey or a World War II Bill Mauldin cartoon in Stars and Stripes. John F. Kennedy had just emerged from two months of convalescence in Naval hospitals after his grueling 17-day experience floundering around in the South Pacific after his PT vote had been demolished. Lt. John F. Kennedy was home from the Pacific, still tanned, his hair floppy and windswept, soulfully getting over his jilting by the girl he'd dreamt of returning home to marry, textile heiress Frances Cannon. She had paired up with the author of JFK's war story of PT109 for *The New Yorker*, fellow Ivy Leaguer John Hersey. Kennedy was rebounding and looking for solace.

"My heart skipped a beat," superstar Gene Tierney later confided.

Born in Brooklyn in 1920 as one of three children of a wealthy insurance broker, Gene Tierney led a happy and privileged early life.

After returning from two years of finishing school and language studies in Lausanne, Switzerland, she was touring a back lot in Hollywood when director Anatole Litvak was struck by her beauty. "You ought to be in pictures," was the sharp-witted director's corny opening line, Tierney swore. He gave her a screen test and took her to see Jack Warner, who offered her a film contract that she would run by her domineering father back east. A hardheaded businessman, her father was insulted by the financial insufficiency of the offer especially since he frowned on the West Coast movie industry to begin with. He saw Broadway as the legitimate theater and did not interfere when his daughter won Broadway bit parts in 1938 and 1939, especially when her brief appearances stirred critics to heap praise on the teenage beauty. In due course Miss Tierney won the starring role in 1940 in the Male Animal, which became an instant hit, making her at age 20 the toast of Broadway,

Theater critics had gone out of their way to extol Tierney's beauty despite the brevity of her walk-on appearances. On one occasion the Variety critic enthused that she was the prettiest bucket- of- water deliverer he had ever seen. Hollywood phenom Darryl F. Zanuck, founder and president of 20th Century Fox, during a performance of *The Male Animal*, left his audience seat and went backstage to offer her a film contract, offering the standard $150 a week for a promising ingenue. She refused. He saw a beautiful woman later that night at the Stork Club in New York City and, not knowing it was the same woman who had rejected him earlier in the evening, made another pitch. This time Tierney accepted – for $750 a week.

DARYL ZANUCK'S 'MOST BEAUTIFUL'

"Undeniably the most beautiful woman in motion picture history," Zanuck said of Tierney, whose green eyes, high cheekbones and exquisite features gave her visage an Asian cast that a faint overbite made even more enchanting. By 1943 she had made 12 hit movies and was a superstar, distinguished by her roles in *The Return of Frank James, Tobacco Road, Shanghai Gesture, Belle Starr. Laura, Leave Her to Heaven, The Razor's Edge, Heaven Can Wait* and *The Left Hand of God* opposite Humphrey Bogart who she said detected her incipient mental illness and very decently fed her script lines whenever she faltered. Suffering from the pressure of raising a retarded child, coping with divorce from Oleg Cassini with whom she nevertheless remained friends and a brutally demanding motion picture shooting schedule, she lapsed into bipolar disorder and was institutionalized at the Institute for Living in Connecticut in 1955. The therapy for mental disorder in the fifties was shock treatment in which electrodes were affixed to the head and body as conduits for jolt after jolt of electricity. Objecting to the shock treatments, Tierney tried to escape but was recaptured and subjected to 27 shock treatment sessions. Once released, she became an energetic spokesperson against shock treatment therapy and helped scrap mini-electrocution as a psychiatric crutch and panacea for dealing with mental illness.

When Kennedy met her, she was already separated from and planning to divorce Oleg Cassini, a set designer at Paramount who after his return from military service took to womanizing. It led to a public scene with Howard Hughes. The multi-millionaire, a collector of Hollywood movie beauties, had started chasing Gene Tierney, who retaliated against Cassini by seeing the wealthy airman, adventurer and movie producer. The Cassinis had a daughter, Daria, who brought them heartache when she was born in 1943 retarded, deaf and partially blind – due to an unlucky turn of fate. Two weeks before she was to start maternity leave, Tierney during her one and only appearance at the Hollywood Canteen had been approached by a female fan who asked for and was given Tierney's autograph. As time would tell, Tierney wrote in her autobiography, the fan, a former woman Marine, was quarantined with rubella but had gone out anyhow, exposing the pregnant Gene Tierney to fetal damage sufficient to cause birth of a retarded child. Tierney said the woman had unaccountably sought her out to volunteer the perplexing information. Seeing the actress's anguished reaction, the woman turned and left, saying not another word.

THE AMBASSADOR BUYS HIS SON JACK A SEAT IN CONGRESS

Kennedy and Tierney began a love affair that lasted for close to a year, ending in 1946 when JFK ran for Congress in the Massachusetts district where his maternal grandfather, former Boston mayor John "Honey Fitz" Fitzpatrick, had once served. The way was cleared when JFK's wealthy father, former ambassador to England Joseph P. Kennedy, met with and persuaded Boston mayor James Michael Curley, the grisse eminence of Boston Irish politics, former governor and four-split-terms mayor of Boston to step aside and not seek reelection, paving the way for Jack Kennedy to go to Washington. Curley had held the invincibly Democratic old 11th District seat for four years and was sure to win it again if he so chose. The elder Kennedy's convincing argument was a million-dollar bailout for Curley of a mountain of debt dogging him from past campaigns and legal bills left over from fighting criminal prosecutions. The cash bonanza freed Mayor Curley to continue throwing his weight around in his favorite political job, mayor of Boston. The Democratic candidate in the district would of course swamp the Republican contender, ensuring that John F. Kennedy's first political job, his stepping-stone to the White House, had been bought for him lock, stock and barrel by his wealthy old man. For banker and bootlegger Joe Kennedy, the money now meant little. It was all a mere bagatelle. Curley, meanwhile, would become the role model for Boston Mayor Frank Skeffington of author Edwin O'Connor's political classic *The Last Hurrah*, a 1956 work of fiction that became a hit 1958 movie starring Spencer Tracy. In the final scene old defeated pro Skeffington walks off alone as bands play and crowds cheer for the young new modern political star, whom Skeffington refers to as "Know-Nothing Nut Boy".

JUST ANOTHER BROKEN PAWN

By then Jack Kennedy and Gene Tierney were history.

Had the young former ensign given up too much to fulfill his father's political dream? How do you walk away from "unquestionably the most beautiful woman in motion picture history?" Must a couple split because their parents go to different churches?

The Tierneys were dyed-in-the-wool Republicans, the Kennedys rock solid Democrats. Is love no more than a bunch of isms and doctrines? It's said that religion and custom interfered. A native of Queens, N.Y. and Green Farms in Greenwich, Tierney ran into a sectarian roadblock when she first took Kennedy to meet her family. The couple met a hostile force, her older brother, Howard "Butch" Tierney Jr. He refused to greet Kennedy in a civil manner, Gene Tierney being Episcopal and Kennedy a Catholic. The two were unsuited, the brother said, rudely urging Kennedy to leave. It's doubtful Kennedy ever forgot the slur. Religion would crop up again when Gene Tierney, after visiting with Kennedy at his family's compound on Cape Cod, Mass., was told, "You know, Gene, I can never marry you." JFK explained that she would be a divorced woman if she severed ties with Oleg Cassini and that, because Kennedy planned a political career which was about to commence with a run for Congress, he could never marry a divorcee. "It's over", Kennedy said. "It is," she replied as lunch ended. She got up and left. The romance was over.

After Kennedy reached the White House, Gene Tierney wrote him a congratulatory note. She later confided that she had voted for Richard Nixon.

"I thought he would make a better president," she said.

She married a second time in 1960 to wealthy oilman Howard Lee of Lee Brothers Oil in Houston, whose marriage from 1953 to 1958 to Hollywood legend Heddy Lamarr had ended in a bitter alimony battle. Austrian born Heddy Lamarr, the veiled nude foreign sensation of the cult classic "Ecstasy" who would one day purr that the only time she ever cared about money was when she didn't have it, meanwhile proved that beauty and brains do mix. A math genius, she turned an inspired dinner conversation in 1938 with a Cal-Tech physicist into a pot of gold. She lipsticked her telephone number on his auto windshield afterwards. He called, they met for parabolas and logarithms and together they patented a technology which is now, hold your breath, the wave of the future called Wi-Fi. The divorce settlement left her ex Howard Lee with barely a few million dollars. He struggled along somehow. Tierney, for her part, had been discharged from the Menninger Clinic in Topeka, Kansas after five years rehabilitation due to mental disorder. As part of her rehab, she was tasked to a job at a five-and-dime in Kansas City where she was discovered selling cosmetics to the delight of an alert reporter who turned it into a national story. Tierney and Lee met on a holiday in Aspen, Col. "Please, not another actress," Lee is said to have remarked to chums, recalling his demonetization at the hands of Lamarr. He and Tierney married and settled down to a life in Houston of gardening, travel and socializing. The duo became accomplished contract bridge players. They kept a second home in Delray Beach, FL. Tierney said they spent 16 happy years together.

She and her husband remained staunch Republicans, giving especially strong support to former Hollywood actor and Screen Actors' Guild president Ronald Reagan from his 1960s days as governor of California into the 1990s.

In 1962 Tierney appeared in the movie *Advise and Consent*, based on Alan Drury's powerful novel about the U.S. Senate. By then, her ex-husband Oleg Cassini was a successful fashion designer famously catering to Mrs. Jacqueline Kennedy. As part of the movie rollout, Tierney and her husband Howard Lee were invited to and attended a White House luncheon. Kennedy had not seen Tierney since a supposed look-who-I-bumped-into chance meet in Paris in late summer 1953, two weeks before JFK married Jacqueline Bouvier in Newport, R.I. During the Paris occasion, Tierney rebuffed Kennedy's proposition that they start sparking again.

Kennedy again took Gene aside at the White House luncheon to suggest that they resume dating. It was as if JFK considered it poor form not to try to make out. Tierney's answer was again no, she said. By that time the proper Mrs. Jacqueline Kennedy had decided the only way to slow down her husband was to fight fire with fire. She collared popular and handsome movie star William Holden for a brief romance, to the annoyance and chagrin of the president, so the story goes. It improved things between the first couple.

"What was Jack Kennedy's charm?" Gene Tierney asked herself more than once. She seemed unable to answer. Unlike many others, she did not see their old post-war liaison as much of a love affair.

"We dated only ten times, and that was before he was in the public eye. It's so old hat now".

THE INGA BINGA REFLEX

Long before young John Kennedy engaged in a brief but serious romance with star actress Gene Tierney he went overboard for a Danish lass described by German Fuhrer Adolph Hitler as a "perfect Nordic beauty".

Inga Arvad, 28, a platinum blonde mother of two who was introduced in 1941 to Kennedy when he was 24 by Kennedy's sister Kathleen, had won a beauty contest in her native Denmark before sharing Hitler's private seating box at the 1936 Olympics.

Kennedy was a Navy ensign in the Office of Naval Intelligence (ONI) stationed in Washington D.C. His father had wrangled the appointment by calling the ONI chief, who had worked at Joseph Kennedy's Embassy when the older Kennedy was ambassador to the Court of St. James in London during the late 1930s. JFK needed the political pull because he had been turned down for health reasons when he tried to enlist in the Army. His job involved helping to write daily information summaries for the Secretary of the Navy.

His sister Kathleen worked with the former Miss Denmark who wrote a column for the *Washington Times-Herald*. Separated from her husband, Inga Arvad was the mistress of Axel Werner-Gren, one of the world's wealthiest men and owner of Paradise Island, which was not yet a resort bridged to Nassau as it exists today. He also owned Bofars Armament Factory that would someday become Electrolux, the vacuum cleaner manufacturer. The competition did not deter the young naval intelligence officer. Captivated by Inga's charm and beauty, Kennedy wooed and won her. Their torrid affair caught on and they were for a time seemingly inseparable.

Inga Binga, as Kennedy called her, complimented him in her column, calling him "a boy with a future". There was one problem with the prophetic Dane. The FBI had her down as a Nazi spy. Britain was already in its second year of war with Germany and had heroically endured German air raids as Edward R Murrow kept folks in the states posted. Werner-Gren, Inga's benefactor, was said to be one of Hitler's top operators in the Western Hemisphere. The FBI led by J. Edgar Hoover gave the case of the Naval Intelligence officer and the seductive Nordic spy top priority by gathering photos, planting room mikes, staking out surveillances, drafting full written reports. Tipped off, old Joe Kennedy was fearful that JFK would blow his political future over a dame as so many before him had done. He swiftly intervened. The senior Kennedy called President Roosevelt who had Kennedy transferred out of naval intelligence – with everyone's thanks – to the P.T. Boat unit in Charleston, South Carolina, where garrison duty would lend enough distance to disenchant the passionate Inga and Jack. Just as pop's influence and money had saved Jack from getting thrown out of prep school at Choate, the godfather had called for and collected just this one last favor.

As a favor to President Roosevelt and Ambassador Joe Kennedy, Hoover swept the near scandal under the rug.

SEXPIONAGE ACROSS THE POND

Although Jack Kennedy was as true blue as the next man, his patriotism sometimes tilted toward exotic foreign beauties with whom he fraternized big time, whether or not they were Mata-Hari honeytraps. The hard-edged men who guarded the eagle's nest were less persuaded by benign intent than they were by errant or erratic behavior that contained the peril of dangerous exposure. Many men can become saps when it comes to a sexy woman. The point was dramatically being driven home by the contemporaneous scandal in Britain that by the summer of 1963 had caused the resignation of War Minister John Profumo as first step leading to eventual fall of the entire Conservative Party of Prime Minister Harold MacMillen. Nor was it the first time that Jack Kennedy had seemed a little too intrigued by Hitler, not for ideas with which he disagreed, but as a political force. He'd shown fascination with the psychotic dictator while he and scholars hired by his father were authoring a Harvard paper, which was turned into the book While England Slept. The title was knocked off from British Prime Minister Winston Churchill's book of virtually the same name at the suggestion of *New York Times* columnist Arthur Krock, who was moonlighting on the project as a favor to papa Joe Kennedy. There is no record that Jack Kennedy betrayed any vital government secrets or that Inga Binga solicited any. But as Director Hoover saw it, chess games were played a move at a time; the pawns know nothing of the chess master's panoramic view. To be safe, wasn't it best to play it safe? Hoover had found that if it looks like a duck and quacks like a duck, it probably is a duck. The young Jack Kennedy was lucky in a wartime atmosphere to have dodged the bullet called fraternizing with the enemy, especially for an intelligence officer whose mission it was to see and discourage security risks. The slogan at the time, with German submarines creating havoc in the North Atlantic shipping lanes: "Loose lips sink ships". U-boats in wolf packs or singly under German Admiral Doenitz in 1941 sank 525 British, Allied and Neutral merchant ships, an average of more than 40 a month, in the North Atlantic Ocean and United Kingdom waters. The Davey Locker tally rose to more than 100 a month in the summer months of 1942. Statistics only hint at the daily horror of merchant ships being sunk crossing the Atlantic during lend-lease's early war years, before and after Pearl Harbor and America's formal entry into World War II on Dec. 8, 1941. The merchant mariners were drawing a premium wage; nevertheless they remain the unsung heroes of World War

II, particularly since they were not so much as classified as being in military service. Two books that treat the almost forgotten submarine war are Nicholas Monserrat's *The Cruel Sea*, 1951, about a British corvette sub-chaser; and *Far From the Customary Skies*, 1953, a story about an American destroyer in the Battle of the Atlantic by Warren Eyster of Perth Amboy, N.J. Was the Axis a menace to the American mainland? Japanese subs surfaced off California and shelled Santa Barbara. Mini-parachutes laden with bombs were floated from launches in the Pacific into Oregon and the state of Washington. Germany slipped saboteurs ashore on Long Island, N.Y. and Atlantic Highlands, N.J. Hitler was close to perfecting an atom bomb to drop on New York City. Victory gardens sprang up, margarine replaced butter, gas and tires and sugar were epis. Housewives braided their hair and took buses to suddenly busy war plants. The author's eight-year old redhead of a brother who lived near three oil tank farms sent to President Roosevelt a sketch of a shield designed to protect merchant ships from mines and submarine torpedoes. Everyone pitched in for the war effort. People were already dying overseas, older guys were signing up and no longer seen, gold stars shockingly appeared in house windows. Volunteer wardens, their WWI helmets chin-strapped in place, scanned the skies as air-raid sirens wailed and powerful searchlights swept across scudding clouds. The Battle of Britain was at America's doorstep; invasion could be a week or month ahead. When J. Edgar Hoover's FBI agents rounded up Nazi spies and broke up the Bund, they were not a sign of collective paranoia. They were national heroes.

PROFUMO AFFAIR & SEXPIONAGE

British War Minister John Profumo was the second biggest fish caught in the Anglo-American net that swept the biggest sex and spy scandal of the 20th Century across the Atlantic from London to New York City.

The second biggest.

The honor of being the biggest fish has somehow slipped by. He's celebrated wildly to this day. He's never been so much as cuffed as a naughty boy. Any other Tom, Dick or Harry would have been docketed, disgraced and dismissed.

The big fish that got away was John F. Kennedy, the biggest presidential security risk in American history.

During his three-year presidency, Kennedy slept with spies and security risks not once in a blue moon, not on the equinoxes, not when the sheep returned from seasonal pasture but every single week of the year.

His rogue's gallery shows only eight of the Kennedy honeys whose harlotry and pillow talk constituted risk to the safety, security and well being of the United States, according to counterintelligence experts and the FBI. Rather than a pardonable adventure here and there, Jack Kennedy's wild abuse of national security precautions crossed a line in the sand that applied to any soldier or sailor, any congressman, any emissary, any defense industry worker, any teacher, any policeman, any postal worker, any federal marshal, any good American.

What did the head of state think he was up to? Had he cracked up?

Some six months after the curtain came down on the Cuban Missile Crisis, Kennedy seemed to be spending more time around his New York City apartment at The Carlyle Hotel and nearby Central Park South than in Washington.

Overwhelmed by a job he had not bargained for, Kennedy gazed at the livery horses for hire across the way at the entrance to Central Park. He had already decided it was time to change horses in midstream. He told himself his attitude shift had nothing to do with the LSD trips he and girl friend Mary Pinchot had taken together. He scoffed at advice that a person's thinking is not the same after an acid trip.

That was the spring that John F. Kennedy gave two remarkable college commencement addresses so moving that even in the Kremlin hard-nosed Commissar Nikita Khrushchev wept. Kennedy's stirring words reminded audiences that "we all breathe the same air". The speech inspired college students and came as a relief to a world weary of wars and shaken by atomic fears. Since the missile crisis, the two Ks had exchanged private correspondence in which each had expressed longings for peace and an end to Cold War hostilities. The outside world did not know they had become pen pals. What the two Ks apparently failed to fully appreciate was how inflexibly hard the two empires had dug in against one another. The sweep of historical momentum, the wars, atrocities, ideological rivalries, vendettas, alliances did not welcome or accommodate notions of abrupt change simply because ephemeral leaders of the two world powers were now on the same wavelength.

In fact history had other plans. Forces were already at work that within a year would destroy or politically neuter both Kennedy and Khrushchev.

Kennedy's conduct did not help. CIA counterintelligence boss James Angleton had wiretapped the continuing Kennedy-Pinchot affair in the White House and their drug use, including LSD. Angleton would later reflect that Mary "had the power to influence foreign policy". She not only had the power, she actually did influence foreign policy by chemically changing her lover's perspective. If she had held a pistol to his head it would have been treason. A drug brainwash was just as persuasive, ameliorated only by the 'victim's' voluntary cooperation.

That spring Kennedy was having a grand time with the ladies.

Like a moth drawn to a flame, he was patronizing two power pros from the same London call girl ring that would in June, 1963 force the resignation of British War Minister John Profumo for his affair with prostitute Christine Keeler. It flared into a tabloid circus once Fleet Street newshawks established that the beautiful brunette had been simultaneously bedding Soviet naval attaché Gene Ivanov, a KGB agent. When British MI5 learned that Keeler's pillow talk with Ivanov touched on the "nuclear payload" of NATO atomic cannon shipped to West Europe, the biggest scandal hit London since King Henry beheaded one of his wives.

Did Jack Kennedy run for cover? Quite the opposite. He had his British-born brother-in-law Peter Lawford introduce him in New York to Mariella Novotny, the no-holds-barred bondage queen of the Soho strip joints. Novotny, the teenage wife of a rich 56-year-old S&M pervert and London antique shop owner, was famous for her 'Feast of the Peacocks' orgy in her Hyde Park apartment in 1961 after she had fled a White Slave indictment in New York on the Queen Mary. Guests at her dinner orgy said a masked but unidentified cabinet officer who greeted society guests was clad only in an apron and bowtie, an absence of suitable garb which would eventually inspire a 2,000 word special FBI report waggishly titled 'Operation Bowtie'. He asked guests to whip him if dissatisfied with his service. Wearing a black corset, Mariella later romped in bed with six naked men. The 'Man In The Mask' B & D party involved members of Parliament, thus entitling her to be known as the 'nation's chief whip', Novotny joked.

Jetting back to New York City accompanied by "aging actress" Suzy Chang, 27, Mariella was booked by Lawford to entertain Jack Kennedy. Lawford suggested something out of the ordinary and spicy, so Mariella and Chang dressed as nurses in their room in the ritzy Hampshire House, 150 Central Park South, for a three-way with JFK. Mariella later told FBI probers she engaged in sex with the president three more times. Chang said she never singled with Kennedy and was not attracted to older men. London newspapers referred to the stateless NYC-born Chinese girl as an international spy.

KILGALLEN SPARKS PROBE

The sex romps might have remained a secret except for the fact that *'Voice of Broadway'* syndicated columnist Dorothy Kilgallen spotted JFK sharing a booth at NYC's famous 21 Club with Suzy Chang. In a June jotting in her flagship *NY Journal* American column, Kilgallen by name mentioned the international call girl who was seen "with a high level elected official". Her item left JFK unmentioned. Up to that point, the FBI had shown little interest in the London scandal.

Attorney General Robert F. Kennedy read the gossip item and changed all that. Anxious to kill the story, Bob Kennedy placed a telephone call that Sunday afternoon to order the Justice Department to initiate an immediate investigation. He added, whether truthfully or not, that the president himself "has expressed concern." The call surprised Justice officials because such an order never before had come on a Sunday.

By Monday, FBI agents were all over the case. They interviewed Suzy Chang who sent them to Mariella Novotny. The Czech born-and-raised beauty told them everything.

Among fellow call girls identified by Miss Novotny was a co-worker and madam in New York City named Ilona Bata, a Hungarian who was said to be a KGB spy. Bata and Novotny often went on jobs as a team.

Getting interim updates, Hoover muttered to close deputies that he was sick of the president and 'his $200-a-night whores.' By the fall, third-ranking FBI deputy William C. Sullivan's counterintelligence division issued a 2,000-page report. It was titled 'Operation Bowtie' and signed off on by Director J. Edgar Hoover. The lengthy report concluded that the connection between the Keeler scandal in London and New York and Washington was "too tenuous" to endanger the American presidency.

Those who saw Hoover under every bed must now reflect on why the FBI director, as late as September 1963, signed off on an obvious whitewash protecting JFK. He signed the document but had it up to his eyeballs with the president's misbehavior. He would need just one more provocation. It was already in the works.

THE INDOCHINA 'DRAGON LADY'

The Kennedy assassination was all about entanglements with women, yet they are given short shrift in the reprises.

One with whom Kennedy did not have an affair but probably should have was Madame Nhu, the fiery first lady of South Vietnam. The point would have been to diplomatically persuade the 39-year old pepperpot to please shut up.

Nicknamed "dragon lady" after the cartoon character in the Terry and the Pirates comic strip, the imperious and outspoken lady who ran the presidential palace in Saigon was the wife of Ngo Dinh Nhu, an Air Force pilot who headed South Vietnam's special forces and police for his older brother Ngo Dinh Diem, the elected President from 1955–63, a bachelor who deferred to Madame Nhu as the country's official hostess. The brothers had been put in place by General Edward G. Lansdale for the U.S. Central Intelligence Agency in 1955 after he recruited Diem from the Maryknoll seminary in Lakewood, N.J. at the urging of Francis Cardinal Spellman of New York City and Sen. Mike Mansfield, D-Montana, Senate majority leader. As an American client state, South Vietnam's army (ARVN), advised by 16,000 Green Berets and American support troops, was at war to prevent a takeover by Viet Cong infiltrators from the north.

The young, wild and irreverent Saigon press corps had tagged Madame Nhu as the "fourth multi-millionaire in the world". Clad in a form-fitting ao dao sheath modified by her own fashion change to add décolletage for her crucifix, the spitfire dominated the presidential palace, twice surviving coup attempts. In 1960 her ridicule of Buddhists provoked ARVN paratroops to attack the palace. Citing the oligarchic dictatorship run by the Nhus, Diem and their brother Archbishop Ngo Dinh Thuc, the mutineers assailed job and military preferences accorded to Catholics, to members of the Nhu's two secret political clubs and to Central Highlanders. In 1962 the palace was bombed and strafed by two airmen from General Nhu's own air force. Madame Nhu tumbled down a second floor bomb hole, suffering minor injuries. Her husband and children and Diem were uninjured.

She had suffered worse. Married at 18, she was 22 in 1946 when, as a young mother in Hue, she was taken prisoner together with her baby daughter and mother-in-law by Ho Chi Minh's advancing rebel army. The Communist cadre missed Nhu and his brother Cam but captured their older brother, Ngo Minh Khoi, whom they buried alive. The Viet Minh blew up Madame Nhu's piano, which they suspected was harboring a radio, and then exiled the women to a remote village where they were held for four months on a daily diet of two bowls of rice apiece. They were freed by the reoccupying French army and went to live in Da Lat, then known as another Shangri La, happy years during which Nhu edited a newspaper.

UNDER THE MANGO TREES

As a legislator alongside her husband, she was a moral crusader who had pushed through a soon-to-be unpopular "family code" that banned divorce, drugs, dancing, sexual fraternization, gambling, contraceptives and abortion. It prohibited brothels and opium dens. The joke was that people were allowed to use salt and pepper on their food if they chose. She thought of herself as an empress and was accustomed to a glamorous life not least of which was command of a magnificent summer retreat called the White Palace, built by a royalist French architect between 1898 and 1916 on a rise overlooking the South China Sea. The pearl-studded retreat was in the class of Newport, R.I. millionaire "cottages", replete with a garden adorned with Greek mythological statues among the avocado and mango trees. It had been the residence of Indochina's last emperor, Bao Dai, a distant relative of Madame Nhu. Palace Number Three was in the Central Highlands, less than a one-hour flight from Saigon's Tan Son Nhat Airport. The art deco home surrounded by hills and pine forests had been the retreat of Bao Dai, a hunter attracted by game in the forests, including at one time tigers and elephants.

Her imperious ways by 1962 caused her parents to disown her. Her father, a patrician lawyer who had been appointed South Vietnam's ambassador in Washington, resigned with sharp words against his daughter. Her mother followed suit, resigning as Diem's observer at the United Nations.

Madame Nhu was in Beverly Hills, California on an international speaking tour to drum up support for President Diem and his brother, her husband Gen. Nhu, when the two leaders were murdered during a military coup in the South Vietnamese capital of Saigon on Nov. 2, 1963 — three weeks prior to the assassination of President Kennedy.

"He will pay," she vowed, excoriating President Kennedy for going along with the coup by General Van Minh and other Buddhist tank unit commanders. They had circled the presidential palace and during the bombardment got Diem and Nhu to surrender with a guarantee of safe exit, only to shoot them before daybreak.

The coup, not the murders, had been engineered by CIA Station Chief Lou "Black Luigi" Conein, who had paid the mutinous generals $41,000 on behalf of the U.S. government for the coup d'etat overthrowing America's longstanding ally.

During General Lansdale's long and difficult empowerment and training of Diem, Conein had been Lansdale's right hand man. Born and raised until age five in Paris by his widowed mother, Conein was farmed out to her sister in Kansas City where he was raised by his aunt and her husband, an old World War I veteran of the Argonne. Conein at the onset in Europe of World War II returned to Paris from where he joined the French army in 1939. Once Germany invaded and quickly defeated France, Conein returned to the United States where he enlisted in the U.S. Army. His bilingual skill and European background led to recruitment by the U.S. Office of Strategic Services (OSS). He was parachuted into France where he worked with the maquis. His outstanding war record — silver and bronze stars and a purple heart — brought him into contact with drug rings in Vichy France and the Marseilles waterfront, where he made such firm connections with the Corsican Brotherhood that in post-war years he would be warmly welcomed into one of its fraternal groups. He would tell people that unlike the Sicilians whose contracts were limited to the United States and bordering countries, Corsicans operated worldwide. "They'll go anywhere," he said. Once the war ended, he remained in intelligence, joining OSS actions in Indochina against Japanese diehards before joining the then new CIA infiltration of spies and saboteurs behind the Iron Curtain in East Europe. The 44-year-old U.S. Army sergeant was a Black Ops specialist, a hard drinker who remained in touch with his superior Lansdale despite the latter's transfer back to the states in 1961. There are some students of Dealey Plaza who believe Conein was in the crowd on the fateful day. Though the photo IDs are imperfect, time would tell that Conein was no stranger to several CIA operatives who admitted they were party to the JFK assassination. The man thought to be Conein in Dealey Plaza was a dead ringer for the CIA man. An investigation concluded that the Conein lookalike was a postal worker using his lunch break to watch the presidential visit.

When President Nixon was sinking into hot water in 1972, he formed a squad of killers whose ostensible purpose was to hunt and assassinate international narcotics dealers. Among the special band were Frank Sturgis and E. Howard Hunt, both of whom became so entangled in the Watergate investigations and prosecutions then obsessing Washington that they had very little opportunity to hunt drug traffickers.

Oddly, a big name from the Kennedy Vietnam era surfaced with the names of Hunt and Sturgis. Nixon named Lou Conein to head the assassination squad.

GENERAL LANSDALE TURNS DOWN JFK

"With America as a friend, who needs enemies?" Madame Nhu said of the Kennedy Administration. She did not mention that repression of Buddhists and her own outrageous remarks had backed American leaders into a corner.

"I will supply the kerosene so they can barbecue themselves," she said of the Buddhist bonzes whose self-immolations captured on camera had inflamed world opinion. Six monks had martyred themselves since the first bonze burned himself a few blocks off busy downtown Tu Do Square on June 11, 1963. *AP* Bureau Chief Malcolm Browne, using his own inexpensive camera, photographed the spectacle that ran in the *New York Times* and many other newspapers, earning him a Pulitzer Prize.

During her international speaking tour and before the Saigon coup, Madame Nhu during a talk to students at Fordham University in the Bronx, N.Y. on Oct. 11, 1963 apologized for her remarks expressing joy about the barbecue suicides of Thich Quang Duc and other bonzes. She said her daughter had heard the barbecue reference uttered at a refreshment stand by an American GI and thought it was worth repeating.

The murders of Diem and Nhu sickened President Kennedy, who turned ashen gray and bolted towards the men's room, according to Gen. Maxwell Taylor, newly named chairman of the Joint Chiefs of Staff, who was with the president when word arrived from Saigon. Kennedy did not want Diem shot, but it was listed as a remote option, tenth on a list, on a National Security Council memo. The murderer was Nguyen Yan Nhung, aide to ARVN General Duong Van Minh. The general succeeded Diem as president, becoming first in a long line of hapless failures whose ineptitude only lengthened the war while throwing the burden into the lap of the United States. Allowing a Buddhist general to take over to pacify a restless Buddhist population did not help things. Instead, it hurt, on the issue of competence.

Lansdale was a fast friend of Diem and the Nhus besides being America's 1954 point man who put them in power. He had been asked by JFK to seek their abdication and handle the coup if as expected they refused to step aside. The spymaster turned the president down, one reason being that he was convinced that Diem should remain in power. The ensuing events, escalation of the insurgency into full-scale war and an ensuing ten-year mortality count of 53,000 American deaths suggests that Lansdale, and Madame Nhu, were right in holding that sometimes the devil you know is better than the devil you don't. It was no era for minority Catholics as heads of state: both Diem and his brother were assassinated, then JFK went down and, five years later, with a good chance of winning the presidency, Robert F. Kennedy, by then a senator from New York, was murdered in Los Angeles. The

Saigon pair was embroiled in a religious war against Buddhists who comprised 80% of South Vietnam's population. There was no sign that religion otherwise played a part in the JFK and RFK assassinations, although latent bigotry cannot be totally dismissed as an exacerbating element in the toxic stew of resentment. Only the avowed atheist caudillo of Havana, Fidel Castro, the most savagely hunted quarry of all, was spared the grim reaper's revenge.

FLAG WAVING WOES

Nuances of the coup meant nothing to America's hotheaded expatriate Cuba Libres who thirsted for revenge for Kennedy's perceived treason. They were reminded that he had refused to use air power to rescue them on the beaches at the Bay of Pigs beachhead in April 1961, leading to capture by Castro's military defenders of more than a thousand invading Cuban expatriates. Now from Southeast Asia came news that an American-backed coup d'état in South Vietnam had caused the abandonment and death of longtime allies. This new political prevarication infuriated the anti-Castro Cubans, reinforcing their conviction that the Kennedy White House was unreliable, and maybe even treacherous. It was another double cross. To focused aspiring liberators of their Cuban homeland, the American White House was an uncertain trumpet. That it was whipped by winds of change in a perilous nuclear age was academic doubletalk. Let university professors argue the pros and cons. The only thing that mattered was to kill Castro and retake Havana.

Madame Nhu was another who had no doubts. A judo expert who had formed a 25,000 member women's paramilitary Special Force brigade in her own country, she was soon on the telephone to tongue lash both Conein and Lansdale. She told them both that they were pussycats, using language that challenged their manhood. She would hear no excuses.

Born a Buddhist to an aristocratic family, Madame Nhu's first language was French. A devotee of the piano and ballet, she spoke Vietnamese fluently. She could not write Vietnamese. As a teenager, she rebuffed her parents' promotions of an arranged marriage to choose Nhu, a bachelor 15 years her senior who called her "little niece" in the custom of the country. He was an archivist and a union leader who had repudiated Ho Chi Minh's overtures to join his communist crusade for independence. Nhu was a Catholic and she converted. One of her husband's brothers, Bishop Thuc, was in charge of the Long Minh papal See who in November of 1960 would be appointed by Pope John XII as archbishop of Hue, the highest Catholic post in Vietnam centrally situated in the old imperial capital on the Perfume River.

It was here in the ancient capital of Hue that the downfall of the Diem government began with a seemingly ridiculous flap over flags. In a ceremony on May 8, 1963 to honor Archbishop Thuc's 25th year as a bishop, enthusiastic supporters hoisted a Vatican banner next to the South Vietnamese flag. Two days later on the holiday known as Vesak, commemorating holy man Gautama Buddha's 2506 birthday, everyone dressed in traditional white. A request to fly a Buddhist banner was turned down based on a national law that said the Vietnamese flag must fly alone. The Buddhists flew their flag anyhow. When ARVN soldiers intervened, a riot erupted. Untrained in crowd dispersal, the soldiers used tear gas and gunfire, killing nine and wounding many more unarmed civilians.

The flame of protest fanned to other cities. In Saigon, Nhu's Special Forces raided the central sanctum and protest center called the Xa Loi Pagoda where they silenced the din of the huge gong that had been ringing incessantly. They rounded and roughed up hundreds of bonzes. Simultaneous raids hit pagodas all over the city. They became infamous as "the pagoda raids" rallying protesters to stage sit-ins and a monster hunger strike that swept the city. Madame Nhu and her husband were convinced Communists were manipulating the swelling Buddhist rebellion and their overreactions served only to foster wider resentment.

The Buddhist uprising broke into worldview with the June self-sacrifice by an elderly, revered Buddhist bonze named Thich Quang Duc as a protest against the Diem government.

The ripple became a wave, persuading Washington's inner corps of pundits and policy makers to turn against Diem. Thinking was that Diem himself was tolerable, but that Nhu and especially his wife had to go. U.S. Ambassador Frederick Nolting was replaced by Henry Cabot Lodge, a Boston Brahmin who had been on Richard Nixon's ticket as vice president when Kennedy and Johnson were elected in 1960. They would get Madame Nhu out of the way by scheduling her for an international speaking tour.

Then the iron fist in the velvet glove was released. The United States announced that economic dollar support on imports would be withdrawn unless Diem changed his ways and dumped the Nhus. Nhu put out feelers to Ho Chi Minh and in one of history's great ironies, new Ambassador Lodge sat down to an ice-breaking meeting in Diem's highland house at Da Lat to talk things over and to suggest that Diem appoint an emissary to the Embassy in New Delhi, India who would start talks with a counterpart named by Ho Chi Minh.

The stubborn Diem, however, using an interpreter, did not concede the point immediately. He would have to be given a chance to save face, the interpreter said, adding that once the meeting had ended, Diem made firm plans to empower the two emissaries to begin peace talks, the subject being federation of South and North Vietnam.

For Ho Chi Minh, it had been an 18-year wait. The 1945 death of President Franklin Delano Roosevelt had jettisoned the plan to push at the time for Vietnam's Independence. Minh had fought with American and British forces to defeat Japan. FDR in turn knew it and strongly favored his independence plan. Apparently outside the loop, FDR's successor Harry Truman let it slide or preferred the French reoccupation initiative. President Truman never answered Ho Chi Minh's cable, and therein lays the genesis of a tragic 25-year war.

THE RACE CARD

The ballyhooed 1963 "March on Washington" did not turn out to be a violent overthrow of the government, as some had feared.

In fact Hoover and the police brigades were delighted when a crowd estimated at 250,000 — eighty per cent of whom were blacks and non-whites — which had rallied around the Lincoln Memorial and Capitol malls dispersed peacefully after hearing a succession of presentations highlighted by Rev. Martin Luther King's "I had a dream" speech.

The Wednesday assemblage, which fell on the anniversary of President Lincoln's Emancipation Proclamation granting freedom from slavery, had been billed as a rally for jobs and freedom by organizers A. Philip Randolph, president of the Negro American Labor Council and a vice president of The AFL-CIO, and Bayard Rustin, a longtime civil rights advocate and among the first of the 'freedom riders' to test the U.S. Supreme Court ban against racial discrimination in interstate travel.

Rustin was in charge of mobilization and logistics which brought into Washington D.C. 2000 buses, 21 trains, 10 chartered airlines and thousands of cars. The largest political rally for civil rights in U.S. history was held free of discord except for a sour note from Malcolm X of the Nation of Islam who mislabeled it a "Farce on Washington". Disagreeing with him was the most prominent white speaker, Walter Reuther, president of the United Auto Workers, UAW-CIO, the most powerful union in the country and one which saw that blacks got a fair share of jobs; and four prominent black civil rights leaders: James Farmer of CORE, John Lewis of Student Nonviolent Coordinating Committee (SNCC), Roy Wilkins of National Association of Colored People (NAACP) and Whitney Young of the National Urban League (NUL).

Hoover's FBI had by then apparently dropped its antipathy toward Rustin as overly liberal. King was still distrusted since years earlier when in his days as a young preacher being trained by identified Communist Party members at the Highlander Folk School in Monteagle, TN. he had been seen as part of an avowed Soviet Comintern drive to internally take over the United States by subversive manipulation of minorities, students and labor. King, the preacher from Birmingham, still had two avowed Communists in his entourage in 1963. He had overcome their influence to mount a true American nativist drive to lift his people and free them from minority oppression and discrimination. Hoover did not like King's secretly recorded indiscretions and wanted the American Negro movement to rally around someone like rally organizer Randolph, 78, who had pressured President Roosevelt in 1943 to ban discrimination in defense industries and President Truman in 1947 to integrate the armed forces.

THE REVOLUTION THAT WASN'T

During the early 1950s there was a teacher in an American intelligence academy named Major Bernard Sweeney who stood in front of the class and branded various prominent people Communists. One of his targets was Walter Reuther, who before organizing autoworkers in the late 1930s in Detroit had with his brother visited the Soviet Union. The redheaded Reuther's family was of German socialist stock, tough and intelligent. Reuther had lost an arm battling anti-union goons in the violent Ford strike in 1939. His leadership of the United Auto Workers, CIO, together with that of his brother, Victor Reuther, and a third brother had blazed a trail for progressive union contracts replete with guaranteed annual wages (GAW), supplementary unemployment benefits (SUP), retirement health benefits, summer recreational opportunities and job pay and benefits that became the envy of the nation's blue-collar workers. A number of people still haven't figured why Reuther never ran for president.

"There is not the shadow of a doubt that Walter Reuther is a revolutionary Marxist", Major Sweeney proclaimed at the CIC intelligence agent school in Baltimore.

A student who had written a college term paper on Reuther challenged the assertion by pointing out that in 1948 Reuther had purged the UAW-CIO of his union's Communist leaders in an open floor fight before decommissioning 11 locals run by Communists. Sweeney had no answer.

LI'L ABNER SURVIVES RED SCARE

In that era of Senator Joseph McCarthy's roundhouse swipes, Major Sweeney tried to tarnish two cartoonists as "reds" or at least "pinkos" because they took sly satirical digs and exuberant mocking punches at the establishment: Al Capp, who did *Li'l Abner*, and Capp's friend Walt Kelly, who did *Pogo*. Capp's ideological transgressions centered on his mockery of Senator Jack S. Phogbottom, who in a cartoon was substituted for him at a speaking engagement by a gas bag and no one noticed the difference, and his indelibly wry socioeconomic take on an American scene in which Abner's hungry Pappy Yokum family in Dogpatch was glad to settle for "two mizzable pork chops". His comic strip sponsor, Scripps, in 1947 briefly censored his cartoon panels, objecting to his portrayal of the U.S. Senate as a conclave of crooks, windbags and fools. The animated critters in the Okefenokee Swamp in Walt Kelly's *Pogo* still haven't figured out in what way they violated the loyalty oath, although Kelly did give Senator McCarthy a going over as a gun-toting bobcat. At its peak, *Li'l Abner*, launched in August 1934 by a virtually penniless Capp under a binding low-pay contract by United Features Syndicate, was read daily seven days a week by 70 million of 180 million Americans. He was syndicated for 44 years, from 1934 to 1977, reaching 900 newspapers in 28 countries around the globe. Capp escaped his nickel-and-dime contract by cartooning a greedy news-service publisher and mercilessly lampooning him until his real employer freed him to syndicate his own work the following year.

Kelly worked for five years at Walt Disney Studios in California where he did animation jobs on *Pinocchio* and *Snow White and the Seven Dwarfs*. He left without taking sides during the Animators' Strike of 1941 and got a job at Dell Comics, helped by Disney's personal recommendation. His *Pogo* gained syndication for 26 years, best known for his animated possum's remark, "We have met the enemy and he is us."

The Columbia University historian Will Durant was on Sweeney's list. Durant, in his upper 60s in 1953, and his wife Ariel, were authors of the 11-volume *Story of Civilization*. The books were prized by many academics. Sweeney said Durant was a Communist. He did not like hearing a dissent from a student that all Durant was really saying in one of his books was that in the showdown between the Soviet Union and the United States, the economy that most effectively produces consumer goods for its people will win. In the McCarthyist paranoia of the day, questioning the mudslinging Sweeney was heresy. Major Sweeney was not dumb but his slanders were more than enough to dwarf those of Senator McCarthy. The Army Counter Intelligence Corps School in Baltimore, Md. eventually got rid of Major Sweeney by the late 1950s after McCarthy's Maoist-type red scare was ended by the U.S. Army at the Army-McCarthy hearings at Fort Monmouth, N.J. in 1954. The unseen hand of President Dwight Eisenhower, the five-star general of the WW II ETO, played a part as Boston Attorney Joseph Welch silenced McCarthy with the line, "Have you no decency, after all, senator?" The McCarthy team's lawyer was Roy Cohn, backed by Robert F. Kennedy.

Yes, the same RFK. Before joining his brother's administration, Bob Kennedy caught a lot of ink as counsel to the

McClellan Rackets Committee interrogating and publicly insulting Teamster boss James R. Hoffa and Chicago Mafioso Sam Giancana, overdoing it, many thought. He had also worked as an associate counsel for the McCarthy Committee, where N.Y. lawyer Roy Cohn did most of the talking. RFK's older brother, future President Jack Kennedy, as a senator sat as a member of the McClellan Committee.

The 1963 March on Washington was a blessing for everyone because it demonstrated that in the United States a revolutionary convergence of minorities, labor and students would not tear down the capitol after all. There would be no Bastille Day or guillotine, no Red Square mobs, no piking of heads at Tower of London. Never were things so ripe for an explosive outburst, a mob scene within the shadow of seemingly vulnerable institutions such as the White House, Congress, the Pentagon, the CIA across the Potomac River.

FBI Director Hoover and Major Sweeney seemed to have overstated their case against progressives and troublemakers. Reuther continued to promote his progressive agenda throughout the 1960s including opposition to the Vietnam War. He died in a small-plane crash in 1970 caused by what was called a defective altimeter. Reuther's daughter suspected foul play, particularly since a year earlier the legendary labor leader had narrowly escaped death in a plane also described as having a defective altimeter. Reuther was a youngish 63 when he died.

TROUBLE IN DIXIE

While the March on Washington went peaceably, there was no end to the racial turmoil still to come in the 1960s. President Kennedy and his brother were regularly pressed by black leaders to advance integration, especially in the south.

The Kennedys eventually became staunch champions of civil rights but they were by no means pioneers.

"What the f—- does he want anyway?" Jack Kennedy said privately to his brother at one point, after he had personally telephoned Alabama authorities to release Martin Luther King after his "Letter From A Birmingham Jail" reached the White House. Bobby Kennedy, who had authorized FBI Director Hoover to wiretap Dr. King, pressed forcefully for integration and voter registration.

The peaceful March on Washington came amid strife in Oxford, Mississippi and Birmingham, AL that would ignite riots in northern cities —rioting that began in fits and starts even before JFK's assassination.

All hell broke out in the fall of 1962 at the University of Mississippi when a 29-year old six-year Air Force veteran named James Meredith became the first black ever to enroll at Ole Miss. Most students at the fine Oxford institution were interested more in celebrating the university's 100th anniversary, which coincided with a tragic loss of southern lives a century earlier. In 1862 during the Civil War, all but four members of the Ole Miss graduating class had enlisted in the Confederate Army, forming the 11th Brigade, CSA. All were killed at the Battle of Gettysburg.

Campus morale was also supercharged by Ole Miss embarking on what would become its first undefeated football team in school history, winning in the nationally powerful Southeast Conference on the way to a New Year's Day victory over Arkansas in the Sugar bowl.

The enrollment, however legitimate, smacked of an ill-timed provocation. The choice of time and place could not have been worse. Some undergraduate chauvinists and racists who were not hard to find in the south in those days staged a protest demonstration against Meredith's enrollment. Former General Edwin Walker, a John Bircher, war hero and America Firster who had reluctantly led U.S. troops to integrate schools in Little Rock, worked to organize protests against Meredith, lending skill, money and organizational talent. Things quickly got out of hand to become a mob scene. In Washington, President Kennedy telephoned Mississippi Governor Ross Barnett seeking activation of the state's National Guard. Barnett refused, as young CBS-TV reporter Dan Rather reported. The Kennedys sent in U.S. Army soldiers drawn from the 82nd Airborne Division at Fort Bragg, NC and the 101st Airborne Division from Fort Campbell, KY. These were troops otherwise girding for combat in Vietnam.

In the ensuing melee, the Army soldiers fired tear gas at rioting students and roughed them up, often in self-defense. Many of the rioters were injured, some from rifle fire. The quietly courageous Meredith would graduate in 1963 and a black girl who matriculated shortly after the Meredith mess would soon be elected senior class president, even after she had refused to carry the school's trademark rebel flag, It was a sign that the University of Mississippi's female student body, and probably most of its students, favored desegregation. Nevertheless, deep scars inflicted in that fall of 1962 would engender fatalities elsewhere before the winter was over.

BIRMINGHAM BLUES

In the 16th Street Baptist Church in Birmingham, AL, which King used as headquarters, a far worse outrage erupted early on a Sunday morning in January 1963. Four black girls, three of them 14-year olds and one a mere 11 were killed due to terrorism while entering the church for Sunday school class. The dynamiting shocked the nation, leading to a national anger to see the suppression of blacks put to an end, there being no place in the American individual or collective conscience for sacrificing innocent teenage children to cultural animosities based on skin color. The dynamite was planted by four white supremacists, extremist members of a local Ku Klux Klan chapter, who were opponents of the desegregation drive by civil rights organizations to rid the country and particularly the southeastern United States of discrimination and second-class status. One of the terrorists had been seen carrying dynamite. He was tried, fined a small sum and walked free. Not until 14 years later when review of FBI investigative field reports identified all four Klanners and their dynamite stash was the Klanner retried and sent to prison for life. All four were eventually caught and imprisoned.

The FBI from that point on stopped playing games with southern racists. No longer could the "aw shucks" good old boys escape consequences or dodge answering questions by turning to folksy digressions about " where the fish are jumping." J. Edgar Hoover reprised the skills that in earlier years had wiped out machine-gun toting bank robbers, broken up the Bund and rooted out Communist spies. Agents infiltrated and harassed Ku Klux Klan klavens, sending violence-prone agitators scurrying for safe ground. The smirking duplicity that lurked behind the faces of too many otherwise smiling rustics and sometimes even gracious southern gentlemen was forcefully if slowly stamped out so that only the known and incorrigible racists were left to fester in their hatreds. The southland, long famous for some of the nicest people in the world, would be glad to shed itself of that turn-like-a-snake viciousness once buried in the ethos of too many of its men folk whenever the subject of race relations reared its ugly head.

President Kennedy would enjoy his finest hour in several stirring speeches elevating national aspirations for civil rights and equality in spirit as well as law.

"Change is the law of life," he intoned in one of his stirring speeches on June 25, 1963, delivered to an adoring crowd in Frankfurt, Germany. Always inspirational with his crackling Boston-accented orations devoid of the letter "r", Kennedy's soaring rhetoric unfortunately lacked one thing that the podium could not provide. He appeared to lack any sound grasp of the power his speeches had. Larded with classical allusions and stirring quotations – many put there by his non pareil speech-writer Ted Sorrensen – JFK's speeches too often ignored the problem of rising expectations, promising more than Kennedy could deliver. The world could not nor would not change overnight. It was one thing to express ideals, quite another to deliver.

"YOU MEAN THEY'RE GOING TO KILL HIM?"

"Oh yeah – it's in the working," replied confirmed racist Joseph

Adams Milteer on November 9, 1963 – 13 days before President Kennedy was assassinated.

Milteer was being wiretapped by Miami, Florida detectives who had planted a 40-pound tape recorder in the Miami apartment of set-up man Willie Somerset, their confidential informant. The telephone talk was between Milteer and Somerset.

Milteer was a known racist from Pitman, Mississippi, a Klansman who gloated over the prospect of JFK's expected demise. He said the hit men would use a high-powered rifle. He did not say the hit would occur in Dallas because he expected that Kennedy would be murdered in Florida, where he was to speak in Miami and Tampa before jetting on Air Force One to Dallas.

JFK had been warned by his brother, Attorney General Robert F. Kennedy, to avoid the southern campaign swing because it was too dangerous. There had already been a rumor of an assassination in Chicago where on November 2 JFK had cancelled a scheduled appearance in Soldiers' Field at a Saturday afternoon college football game between the U.S. Military Academy and the Air Force Academy, two military service teams more commonly known as Army and Air Force.

There are two divergent reasons why JFK cancelled the Chicago trip. One reason was that JFK was needed in Washington due to an overnight emergency development in the Far East. A military coup in Saigon, capital of South Vietnam, had unexpectedly caused the death by assassination of longstanding American ally President Ngo Dinh Diem and his brother, Nhu. Kennedy's White House had authorized CIA Station Chief Lou Conein to pull off the coup. That the coup tank commanders had decided to murder the deposed president was not really part of the game plan and it sickened Kennedy. The second reason for scrubbing the stop at Soldiers' Field was fear that there might be an assassination attempt on the way to or from the stadium. Chicago police had arrested but did not book two men who were carrying high-powered rifles which police thought might have been the same ones stolen a day or two earlier from an Illinois armory. The detained men were released because the weapons reportedly were not held illegally.

A third angle to the Chicago story is the strange arrest of Secret Service Agent Abraham Bolden, then 28, the first black ever to be assigned to the president's Personal Protective Service. The former Illinois state trooper was hired personally by JFK in 1961. Arrested and jailed on testimony of two Chicago counterfeiters he had busted for allegedly trying to shake them down, the Secret Service agent would be convicted in July, 1964 and sentenced by Illinois Judge Sam Perry to six years in jail. One of the counterfeiters later recanted and said he was told to lie by the prosecutor. Perry blamed the frame-up on Mafioso John Roselli, a top mobster in the Chicago Outfit who would surface three weeks later in Dallas as part of the Chicago hit team. Perry always claimed he was framed for repeatedly trying to report that he had overheard Secret Service colleagues, many of them conservatives and southerners, say they did not like JFK and would never take a bullet for him.

After hearing Bolden, the HSCA in March, 1979 concluded that the Secret Service was inadequately prepared in Dallas to protect JFK from a sniper and that the Secret Service had information that was inadequately "analyzed, investigated and used" that might have prevented the assassination.

THE PLOTS CONVERGE

ASSASSINATION RUMORS RUN RAMPANT

As JFK swept through nine states in a week on a whirlwind tour to open his reelection campaign in November 1963, rumors spread widely that he faced assassination attempts.

He said as much to his wife in Fort Worth just outside Dallas before his breakfast talk to Texas businessmen on November 22, 1963.

"It wouldn't be hard for a rifleman in a tall building," Mrs. Jacqueline Kennedy recalled the president saying. In Washington, privy to incoming scraps of information, Attorney General Robert F. Kennedy had warned him to stay out of the south.

They had learned from Miami Police and the FBI that a known racist had been wiretapped on November 9 telling a supposed friend that JFK's assassination was "in the working", undoubtedly by use of a high-powered rifle from a tall building.

That intercept was relayed to the FBI where the head of its Atlanta Field Office called for a rush report on Joseph Adams Milteer, a Mississippian then living in Georgia. The assignment was given to youthful FBI Special Agent Don Adams at a sub-office in Thomasville, Ga. where Agent Adams tailed and then confronted Milteer. Milteer said it was only some loose talk.

Adams worked overtime on the lead and wrapped it up on Nov. 19, when he submitted his report to the Atlanta Field Office. There was talk that Milteer was seen in Dealey Plaza in Dallas three days later. In a speech and You Tube recording many years later, the retired FBI agent said Milteer was not in Texas on the day of the assassination. He checked back and confirmed that Milteer was in Georgia the whole time, Agent Adams said.

There were other leaks separate from the Milteer wiretap, according to Secret Service Special Agent Samuel A. Kinney when he was interviewed in the late 1990s by Vince Palamara for the latter's book *The Third Alternative*. There was a scare on Nov. 18 four days before Dallas while Kennedy was in Florida, Kinney said.

That everyone was on their toes during Kennedy's campaign blitz to Florida is well documented. As time would tell, the renegade Operation 40 team ensconced in a safe house in Miami originally planned to assassinate Kennedy in Florida. It's never been fully documented how many other hit men had the same idea.

PLAN TO INVADE CUBA

The danger signs in Miami centered on JFK's scheduled motorcade and speech on Monday, November 17, at the Inter-American Press Association Conference. The speech contained a brief coded message to secretly signal disaffected militia and army officers in Cuba that the American government supported a planned invasion that CIA point man Desmond Fitzgerald from Washington had scheduled for December 1, 1963. Anti-Castro guerilla exiles armed and ready were based at offshore paramilitary staging encampments in Central America and the Dominican Republic. Fitzgerald, a redheaded Bostonian with a brilliant Far East back-ground, had recently been tasked by the Kennedys to get rid of Castro. As a CIA Inspector General's 1967 report unreleased until 1998 would show, Fitzgerald had met in Paris in late October with Cuban Major Rolando Cubela Sanchez, a Cuban revolutionary hero who had soured on Castro. Fitzgerald had arranged for Cubela to meet in

Paris with CIA Agent Nestor Sanchez on November 22. On that fateful day, CIA Agent Sanchez handed the renegade Cuban a high-powered rifle with a scope and silencer which Cubela wanted and a Paper Mate ballpoint pen fashioned to inject Castro with a fatal dose of Blackleaf 40. Castro's KGB had penetrated the plot, but it was not due to any double agentry by Cubela. He would continue his efforts to oust or kill Castro until 1966, when he was tried in Cuba for treason for which he served 13 years in prison. A celebrated rebel who was first to seize the presidential palace from dictator Fulgencio Batista on Jan. 1, 1959, Cubela was spared execution only because Castro was unwilling to put to death a fellow revolutionary hero for fear it might cause an uprising.

In Miami following cancellation of the motorcade, Kennedy gave his speech to the Inter American Press Conference indoors and without incident. This was the speech that included the coded message about White House support for the upcoming Dec. 1 assault on Cuba. Perilous undertakings involving the cagy Castro were afoot. Castro had already served notice he was aware of the Kennedy and CIA maneuverings when in late September he called an Associated Press correspondent aside at a reception in the Brazilian embassy in Havana to offer a veiled warning that those who would try to "threaten others are not themselves safe." The warning factored into LBJ's post-Dallas confidential remark made to his aide Jack Valenti that "the Kennedys were running a goddamned Mafia operation in the Caribbean but Castro got to them before they got to him." It sounded good at the time, but LBJ was not telling everything that he knew.

The next day, a Tuesday, the president helicoptered from Miami to McDill Air Force Base on outskirts of Tampa, where he was joined by his personal pal, Sen. George Smathers, D-FL in a presidential limousine. Tampa is the ancient pirates' cove near the Gulf of Mexico known as the lightning capital of the world because of the natural fireworks that at times flash across Tampa Bay. The president witnessed the launching of a huge Polaris missile at McDill – the same type of ICBM that was primed to strike Havana during the Cuban missile crisis the previous October.

BAIT DANGLED FOR BOUNTY HUNTERS

The long highway drive to Tampa proper did not detour into the outlying Cuban exile enclave known as Ybor City, which was famous for Cuban cigars and the bolita numbers lottery run by Tampa Mafia boss Santo Trafficante, a conniver in the Chicago Outfit's major role in killing Kennedy. Trafficante was a double-dealer who sometimes dealt secretly with Castro because Fidel had not executed him and had released him from a Cuban prison after having closed his Havana casino hotel. He became notorious for before his imminent death while driving in the back seat of a limo telling his lawyer, Teamster attorney Frank Ragano of Washington D.C. who was also counsel for Teamster boss James R. Hoffa, "We shouldn't have killed Giovanni – we should have killed Bobby." The remark smacked of doubletalk, because Trafficante at another point was quoted by Ragano as advocating killing a snake by cutting off its head, the same old underworld saw used by his gumba, Carlos Marcello. Ragano said Hoffa was tired of being hounded by Bobby Kennedy's Justice Department "Get Hoffa Squad" and had told the lawyer to relay word to Trafficante and Marcello that, "It's time to kill Kennedy."

Marcello had personal reason to hate Bob Kennedy. The attorney general had grown impatient with Marcello's nine years of court stalls blocking deportation. He had his men kidnap the tomato wholesaler, slot machine distributor and motel owner. They unceremoniously dumped the reputed New Orleans Mafia boss in Guatemala, forcing a long walk to Guatemala City. Marcello swore revenge, but a wiretap in his highway hotel revealed nothing about any assassination. Marcello did crow to a prison yard squealer later that he had taken care of the Kennedys – typical braggadocio that gained some credence because tons of intrigue was later found to have swirled around Marcello's bailiwick of New Orleans.

SUN BELT MAFIOSI TEMPT BOUNTY HUNTERS

Assassination researchers point to widespread informal reports that Trafficante and Marcello had dangled bounties as high as $40,000 on the president's head – a small fortune which could buy as many as two new houses or more in a good suburb in the early 1960s.

As the leading underworld figure in Florida outside of "open city" Miami, Trafficante had narcotic connections to the Corsican Mafia in Marseilles, France. Researcher Steve Revele speculated that the Mafia went overseas to recruit a stone killer and drug dealer named Lucien Sarti, age 32, an international killer-for-hire, to take the contract in Dallas. In Marseilles, the southern French port city where opium from Turkey and Indochina was processed, the contact was Antoine Guerini who had a waterfront dive from which he ran the Corsican mob. He was told to put out a contract on "the biggest vegetable" in the United States and offered the hit to Christian David, who would become Revele's information source. When told the hit would be in the United States, Christian said he turned it down because it was too dangerous. It then went to Sarti who would go anywhere and hit anyone if the price was right. Revele was told by David that Sarti was prone to violence and thought nothing of using explosive bullets.

When faced by Revele about cold-blooded cruelty, Christian replied, "It's not about sympathy." He said it was a job just like any sniper.

David said he heard details of the assassination first hand from Sarti at a bar where the drug traffickers hung out together in Buenos Aires, Argentina a few months after the event.

CORSICAN BROTHERHOOD IN ON HIT

The story about three Corsican assassins in Dallas told to researcher/author Steve Revele suffered when it was proven that Sarti's named fellow Corsican killers could not have been in Dallas because they were in fact in prison in France on Nov. 22, 1963.

Sarti's alleged two sidemen could have been two others but Revele was stuck with discrediting information overload – an occupational hazard when trying to unravel a mystery hoary with age and fraught with contradictions many of which were deliberately planted by dissimulation experts. Supporting evidence inescapably scant for his book and 1988 TV documentary *The Men Who Killed Kennedy*, Revele's story said that Sarti and two other hit men flew into Mexico and crossed the Rio Grande at Brownsville, Texas, where they were met by a Chicago mobster, presumably John Roselli. They holed up in a Dallas safe house and laid low there for two weeks after the assassination before flying to Montreal in a private plane, the story went. It further said that Sarti did not fire from the Elm Street triple-overpass because people were there so he went instead to the fence atop a grassy area from where his shot blew the president's scalp off. Asked whether Sarti was in disguise, Christian David was hesitant before saying such jobs always require a disguise and then agreeing that the assassin wore a police uniform. This coincided with the so-called famous "badge man" on top of the grassy knoll captured by luck in spectator Mary Moorman's snapshot. Once the photo was enhanced years later, it showed the outline of a killer wearing a badge. Revele's crucial source, Christian David, a convicted heroin dealer, was angling for release from prison. He coyly promised Revele he would reveal more by releasing a secret document that was being held by his lawyer pending his eventual release from prison in France. The informant Christian David is now out of prison and hasn't been heard from. After years of research, Revele finally gave up the chase and took a job as a Hollywood scriptwriter, contributing to the motion picture *Nixon*. The French Connection had become unresolved history.

In May 1971, President Nixon announced a war on international heroin dealers. He formed a killer squad of 15 former CIA agents headed by Lou Conein, the veteran French-speaking former Saigon CIA station chief and old OSS French maquis resistance hand from World War II. The Marseilles gang loved Conein, so much so that they had awarded him a medal and conferred on him lifetime honorary membership in the Corsican Brotherhood, a recognition that Conein prized highly. The veteran soldier was remembered as the longtime right-hand man in southeast Asia of legendary CIA superspy General Edward G. Lansdale and who was — after Lansdale came home to the Pentagon – the CIA man who on orders of the National Security Council and White House engineered the Nov. 1, 1963 coup that left America's old ally Diem and his brother improvidently dead. The murdering was becoming contagious.

Given a new license to kill by President Nixon eight years later, Conein lost no time tracking Corsican heroin dealer Sarti, a suspect in the JFK assassination. On April 27, 1972, while sportily clad Sarti was partying with his wife and some pretty disco girls outside a club in Mexico City, Sarti engaged in a shootout with and was gunned down by drug enforcement agents and Mexican police. One of the suspected Dealey Plaza riflemen was silenced forever. Many said good riddance. Others rued loss of a key to help unlock the mysteries that remain.

TAMPA DEATH THREATS

By the time on November 18 that JFK reached the University of South Florida nestled among tall highway buildings off the freeway in Tampa, his road route had been scrambled for safety purposes. The FBI had tracked a series of five death threat letters sent by three young men saying they would shoot the president because of his association with Martin Luther King, a civil rights leader promoting desegregation. The FBI posted a wanted bulletin for John Warrington, 20, a slim white male, who had said if he couldn't get a gun he would figure out some other way of killing Kennedy. Police Chief J P Mullins stationed policemen armed with rifles on all overpasses along the motorcade route. The Secret Service, meanwhile, was hunting for a Cuban rifleman who they considered a far more serious threat. The UPI ran a story in the *Tampa Tribune* about the death threats, but it did not appear until Nov. 23,with a follow up the next day in the *Miami Herald*, both coming after the assassination. On Nov. 19, Dallas police arrested a young white male machinist who had told two girls he would shoot Kennedy on November 22 from a vantage point near the International Trade Center which was near the machine shop where he worked. A full-page ad later tracked to a front group sponsored by oil baron H.L. Hunt in the *Dallas Morning News* on Friday, Nov. 22 carried a big bold anti-Kennedy wanted headline: Treason.

There were other perils to worry about. Madame Nhu had lashed out at Kennedy furiously after the Saigon coup ousted and caused the death of President Diem and his brother, her husband. In September Attorney General Robert Kennedy had paraded veteran Mafioso Joseph Villachi before television cameras to lay out the mechanics of what was revealed for the first time to be an Italian/Sicilian underworld called Cosa Nostra, meaning "Our Thing", a shade different from what had always been known as the Mafia. Vilachi supposedly had revealed a lot of underworld secrets, which did not enchant the mob bosses. It was known that the FBI and Bobby Kennedy were running wiretaps widely and that the Kennedys even while forcing a rollback in steel prices had bullied leaders of the steel industry by use of the blackjack tool of pulling their income tax returns. Kennedy had also spoken openly about replacing the Federal Reserve banking system – a potentially revolutionary change in the money system that recalled Andrew Jackson's struggles and would presage President Nixon's problems after he abandoned the gold standard.

The president in 1962 had been seen openly on TV to be fooling around with movie icon Marilyn Monroe before she overdosed and died. The 36-year -old was still cherished by a generation of Korea vets who loved her for her good-skate ways displayed in the Frozin Chosen on her tours with comedian Bob Hope in the 1950s and for her musical comedy talents.

NATION TORN BY TURMOIL

The Profumo Affair in London had sullied the reputation of a longstanding ally and toppled the government. At the same time, the same call girl ring was rumored to be active in New York City and an Iowa newspaper had accused New Frontiersmen in the executive branch of government of patronizing prostitutes. The defection of British superspy Kim Philby in the summer of 1963 to Moscow not only left the United States with egg on its face, it left people to fret about just how badly the nation might be faring in the Cold War vis a vis the Soviet Union. Still fresh in everyone's mind were the terrible tension of the Cuban missile crisis and the threat of nuclear war. Cuba remained a festering sore, leading tough ex-vets of wars in Europe, the Far East and Korea to wonder what was so hard about flipping one little Caribbean thorn in the nation's side. Drug use was mushrooming and a new scourge called LSD or acid was bending minds all over the place as mindless millions seemed content to do little more than twist the night away.

Racial clashes and desegregation protests flared throughout the south and sparked mini-riots in northern, eastern and western cities where the whites believed there had been no institutional segregation. Stormy protests were on the verge of erupting into riots in the inner cities that would destroy the woof and warp of urban America as the supermalls and big box highway stores displaced the mom-and-pop shops so dear to older generations and young folk as well. The price of uhuru in 1960s America was to become entire streets ruined or burned to the ground and in 1963 a great many people could see it coming, much to their chagrin.

'Surging crowds and squealing women surrounded a smiling Kennedy wherever he went but the background static from recurring assassination threats was so pervasive and unusual that clearly the tour should have been cut short. As if he had a death wish, JFK would not heed the warnings.

The Cuban tinderbox cut both ways, breeding bands of armed men intent on having their way. Southern male blue-collar workers and redneck rustics, young and old, were driven to frenzy by the desegregation threat to their cultural dominance. They blamed and scapegoated Kennedy for an evolving social revolution in which he was little more than a cork bobbing on the waves – though admittedly an eloquent cork. Everything was Kiplingesque: boots, boots, boots, boots, marching up and down again.

A Democratic National Committeeman, Marty Underwood, sensed the danger. He told researchers that he had been hearing all kinds of rumors as little as 18 hours prior to and right up until the end that JFK would be assassinated in Dallas. He told Kennedy personally about the threats, voicing his concern. Underwood said Kennedy was touched personally by his concerns, but graciously brushed them off as perhaps a bit overblown. Underwood said JFK had spoken to Rep. Henry Gonzalez, the congressman for San Antonio, who had learned through his two brothers of dangers and then told the president there was no need to worry because he had been told that the Secret Service knew of the threats and had taken care of everything.

Kennedy's all-day whistle-stop type tour in Tampa reached out everywhere: The Steelworkers' International Union, the Chamber of Commerce, and the Al Lopez ball field. At the University of South Florida, the president gave his fifth talk in nine hours. The host presented a puzzled JFK with what looked like a teddy bear but Kennedy was gracious enough to crack a broad grin, accepting it as some sort of replica of a mascot.

NAGEL WAS ARMY INTELLIGENCE AGENT

In his 1992 book *The Man Who Knew Too Much*, a biography about an American military "floater" and double agent who wrote to J. Edgar Hoover in September, 1963 warning of a plot to assassinate President Kennedy, author Dick Russell cites Agent Richard Case Nagell's recollections of the professor in civilian clothes in an Army Intelligence academy who wildly labeled various people as Communists. The recollection was a test of Nagell's credibility. He passed since only someone who was actually there could know of the weird professor who liked to pin the red label on well-known public figures and celebrities. Going far beyond redbaiting Senator Joseph McCarthy, the professor's targets included several media news stars, none of whom had ever been publicly accused of undermining the Republic or promoting Sino-Soviet Communism. The recollection by Nagell said he did not know the professor's name. Nagell's reference to the professor's odd en camera accusations does establish Nagell's bona fides, proving he had been a student at the Army Intelligence School as he claimed. Nagell said he had worked for the CIA and doubled as an agent for the KGB, making him a "triple agent", as he described it, his loyalty being to the United States.

Such confused identity passes as cleverness in the intelligence trade where not everyone is who they say they are. Although the CIA may bankroll "floaters" such as Nagell and step in as control agents or case officers, Nagell appears to have been an Army Intelligence FOI (Field Operating Intelligence} "floater", a status achieved by completing a successful tour of duty and then being reenlisted by the SAC of his office in that particular city or by the regional command. He would acquire a "cover" occupation, and be freed of daily investigative and reporting chores. The undercover agent would be assigned to penetrate a suspect organization or group and made to report to a referenced and unidentified secret "control agent" whom he would never meet face-to-face, restricting communication to safe phones and coded messages. The control agent would use a nom de guerre so that his identity would remain unknown to the field agent. All very hush hush, like two Capricorns having an eye duel.

Nagell said he got involved in the fall of 1962 in Mexico City with a group of violence-prone Cuban exiles that was talking about assassinating Kennedy using anger over the Bay of Pigs disaster as a pretext and then blaming the proposed assassination on Cubans and Russians in hopes of starting a war. The instigated war would then enable the anti-Castro Cubans to regain control of Cuba. Nagell mixed with two firebrands he knew as "Angel" and "Leopoldo" who were tentatively identified as Sergio Arcacha Smith and "Q", the latter being Carlos Quiroga or Rafael "Chi Chi" Quintero, who were part of the Alpha 66 movement to oust Castro. His penetration took him with "Angel" and "Leopoldo" to New

Orleans and Miami, then back to Mexico City where at the Luma Hotel he met Lee Harvey Oswald as well as a beautiful prostitute, Maria Del Carmen, a Cuban G-2 KGB agent who was also on the CIA's payroll. He suggested that Del Carmen was helping to promote the Alpha 66 project while simultaneously tattling to Castro's G-2 agents.

Nagell's tortuous tale is significant because "Angel" and "Leopoldo" knew and helped renegade CIA Agent David "El Indio" Sanchez Morales, key man in the Operation 40 outfit based in Miami. Morales was field point man for one of the key assassination squads — the one involving anti-Castro Cuban exiles and a renegade CIA faction. This was the Kennedy-hating bitter anti-Castro gang which retaliated against Attorney General Robert F. Kennedy for, immediately following the Cuban Missile Crisis, ousting CIA legend William King Harvey, the no-nonsense, salty-tongued chief of the covert $50-million-a-year Task Force war against Castro known as Operation Mongoose. The knives-in-their-teeth Cuban exiles and their CIA handlers bridled at what they described as "being sold out by the Kennedys again" and were infuriated by the scapegoating of their boss, "Two Gun" Bill Harvey. Gen. Lansdale had named the project after a ferret-like mammal in south Asia noted for its quickness and agility in killing snakes and rats. The snout-nosed and long-tailed mongoose was said to have 33 attack modes. Lansdale had proliferated so many code-lettered ad hoc organizations in the Sun Belt – A/R Rifle, Operation 40, AMLASH, Alpha 66, ad infinitum — that no one could figure out one from the other, which insiders said was just the way the celebrated spymaster wanted it. President Kennedy was a big fan of unconventional warfare who at first was so taken by Lansdale's imaginative plans that he privately referred to the general as "America's James Bond".

The Operation Mongoose secret assaults and assassination attempts against Castro were initiated in the second half of 1961 and continued during 1962 until the para-military phase was abruptly cancelled by the Kennedys as part of a sub rosa deal with the Soviet Union's Premier Nikita Khrushchev to defuse the

October, 1962 missile crisis. Three of Harvey's seven pending midnight infiltration commando raids had proceeded past the deadline. RFK considered this a case of insubordination and a perilous one, since the Kremlin would see it as a breach of an accord newly agreed upon. History has never clearly shown whether the bull-headed Harvey was making his own foreign policy – telling the Kennedys and the Kremlin to get lost – or whether RFK did not factor in that the horse had left the stable and overreacted by targeting Harvey. Harvey was transferred to Rome to become station chief, a soft assignment. However, to Castro-haters girding for new assaults on Cuba, the reassignment was tantamount to a demotion signaling an end to Harvey's noteworthy CIA career.

OPERATION 40 MAKES COMEBACK

It is proverbial in the intelligence world that the two common motives for abandoning flag loyalty or defection are personal gain and ideology. At least as common is the motive of revenge. Ideology was heavily shaded in as a general background motif for the Operation 40 stampede into Dallas, but it was vengeance that whipped the fury of participating members. Operation 40 was the original anti-Castro task force of 40 members that first met secretly in January 1960 to thwart Cuban caudillo Fidel Castro's sudden shift from liberation hero to Soviet hemispheric menace. The Operation 40 task force was headed, in that final year of the Eisenhower administration, by then Vice President Richard Nixon, who would after his defeat by Kennedy in November 1960, turn over the reins. The group would go on to sponsor the ill-fated Brigade 2506 manned by Cuban exile invaders who were defeated by Castro's army at the Bay of Pigs disaster on April 17, 1961.

The Bay of Pigs invasion was code-named Operation Zapata after a Cuban province and CIA asset Zapata Oil Company, in which future CIA director and president George H.W. Bush was a partner. Using transports purchased in Delaware, the two ships were named the Houston, where Bush lived, and the Barbara, the name of George H.W. Bush's wife. In keeping with CIA mandates, former President George H.W. Bush is not known to have ever acknowledged participation as a corporate asset in the Bay of Pigs CIA-backed operation. GHW Bush was a graduate of Yale where he played varsity first base and was a member of a secret undergraduate institution called Skull and Bones, a springboard to stardom in first the old OSS and later its successor CIA. The son-in-law of a former U.S, senator from Vermont, he was unsuccessful in running for public office until winning the vice presidency in 1980 as Ronald Reagan's running mate. He had once sought a Texas congressional seat without luck. He was nonetheless appointed CIA director for a year in the mid 1970s and was so well regarded that he was named running mate for vice president Ronald Reagan as Reagan/Bush swept to victory in 1980. Bush was elected president in 1988 and served one term before losing a reelection bid in 1992.

An interesting sidelight to Bush's speculated role as a CIA asset in the early 1960s was the fact that in an FBI memo a George Bush was mentioned as having been briefed by FBI Director J. Edgar Hoover on the JFK assassination the next day. Bush was once asked about it and reportedly said it must have been a different George Bush.

SPYWORLD'S E.H. HUNT ADMITS PLOT TO KILL JFK

In a confession on his deathbed in 2004, agency superspy E. Howard Hunt said the plot that was code-named "The Big Event" was hatched in a Miami hotel room in league with Frank Sturgis. They talked a minute after the orchestrated departure of David Sanchez Morales. Bill King was already "on board", Sturgis said. Morales was the CIA's top assassin in Latin America. Hunt and Sturgis went to Dallas as "benchwarmers", a baseball term meaning substitutes who would come off the bench if needed. Both would be arrested and imprisoned some ten years later in the Watergate scandal, ex-Marine and CIA hit man Sturgis as one of the Nixon White House "plumbers", Hunt a schemer and paymaster.

The intersection of Oswald with Nagell was germane for reasons other than direct field verification that Oswald was an intelligence agent. Nagell said he and Oswald at one point were target shooting in a northern Mexico desert. "He couldn't hit the broad side of a barn," Nagell said of Oswald, typifying his accuracy level as "Maggie's draws", a military term used to describe a shooter who not only couldn't hit the target rings around a bulls eye but couldn't even hit the target itself.

Author Russell said when he last spoke to Nagell by telephone a year-and-a-half after publication of the Nagell biography. Nagell said he hadn't even read it. The author found that to be surprising. He said that Nagell, 65, who had eluded several assassination attempts according to the book, was found dead a week later in his rundown apartment on the fringes of Los Angeles. The cause of death was certified as a heart attack by the Los Angeles coroner's office.

Agent Nagell was an element in the mystery man portrayed as an all-knowing Black Ops supply operative in the Oliver Stone movie JFK except that New Orleans District Attorney James Garrison had met him not in the Washington D.C. mall but in New York City's Central Park. The character played by actor Donald Sutherland spouted the views of real-life Colonel Fletcher Prouty, a former aide of Pentagon General Ed Lansdale. Nagell was a decorated Korean War veteran who after being injured in a stateside plane crash was recruited into the Army Counter Intelligence Corps and then its covert Field Operating Intelligence (FOI), which he told author Dick Russell was CIA.

There is nothing to verify FBI acknowledgement of floater Nagell's cryptic letter sent from the southwestern U.S. in September 1963 to the office of the FBI director in Washington D.C. warning of plots to assassinate President Kennedy. The message, which was partly coded, might have been treated as a crackpot letter many of which are sent and received. It could have contributed to but was not the trigger for the telex received at the

New Orleans FBI office warning five days before the assassination; that came from the Miami Police Department Intelligence Division's wiretap of racist Joseph Milteer's remark about a JFK assassination: "It's in the working."

SIZZLING MIAMI MELTING POT

"It's the dispersal problem," CIA Director Allen Dulles said. "The refugees – that's the real problem." He spoke of destabilizing wars generally, Cuba specifically.

At least 250,000 Cubans emigrated to the United States between January 1, 1959, the day Fidel Castro's revolutionaries took power, and 1964. A *Miami News* story in March of 1962 reported that 8,000 had arrived in a week. The first mass refugee exodus occurred during Kennedy's 1000 days in office.

It was a constant stream, 841,000 in South Florida and 142,000 in Hudson County, N.J., according to one updated survey many years later.

The influx changed the city of Miami. As immigrants do, arrivals from Cuba clustered in insular neighborhoods, gradually expanding outwards. Bodegas sprouted overnight, cigar stores doubled as corner hangouts, gossip filtered through every coffee shop. Masons and carpenters and workmen hustled a day's labor. Prostitutes walked designated alleys. Castro took from the middle class, gave to the peasants. He confiscated private property, empowered state regulators. The merchant class fled to Miami.

This was not Miami Beach or upscale North Miami, touristy Collins Avenue, the luxurious Fontainebleau and Eden Roc Hotels, the cobblestoned Lincoln Road shopping plaza, the chi chi South Beach to come. It was the bustling, music-filled, elbow-rubbing, smoke-filled mix of crowded inner city, an expatriate culture animated by the single unifying idea of regime change in Cuba. It was the crucible of counter-revolution, the forge of vengeance, the birthplace of the Miami-Havana War. Cubans knew how to dance and they would dance until Castro was dead.

The purpose of life was to recapture Havana.

"People do not realize the level of violence that exists in Latin America," said Meredith Vieira in her *Miami Herald* days, before becoming a network news star.

It did not escape notice of the Cuban emigres that Castro rounded up and imprisoned thousands of his real or imagined enemies. It was more than rumor that Che Guevara had personally executed dozens of regime foes. A Batista police agent and Air Force security chief named Francisco Fiorini who had sided with Castro's revolutionaries was forced to prove his allegiance to Castro by personally executing more than 150 condemned prisoners.

When Castro turned Cuba into a Soviet Communist state within a year of his takeover while railing against "the colossus to the north", Fiorini fled to Miami where he rented a plane at Opa Locka Airport and bombarded Havana with leaflets calling Castro a traitor and a Communist. Fiorini under his legally changed name, Frank Sturgis, would emerge as a prized CIA asset of CIA Latin American expert E. Howard 'Eduardo' Hunt and eventually, for reasons related to a Kennedy switch to spare Castro, personally take part in what they called "The Big Event", killing Kennedy in Dallas.

BIGGEST BUSINESS IN FLORIDA

Before and after Castro took power, gunrunning to one side or the other was good for a fast buck. Lou Lupinik of Chicago, an Army CIC Korean War veteran who finished flight school at Opa Locka Airport in Miami, turned down an offer to hop the strait with a load of guns and munitions for $10,000 – enough to pay half the cost of a nice split-level house. Why did he turn it down?

"If they caught you, they cut your cojones off," the future United Air Lines pilot said.

Before and after the unsuccessful Bay of Pigs invasion of Cuba in April 1961, Miami was an armed camp. Some 1200 anti-Castro guerillas comprising Brigade 2506, sponsored and funded by a CIA front dubbed 'Operation 40' for the 40 Cuban renegades and U.S. officials who founded it in January, 1960, were held in Cuban prisons until the Kennedy administration bailed them out by paying off Castro. They returned to Miami, mixing into cliques and squads newly recruited into juicy jobs as guerillas in the vastly expanded CIA project out of Washington known as Operation Mongoose, funded at fifty million dollars a year. Its headquarters on the campus of the University of Miami became the biggest CIA station in the world, headed by 200 CIA case officers and agents and at least 2,000 contract employees and casuals.

"It was the biggest business in Florida," according to ex-Marine and drillmaster Gerald Hemming, a soldier-of-fortune who was stopped by police wandering around two blocks from Dealey Plaza shortly after the assassination. Hemming and Sturgis, two Cuban brothers and a German blonde named Marita Lorenz, an ex-Castro mistress, drove in a two-car convoy carrying rifles, scopes and ammo from Orlando Bosch's safe house in Miami to Dallas where they met E. Howard Hunt, and then Jack Ruby, according to an account by Marita Lorenz given to the FBI in New York City. She said she sensed it was all too big for her so she took a plane back to Miami the day before the assassination. At the time, neither the FBI nor the Warren Commission staff believed her, but Hunt verified her story in his deathbed confession. Hunt said he and Sturgis were there only as "bench warmers". Sturgis later caught up with Lorenz in New York City and told her to keep her mouth shut or she could get hurt.

"You should have been there," she said Sturgis told her. "We made history. That was the day we killed the president."

CHANGING HORSES

The mutiny by CIA funded Operation 40 and other renegade elements in Operation Mongoose's 33 branches was triggered by change in Kennedy Cold War plans, resulting in bitterly resented official government attacks on the anti-Castro guerilla army.

ATF and Customs agents rousted anti-Castro soldiers on No Name Key north of Key West, demanding to see proof that their weapons were licensed,

FBI agents raided the guerilla camp at gunrunner Mike McLaney's storage bunker on the north shore of Lake Pontchartrain in New Orleans, taking down the names and publicizing the arrest of twenty guerillas who were drilling, target-shooting and working detonation scenarios.

Bobby Kennedy demoted William King 'Two Gun' Harvey, CIA chief of Operation Mongoose, for failing to halt in midstream three of ten secret sea craft sabotage launches against Cuba that had been in the works until Kennedy negotiations with Khrushchev secretly pledged hands-off Cuba.

U.S, Navy gunships attacked a privately-funded CIA gunboat, killing three anti-Castro Cubans on board. When ex-Flying Tiger millionaire anti-Castroite William Pawley III learned what had happened, he committed suicide in despair.

At every turn, alphabet agencies were turning the screws, criminalizing what had been a patriotic project called Operation Mongoose organized by Pentagon General Edward G. Lansdale in collaboration with Bill Harvey, the CIA point man, The project had been fully authorized by President Kennedy and the National Security Council. Kennedy had dubbed Lansdale "my own James Bond". Both JFK and RFK knew all about the official project they were now undermining.

This time the Kennedys were not waffling. They were attacking their own troops to honor their pledge to Khrushchev: Castro was off limits. The irony of this apparent détente was the zigzag that followed. Within months and throughout 1963, the Kennedys authorized a new player, the CIA's Desmond Fitzgerald, to head a repositioned task force to assassinate Castro. Fitzgerald's agent on the very day that JFK was assassinated was in Paris meeting with Rolando Cubela, a revolutionary hero who was disgusted with Castro and who was handed a poison pen and a high-powered telescoped rifle with which to kill the Cuban president. Fitzgerald also had plans for his task forces in the Caribbean to invade Cuba again on December 1, 1963.

As Irwin Shaw chronicled the rise of McCarthyism in his 1951 novel The Troubled Air, "watch out for the bomb bursts, treetop level – the wounds of peace are upon us."

FRAGGING IN DALLAS

In war the act of fragging – harming or shooting an overzealous or doltish superior – is not as rare as most people might imagine.

It's ordinarily justified, or it wouldn't happen.

A new leader who comes in and takes charge acts as if he knows everything. He's too bossy. Too gung ho. Partial and unfair. An unqualified bungler. He forces foolish risk, endangers lives. He's a lousy leader.

What to do? What else is there? Take him out. Frag him. Frag as with a grenade. Or rifle fire.

A heroic combat death? Battlefield wound? A purple heart. Maybe a bronze or silver star. Why not --- God bless us all.

A tragedy?

Of course – a tragedy born of necessity.

We're taught hierarchies. Obey the law. Obey the boss. Follow the leader. Eat your peas.

In civilian life it passes for good order.

War is different. Life or death. Struggle. Survive. The Law of the Jungle. War movie propaganda does not change life in a foxhole. Life is real and life is earnest. The grave is not its goal.

They say soldiers are willing to lay down their lives for their country. They may say it but it's just talk. Never met a man who would gladly give up his life for a symbol. He might as last resort. Who wants last resort? Take some stupid suicide hill where goats will graze tomorrow? You take it, sir.

Same goes for reckless or feckless superiors. Got tanks that save lives? Use 'em. Air cover to pin the bums down? Yessssssss! Go home with the guy who brought you? You bet.

There is no entry for the term fragging in Webster International's super huge 1934 dictionary. The passage of time would bring World War II, Korea. Indochina. Cuba, the Cold War. In 1994 – sixty years later – the words frag and fragging are listed in a much smaller Webster as U.S. Army and Marine Corps slang for injuring or assaulting an unpopular or overzealous superior with a fragmentation grenade. Please – perish the thought.

JFK?   Think Bay of Pigs.   Think Hispaniola.   Think Saigon.   Think Cuba.

Think fragging in Dallas.

MARY REDUX

Dr. Leary, again, in his autobiography Flashbacks:

"Ever since the Kennedy assassination I had been expecting a phone call from Mary. It came around December 1."

Leary could hardly understand her. She was either drunk or drugged or overwhelmed with grief. Or all three.

"They couldn't control him anymore," she said of Kennedy. "He was changing too fast."

There was a long pause, Leary wrote. Hysterical crying. He spoke reassuring words. She sobbed.

Mary said, "They've covered everything up. I gotta come see you. I'm afraid. Be careful."

Leary said the line went dead. "Worried, I could do nothing."

Leary was in India, a leg on a worldwide tour, in 1964. He did not know that Mary Meyer had been murdered during his absence, on Oct. 13, 1964 — less than a year after JFK's assassination. After returning to Millbrook in June of 1965 he yearned to see her. Had she phoned while he was on his world trip, he asked. No one had heard so he tried directory assistance. Finding no listing in Washington D.C., he called the Vassar College alumni office in Poughkeepsie, N.Y. The alumni office secretary broke the news:

"I'm sorry to say that she is, ah, deceased. Sometime last fall, I believe.' Leary and his fellow LSD tripper Michael Hollingshead resolved to find out what had happened to her. On their next trip into the city, their friend Van Wolfe contacted a friend at the New York Times who sent them a manila envelope containing file clippings from the newspaper's morgue.

Leary wrote that he was stunned to learn that Mary had been married to and divorced from Cord Meyer, whom he described as "...my nemesis from graduate school days, who now turned out to be a top spook. My head was spinning with ominous thoughts." Astounded that the murder of a friend of the Kennedys had brought so little inquiry or public outcry, Leary had Van Wolfe check police intelligence sources in D.C. who told him a lot of people there felt it was a professional hit.

ONE OF 'BIGGEST COVERUPS'

"Two slugs in the brain and one in the body. That's not the modus operandi of a rapist. And a mugger isn't going to shoot a woman with no purse in her hand," Leary recalled Van Wolfe saying. "It's gotta be one of the biggest cover-ups in Washington history. It's too hot to handle. Everyone comes out looking bad. Some people say dope was involved. So the truth could hurt everyone, all those powerful people. No one wants the facts known." Leary and Van Wolfe decided they would investigate and write a book if they could find a publisher big enough to handle it. They never followed through.

At that time in 1965, there was no public disclosure that the murdered woman had been the mistress of the late President John F. Kennedy. Scanning news clippings describing Mary as a friend of Jacqueline Kennedy, Leary still did not know that Mary's mystery lover had been the president. Nor did he know that Mary had trysted 33 times in the White House with President Kennedy between January 1962 and November 1963 during which they smoked pot and used other drugs. *Washington Post* executive James Truitt and his wife had been confidantes of Mary Meyer. At the time Truitt had been a high level assistant to Philip Graham, owner and chief editor of the *Washington Post.* Truitt was equal to or higher than Ben Bradlee, a JFK partisan who would become executive editor of the *Post* in 1968 after its control passed to Katherine Graham, the daughter of the *Post's* preceding owner. She had won control in court after Philip Graham's death when celebrated criminal defense attorney Edward Bennett Williams, lawyer for Philip Graham's estate, testified that the deceased editor had not been of sound mind when Williams took his dictated will disinheriting Graham's wife and wresting away her stock in the newspaper. Katherine Graham won the will struggle and sent her estranged husband's Australian newspaper girlfriend packing.

According to Leary's memoirs, his discovery of Mary's mystery lover did not surface until 13 years after he last spoke to her. A headline in the *San Francisco Chronicle* caught his eye in February 1976: NEW JFK STORY – SEX, POT WITH ARTIST. In interviews with the *National Enquirer, Associated Press* and *Washington Post*, former journalist James Truitt told of supplying drugs to Mary Meyer.

"I lit a Camel, walked to the window, and looked through the bars on San Diego Bay," Leary wrote. "So it was JFK that Mary had been turning on with. Once again I sensed that Mary Meyer's life and death were an important part of modern history."

The Justice Department has a long history of dealing harshly with violators of laws relating to espionage. Its major form is any overt act giving aid and comfort to an enemy of the state.

Spying for the enemy is banned by the Espionage Act of 1917, as amended periodically over the years. It's treasonous to sell or convey state secrets. Vital defense information is protected by its classification as top secret, which is stamped on literally millions of Security Act documents. Sensitive armaments and facilities are off limits, at risk of being shot or arrested.

Except when an Act of War is passed by Congress, or a statutory scheme explicitly defines prohibited acts, espionage is partly in the eye of the beholder. The First Amendment rights to free speech, press, religion and assembly are sacred parts of the Bill of Rights without which the U.S. Constitution could not have been passed in the first place. Proponents of laws binding everyone to the security of the state are not fond of the Bill of Rights, but theoretically they are bound by it, like it or not. Patriotism is a fine concept in principle; in practice it tramples on the equally fine concept of opposing a police state.

When Mary Meyer desperately told Dr. Leary a snitch had blown her brainwashing project, she was on the hook for espionage.

Was there any doubt? The filing of criminal information with the Federal Bureau of Investigation predictably invited a round of investigations during which FBI agents gathered information, filed field reports, took depositions and assembled witnesses. They obtained search warrants and gang raided homes and offices of useful witnesses and suspects. Once the train leaves the station, only powerful inside forces can slow its momentum or bring it to a halt.

Knowledge of a conspiracy by a self-described cell of influential Washington officials to brainwash by use of LSD to influence foreign policy would constitute a prima facie case of espionage, activating the FBI's counterintelligence Division Five headed by William Sullivan, third ranked behind Director J. Edgar Hoover, and the CIA's chief of Counterintelligence, James Jesus Angleton, a law unto himself given free rein within the Company.

"INFLUENCING" FOREIGN POLICY

Angleton's wife was best friends with fellow Vassar girl Mary Pinchot. Angleton, himself, was very friendly with Mary. Angleton would later acknowledge that Mary's affair with President Kennedy "could influence foreign policy". He never said whether his wife was one of Mary's "nine women" who introduced use of LSD to their husbands, which would have meant that Angleton himself could have been "brainwashed" or "utopiated". He did express enduring antipathy toward JFK, archly threatening at offices of Accuracy in Media (AIM), usually after drinking too many martinis, "to expose the real Jack Kennedy". He gravitated towards AIM, a think tank headed by Brent Bozell, son-in-law of

Conservative Review owner William F. Buckley, after being offended by an excellent Angleton biography by journalist William Martin called *A Wilderness of Mirrors*.

The ferocity of FBI agents in pursuit of spies was no less intense in May of 2013 than it was fifty years earlier.

In pursuit of a State Department employee's 2009 leak to the press of top secret information about North Korea's nuclear plans, FBI agent Reginald Reyes' affidavit seeking a warrant said there was evidence that reporter James Rosen broke the law "either as an aider, abettor and/or co-conspirator" when Rosen in 2009 wrote a story for *Fox News*. The story said U.S. Intelligence issued official warnings that Pyongyang would likely respond to U.S. sanctions with additional nuclear tests. Rosen in the past during the Clinton administration had held a high cabinet post in the State Department. His wife, Christiane Amanpour, was a veteran war correspondent for *CNN*. The two enjoyed wide respect, raising eyebrows when James Rosen became the target in the FBI search for the mole, a Korean State Department employee with whom Rosen was friendly. Rosen's story proved accurate; North Korea did respond with nuclear tests.

The furor raised a press firestorm that prompted the Department of Justice to deny any intention to prosecute Rosen. The episode did curtail his ability to freely pursue his profession, however, since his communications and e-mails were subjected to search and seizure.

The FBI crusade to nail moles and to plug leaks surfaced in another instance when the DOJ subpoenaed phone records for 21 phone lines used by 100 AP journalists over a span of two months, according to the Associated Press.

Federal investigators went wild when a series of leaks at Fort Meade, Md. showered secrets all over the Internet universe. The National Security Agency (NSA), the super secret "Big Ear" at Fort Meade, is known for routinely monitoring international telephone traffic. It's been doing so since the 1950s, according to soldiers who worked there and stories about arrested spies.

During trial of Army PFC Bradley Manning at Fort Meade in June 2013, Captain Joe Morrow accused the soldier of harvesting and distributing on the Internet thousands of documents that became available to the nation's enemies so as to "put the lives of fellow soldiers at risk". The defense described Manning as an idealist who saw injustice in Iraq and wanted to bare the violence against civilians caused by the Iraq War. Manning was convicted and imprisoned.

Still another target of espionage was former NSA contractor Edward Snowden, who claimed he was motivated by humanitarian concerns when he breached Security restrictions by unauthorized release of massive government telephone surveillance programs. He fled to Hong Kong to escape arrest, and continued to move ahead of authorities to promote his views. In Dublin for a conference on June 15, 2013, Attorney General Eric Holder vowed that Snowden would be punished once he is caught.

The tension between freedom and security is unending. A *New York Times* editorial espoused a soft landing for Snowden, whose espionage breached a contract trust which yielded him $175,000 a year. His proof that the NSA "Big Ear" was wiretapping foreign leaders had a nasty ring to uninitiated believers in a world of sweetness and light. His crusade for privacy might be an overdue gesture, while raising red flags from those entrusted with ensuring a safe and sane world. A far clearer call is the case of peace protesters outside Fort Bragg who were jailed for anti-war protests. They should be freed immediately and praised for putting peace over war as a foreign policy, civil libertarians insist. Polls show most Americans agree.

Hoover did not comment about Kennedy's not one but two separate and distinct major sexpionage indiscretions in 1963 or their implications for national security.

OUTSIDE THE BOX

Instead, he contacted important enemies of the Kennedys to advise that were they to take action to remove a malfunctioning president, who was he to argue? Beyond doubt, J. Edgar Hoover in months prior to Dallas wanted the Kennedys to disappear. His personality clashes with the Kennedys, especially Attorney General Bob Kennedy, in and of themselves might not have pushed him over the edge – he had weathered a stormy relationship with President Harry Truman a decade earlier without going outside the box to prevail. With Jack Kennedy it went much further. Not only was a hostile and arrogant Bob Kennedy waiting in the wings to seize power, the president's outrageous sexpionage adventures were, objectively, a compromise of national security. His breaches of conduct were institutional. The special problem was how does one rein in a riderless horse, especially if his stablemate is wilder still. There was only one course of action, anathema though it might be.

Get rid of him.

Contrary to speculation over the years that the FBI went into the tank prior to the JFK assassination, the evidence does not support such theories. The Department of Justice, headed in 1963 by RFK, attorney general, and the Federal Bureau of Investigation, while guarding federal law generally, did not see itself as primary protector of the president, a role assigned by law to the Secret Service's Presidential Protective Service of the U.S. Treasury Department, a separate and independent cabinet department.

The FBI had fielded a number of alerts about possible assassination attempts in months prior to the actual assassination. While the volume of static with respect to JFK had far exceeded threats of domestic violence experienced under previous presidencies of Dwight Eisenhower and Harry S. Truman, assassination threats were by no means rare. During JFK's 1000 days in office, authorities had counted approximately 800 threats against JFK, most of them from unfelonious cranks. There had been remarkably few actual assassination attempts in the United States during the violent, war-ravaged 20th Century.

ASSASSINATIONS A RARITY

Until John F. Kennedy, three of 34 presidents had been assassinated, only one in the 20th Century. There were two victims in the last half of the 19th Century. Abraham Lincoln was shot by actor John Wilkes Booth acting for a Maryland-area group of conspiratorial Confederate sympathizers and John Garfield in his second term was shot in a Washington train station by a political supporter who was aggrieved because he was not rewarded with a job as consul to a European nation. There was no Secret Service shield in those days.

McKinley was the only 20th Century victim before Kennedy, cut down in his second term by anarchist Leon Czolgost. McKinley was moving the country toward internationalism, the Pan American Exposition in one sense being a vehicle to promote world trade that the Mark Hanna Republican machine out of Ohio welcomed as an expanded market for American manufacturing goods. McKinley had also expanded American frontiers, winning the Spanish-American War that brought Cuba, Puerto Rico and the Philippines into the ambit of the United States. Inflamed by a cause, his assassin had embraced an ideology that didn't believe in government, period.

Czolgost was an anarchist inflamed by an international sociopathic wave that had also targeted heads of state in Europe and Russia under the banner of Nihilism.

Teddy Roosevelt, after serving out McKinley's three years and a four-year reelection term, later survived an assassination attempt in Milwaukee, Wisconsin in September 1912 when as head of a third-party Bull Moose independent ticket he helped oust his old friend and political protégé President William Howard Taft, only to ensure the election of Democrat Woodrow Wilson. Teddy Roosevelt was saved because he was "longwinded and myopic," a biographer observed, because the bullet that lodged in his chest was deflected by a double-folded 50-page speech and his steel reading-glass case. Roosevelt recovered quickly and still had the bullet in him when he died many years later.

In the intervening forty years, the only sitting president targeted for assassination was President Harry S. Truman, in both instances for international political reasons rather than ad hominem hatred. In 1947 the Secret Service acting in concert with British Intelligence intercepted letter bombs mailed to both British regents and Truman by the terroristic Stern Gang in Germany at a time when Britain was reviewing its mandate in Palestine. The gang wanted an independent Israel and got it in 1948, with Truman's support. Again in 1951, two Puerto Rican nationalists tried to assassinate Truman over an international issue involving independence and sovereignty. Living at Blair House while the White House was undergoing renovation, Truman escaped a confrontation when White House police and Secret Service stepped in. The ensuing shootout on the lawns of the White House killed one assassin and mortally wounded the other. The gun battle, depicted boldly on front pages of New York tabloids and other newspapers, cost a White House policeman his life.

The two Truman assassination attempts demonstrated the extremism that could be mustered by unhappy ideologues obsessed by a foreign policy cause. Analogy is obvious in the Kennedy case, in which the Miami expatriate Cubans were in high dudgeon to depose Fidel Castro for using the island's revolutionary tradition as a foil for his Marxist march into the Soviet bloc. Frustrated in its counter-revolution by the Kennedys' zigzagging, the backlash redirected venom towards the Kennedys themselves.

The 'time warp' club that disingenuously portrays designated patsy Lee Harvey Oswald as a frustrated loser ignores the fact that Oswald – whose 118 IQ was the same as JFK's – had by the age of 24 achieved more than most people. The "Oswald did it" time-warpers stigmatize him because he was poor and raised in a fatherless household, like 40% of Americans today. He is impugned because his hard-working mother while he was growing up moved 15 times, including a stay in New York City where Oswald spent a lot of time in the city's wonderful libraries reading while playing hooky. Like his brothers and thousands of average Joes motivated by stirring stories from World War II and Korea, he joined the U.S. Marine Corps for a four-year hitch, educating himself by reading while he went through boot camp. How many of his critics have withstood the rigors of boot camp? Rated well for technical competence, he underwent radar training before being assigned to the U-2 flyover reconnaissance base in Atsuggi, Japan, which doubled as the largest CIA station in the Far East. By the time Oswald was reassigned to El Toro Marine Corps base in California, he was teaching himself to read, write and talk Russian. Was anyone listening? Did any of his detractors ever teach oneself a second language, let alone Russian?

He was so unique that the Office of Naval Intelligence (ONI), the intel branch for the Marine Corps, recruited him for a special fake-defector project, gave him an early discharge and infiltrated him into the Soviet Union, where he spied for the United States for two years, worked in an electronics factory and married a Russian girl who because of his linguistic skill thought he was actually a Russian. He was allowed to return to the United States without penalty, without harassment and without trial for treason only because he had been spying for the United States all along.

During his teenage years, Oswald's favorite television program was "I Led Three Lives", a popular dramatization of FBI Agent Herb Philbrick's storied undercover career. "He never missed an episode. He just ate it up," a friend said. It was unsurprising that the secret agent's hair-raising exploits would capture the imagination of a teenage boy from a military family.

When he grew up, Lee Harvey Oswald led three lives: his own, Communist spy, and most of all, American secret agent.

Lee Harvey Oswald was neither hero nor villain. He was checking footprints of the herd when he was overrun by the stampede. He was in the wrong place at the wrong time.

CAMELOT

A Broadway production based on the Arthurian legend of *Camelot*, that launched in 1960, coincidentally spanned the Kennedy White

House years. It led Mrs. Jacqueline Kennedy in a post-assassination interview to expropriate the title *Camelot* as supposedly descriptive of Jack Kennedy's administration – although no such pretense existed while he was alive and until then apparently resonated nowhere except in the widow's imagination. It did catch on and, in the maudlin memories of millions, conferred on the Kennedy years a magnificence undeserved by the randiest president in American history.

In Washington, there was a 'show biz' flair to everything the rich and photogenic Kennedys did, whether it was lovingly playing with their two toddlers, Caroline and John-John, or taking TV viewers on an inside tour of the White House, as the president's youngish and cultured wife Jacqueline breathlessly did.

Stylish, nicely-dressed and good-looking, the Kennedy couple had already become matinee idols by September of 1963, when Walter Cronkite with JFK's unseen help introduced on CBS-TV a nightly half hour news program, the first such regular series in television history. Instead of Ernie Kovacs or Steve Allen or Bob & Ray or Kukla, Fran and Ollie comedy skits, viewers could tune in to a steady diet of news dominated by doings at the White House and in government. Could the GOP top this?

The Kennedys' Hollywood touch left everyone else scratching for publicity crumbs. It was Kennedy this, Kennedy that. The dour Pennsylvania Republican, Hugh Scott, had during the 1960 campaign documented that then Sen. Kennedy had missed one third of Senate sessions during his eight years in the upper house. Water off a duck's back – no one seemed to care. A fellow WWII Naval officer, Sen. Harrison A. 'Pete' Williams, D-NJ, handsome and intelligent, a talented junior senator and gifted speaker who stood for labor and the underprivileged, was eclipsed by the Kennedy magic.

Although Williams would remain a member of the 'Kennedy Club' through the years, his otherwise likely ascent was blocked by 'the Kennedy dynasty' – Sen. Bobby Kennedy's 1968 race for the presidency, for example. Williams, an advocate of putting curbs on spiraling Pentagon spending, or brilliant anti-war Senator Eugene

McCarthy, D-WI, who had proven LBJ's vulnerability by defeating President Johnson in the New Hampshire Democratic Primary, were somehow automatically swept aside once Bobby Kennedy jumped into the race. It was as if the Kennedys walked on water.

In 1963 the nation was still doing the twist, the most vigorous and durable dance rage since the jitterbug made its debut just prior to start of the Second World War. The twist came out of the south, originally spotted by Hank Ballard watching teen-agers in Tampa, Fla. He took it to Detroit in 1958 but it remained local. Before long, basketball fans at the National Invitation Tournament (NIT) in Madison Square Garden went wild when the Memphis State cheerleading squad at halftime performed the twist for them. The biggest push came from Dick Clark's American bandstand that aired every Saturday morning from Philadelphia. Chubby Checker's 'Twist and Shout' shot to the top of the Billboard charts in September 1960 and, for the first time ever, repeated as Number One in February 1962. You could go to The Hialeah Club on Atlantic Avenue in Atlantic City in 1961, take a big white bath towel supplied gratis, and learn the twist by simulating the act of drying off your backside to the music.

As proof that the twist craze lasted, Carousel nightclub owner Jack Ruby was promoting and peddling what he called a 'twist board' as a sideline when on November 23 he visited offices of the *Dallas Morning News*, just a day before he murdered Lee Harvey Oswald.

That fall Alabama Governor George Wallace made a big show of blocking the auditorium doorway at the University of Alabama to protest forced integration of the university. Televised nationally, Wallace meekly stepped aside when federal troops told him to move or get carried off. The university in Birmingham has been integrated ever since. Wallace in 1968 launched a third party Independent campaign for president which was terminated when he was shot up close by an assassin. It ended his campaign and left him crippled for life.

By the fall of 1963, local draft boards were stepping up forced recruitment, reclassifying warm bodies 1-A and shipping draftees off to boot camp to prepare them for service in South Vietnam and the Far East. The widening war was no longer satisfied with volunteers and Special Forces.

Bob Dylan's 'Blowin' In The Wind' made its debut. The TV show *Hootenanny* featuring folk music died out and the California sound came in as The Beach Boys' surfer music enjoyed a surge of popularity. Still to come was the British Invasion in 1964 by 'The Beatles', the smashing success of 'The Rolling Stones', a whole new genre of twangy guitars and hirsute musicians rocking to new sounds. Musical variety shows were being conceived led by ABC-TVs Saturday night *Shindig* to be copied a few months later by NBC-TVs *Hullaballoo* featuring an athletic blonde caged go-go girl named Lada Edmunds Jr., a role model for young girls who was last heard from while running a fitness center in upper Bergen County, NJ into the 21st Century.

Trussed in a surgical corset and brace for his weak back while seeing three different doctors for Addison's Disease and other diagnosed serious ailments, Jack Kennedy had to be content with smoking a cigar and watching the sports seasons change.

Described in childhood by his mother, Rose Kennedy, as a "very, very sick boy", Kennedy was a biologic basket case whose survival to the age of 46 was little short of medical magic. He seemed to be held together by spit, wax and baling wire, a straw man from Oz pumped up on steroids, amphetamines and testosterone. He did not look debilitated, but his pitiful health should have barred him from pursuing the stresses of presidential campaigning and the draining demands of the highest office – for his own sake.

He took testosterone that gave him the strongest libido he had ever seen in a man, according to his friend Sen. George Smathers, D-FL. Jack Kennedy had suffered every childhood disease including scarlet fever and was clinically anemic throughout his teens. Steroid shots given to him since he was 17 were thought to be have exacerbated Addison's disease by the time he was 30, requiring daily cortisone shots to address the adrenal deficiency, according to historian Robert Dalleck in his 2004 book

An Unfinished Life: JFK, 1917–1963, Kennedy suffered either from autoimmune deficiency or type-one diabetes, gastroenteritis, excess digestive disturbances and urinary tract infections. During the years of his presidency he used testosterone therapy, which Senate colleagues said made him randy as a bull.

He sought alternative therapy for chronic back pain which he found in a cocktail dosed out by Dr. Max Jacobson of NYC, better known as 'Dr. Feelgood', a smallish East European who spoke accented broken English. Kennedy was warned that Dr. Jacobson's speedball concoction of amphetamines, megavitamins and other secret ingredients might not be kosher.

"I don't care if it's horse piss," Kennedy replied. "It works."

Kennedy had a greenish bronze pallor and a bushy mop of hair attributed to all the cortisone and other shots. He seemed to have a chronic tan, a mix of Florida sun and medicines. The hormonal chemicals added 30 or 40 pounds to his normal 160-pound weight during the 1960 presidential campaign. His mother said she secretly preferred his lean look to the widening facial bloat that she perceived.

JFK's ODDS OF LIVING OUT A SECOND TERM

In Vegas they make book on sports. They do not advertise the odds on public figures living or dying.

If they did, John F. Kennedy's chances of healthily surviving a second term given knowledge of his medical condition would have been 10-to-1 against.

Maybe that's too generous. How about "no price" —- meaning there's no action on that because there was no chance he would make it through. JFK was a medical basket case whose natural life was coming to a close. He was on the verge of dying from dozens of dysfunctions and galloping adrenal and organic pathologies. He was a virtual dead man.

Frivolous? Not really, not when in fact in 1963 you had one of the world's top bookies figuring the odds. That would be the Chicago Outfit's Sam Giancana, the world's biggest betting layoff broker for sports. He'd already been hounded and humiliated by the AG's bloodhounds.

Giancana would make sure he got it right because the stakes were sky high. When JFK died, his brother Robert F. Kennedy would take power and within a year move in as president. It was the ultimate nightmare because as JFK's attorney general Bobby Kennedy had already demonstrated his ruthlessness. Not only crime busting, but fanaticism beyond comprehension.

The mob could work it out with Jack Kennedy as president, but could not allow his arrogant kid brother to take charge. RFK would certainly seize power once JFK died the natural death the older brother was already facing. There was only one answer.

JFK's departure had to be speeded up while there was still time. If he were to die now Vice President Lyndon Johnson would succeed and Bobby Kennedy would be out in the cold. The dynasty would end before it got off the ground.

It was time to stop talking. The order went out. Make the hit.

MARY'S DRUGS 'INFLUENCING' JFK FOREIGN POLICY

In looking back, the enigmatic CIA counterintel chief James Jesus Angleton would tell journalists that his wife's best friend Mary Meyer's psychedelic liaison with President Kennedy may have "influenced foreign policy".

Customarily coy and evasive, orchid-cultivating Angleton did not belabor the obvious. Given her personal mission to "brainwash" JFK and national leaders by use of LSD, Meyer was working methodically in secret to defuse the Cold War mentality that she said dominated the nation's capitol in the early 1960s.

She was also stepping across a not so invisible line. As a government super-agency, the CIA in the name of fighting for freedom and the United States, had arrogated to itself a bizarre laboratorium of secret LSD and drug experiments that went far beyond normal parameters of governmental function. The statute-loving Justice Department and FBI agents who enforced federal law often looked the other way when sanctioned CIA projects were involved, but did not relinquish its powers. Undercover CIA spies, informers, sting artists were subject to the same laws as anyone else. They could be and sometimes were busted, doing time for using and moving drugs.

If Mary were "influencing foreign policy", as the CIA's counterintelligence chief euphemistically put it, the next question hard-eyed Justice Department lawyers and U.S. Attorneys in every state were obligated by oath to ask, was whether she was "undermining foreign policy" —- which would take them squarely into a question of espionage – a legal half-brother of treason.

The summer of treason, 1963, was already flourishing, as we have seen. In London the Profumo 'sexpionage' scandal was in process of destroying Prime Minister Harold MacMillen's Tory government — institutionalized since 1950. In Moscow, double-agent defector Kim Philby was collaborating with his KGB handlers, forcing vast redeployments and code changes in the worldwide anti-Communist security apparati. Gaining momentum was an air of blithe spirits and liberal orthodoxy, a widespread eagerness to dis fuddy-duddies and lampoon super-patriots, tarnished with the broad brush stigma of discredited 'McCarthyism'. Not until 1998 would Senator Daniel Patrick Moynihan, D-NY, a trusted liberal, pull the genie known as the Venona Intercepts out of a bottle, proving in the process that government wiretaps of Soviet cable traffic since World War II gave credence to some of the things that McCarthy had been saying – as insisted over the years by William F. Buckley of the magazine National Review. The pill revolutionized the nation's sexual mores, uninhibited popular dance crazes such as the twist and the monkey swept the nation to the beat of war drums from Vietnam and the imagined drone of SAC B-29s primed 24-hours-a-day to blow the world to kingdom come. Like Al Capp's comic strip schmoos in *Li'l Abner*, colonies of druggies metastasized across the land, contaminating society with sleepy-eyed mindlessness. Or so it seemed to people clinging to 'old-fashioned values'. Was it all part of a big conspiracy?

By the time President Kennedy went on his college graduation speech tour in June 1963, he was 16 months into his conspiratorial plot with his lover Mary Meyer to change official Washington's Cold War thinking by use of "utopiates", as she and LSD guru Dr. Timothy Leary called the drugs. She had sought out Dr. Leary for information on how to conduct LSD sessions safely so that users would not freak out. As the academic pied piper at Harvard's Newman Center and practicing LSD swami at a lavish upstate New York mansion owned and made available without cost by the super-rich heirs of polo great Tommy Hitchcock, Millbrook was a magnet Shangri-La for weekenders from New York City.

While Leary unabashedly urged people to 'turn on, tune in and drop out', he warned that LSD could be dangerous and that mood setting was vital for such sessions, He wanted to proselytize folks into blissful serenity, he said. Mary told him her boyfriend was a very important man but she had never revealed to Dr. Leary that the lover was in fact the president of the United States. She had successfully recruited wives in her inner circle of VIPS to get their husbands to use LSD, cannabis, mescaline and other drugs. She called the group a 'cell'. It was a conspiratorial word, familiar to FBI agents and particularly Division Five core anti-espionage experts. A cell was the ideological combat unit for the worldwide Communist apparatus known as the Comintern. Mary's use of the word 'cell' would in itself be taken as suspicious.

If Mary Meyer were to be put in the dock for espionage, what would be President Kennedy's alleged crime? Nine out of ten prosecutors without knowing who was involved would reply, pro forma: aiding and abetting a felony. As a gesture to majesty, he would be named in the indictment as an 'unindicted conspirator'. That is, if anyone had the nerve to hold the highest elected official in the land to the same standards that applied to everyone else.

How do we know President John F. Kennedy aided and abetted Mary Meyer's utopiate plot to brainwash top Washington officials, including the president himself? Tim Leary's 1985 book based on his diary describes Mary's aggressive project as well as her series of visits to learn how to run LSD sessions, together with updates on her success. White House Secret Service logs document half of Mary's known visits as JFK's mistress, whom she describes to Leary as her 'boyfriend' and 'lover'. The executive editor of the *Washington Post*, Phil Graham, in June of 1963 publicly proclaimed at an editors' convention in Arizona that Georgetown divorcee Mary Meyer was having an affair at the White House with the president. CIA Counterintel Chief James Jesus Angleton would in years to come acknowledge his secret bugging knowledge that Mary and the president used LSD together, after which "they made love and fell asleep". Ever soft on the affair because his wife was one of Mary's closest friends, Angleton did acknowledge, after he and his wife had essentially split up, that Mary's activities had the capacity to "influence foreign policy". He also told reporters he would soon expose the "real Jack Kennedy" — which he never did.

Was Mary a Soviet 'sleeper' agent? Part of a KGB super-plot to subvert the West's leadership defenses in a miasmic quicksand of sex and drugs? Action trumps intent. The girl was a Soviet agent – a honeytrap.

JIM TRUITT'S DIARY

It irked and exasperated Jim Truitt that his former colleague Ben Bradlee was overly prone to double talk on the subjects of John F. Kennedy and Richard Milhouse Nixon. Everything that JFK had done was grand; everything that RMN had done was villainous.

Bradlee was riding the crest of the post-Watergate wave which credited Nixon's 1974 forced resignation to journalistic tenacity by *Washington Post* reporters Bob Woodward and Carl Bernstein guided by Ben Bradlee, the newspaper's executive editor.

Bradlee had always been a Jack Kennedy partisan. Both from Boston and both being Harvard men, their affinity was not unusual. Bradlee at White House receptions often palled around with Kennedy, bonding with him as they ogled girls imported from New York City.

"The girls were always spectacular," Bradlee would say, without acknowledging that the New York City imports were invariably call girls and prostitutes. Bradlee was married to Antoinette Pinchot, eight years younger than her sister, Mary Pinchot Meyer, Jack Kennedy's mistress. Bradlee was a *Newsweek* correspondent in Paris during the summer of 1958 when he met the Pinchot sisters. They had each been gifted $1,000 in mad money by their mother to vacation in Europe where both found new mates to replace husbands of whom they were tired after long marriages. Antoinette met Bradlee while Mary found a rich and rotund Italian playboy with whom she hoped to buy a ranch in Nevada to raise horses. Her husband and father of her sons, Cord Meyer, thought she had cracked up. The fake count backed out leaving Mary distraught. She diverted herself by disporting with an artist and splashing color on abstracts from the time of her divorce into the early 1960s, when she found herself on the White House guest list as a third-party divorcee accompanying the Bradlees.

Despite his deserved reputation as a womanizer, Jack Kennedy's rather flagrant affair with the blonde divorcee from Georgetown coincident with cascading events leading to his assassination remained unreported until a dozen years after JFK's death. Nor was there mention of the affair when Mary was murdered 11 months later just as the Warren Commission report was being released. The long delayed disclosure came from James Truitt, who along with Ben Bradlee was one of the two top aides to *Washington Post* owner/editor Philip Graham, the man who while drunk had early in 1963 openly described the president's affair to a room full of national newspaper editors only to be totally ignored.

Truitt, in February 1976, spilled the beans about Kennedy's two-year affair with Mary Meyer, who had been murdered while exercise walking on a quiet lane known as the towpath next to a canal in Georgetown, the Washington D.C. suburb where she lived. Upset with what he considered the hypocrisy of ex-colleague Bradlee's moralizing about Nixon's Watergate downfall while remaining silent about the Kennedys wiretapping and misuse of

IRS returns, Truitt granted the scoop to the *National Enquirer* followed by *Associated Press* and *Washington Post* interviews during which he revealed that Kennedy and Meyer trysted more than thirty times at the White House using marijuana and other drugs which he, personally, as a favor to Meyer, supplied for their use. Truitt said he and his wife were among Mary's best friends. She confided details of her illicit affair and regular pot smoking at the White House while the president's wife was out of town. Truitt, for some bizarre reason, kept a diary of Mary's affair. The marijuana use was enhanced by other drugs and Kennedy once remarked to Mary, "This isn't like cocaine. I'll get you some of that", according to the ex-*Washington Post* newsman.

Why did newspapers ignore Jack Kennedy's sexcapades and satyriasis?

"We didn't know," said Helen Thomas, the veteran *United Press International* (UPI) White House reporter many years later. Kennedy enjoyed jollying Thomas during press conferences and she was clearly infatuated with Kennedy's charm and wit. Thomas was a young woman and an outsider. Veteran journalists such as the Alsops and other columnists covered up his capers.

WASHINGTON MERRY-GO-ROUND

While Mary Meyer did not name names in telling Dr. Leary about a "power struggle" in Washington, we learn from other sources that it centered on strife between the husband and wife owners of the Washington Post. Mary's 'friend' whose drunken outburst at a press banquet in Arizona about Kennedy having an affair at the White House with Mary Meyer had very little meaning to Dr. Leary because he did not know that Mary's boyfriend was the president.

Leary's diary as outlined in his autobiography published in 1985 makes no further mention of Phil Graham and his psychiatric woes – not even a word about Graham's shotgun suicide the day he went home after weeks in a mental asylum. Nor did she mention that her peregrinations in promiscuity had included a brief fling with Graham before he went middle age crazy with his marriage-busting young Australian journalist for *Newsweek*, which he owned.

By the time Kennedy called for world peace at the college commencements in early June of 1963, events portended wrenching changes in the Cold War.

On June 5, the Profumo scandal in London exploded when War Minister John Profumo resigned in disgrace. He admitted he had lied to the House of Commons by denying his affair with femme fatale Christine Keeler, a 25-year-old London party girl who was also sleeping with the Soviet naval attaché, a Communist spy who sought secrets about the 'payload' of NATO atomic weapons.

The scandal fallout would topple the Conservative government of Prime Minister Harold MacMillan ending its 12-year run and allowing the Labor Party to next prevail, Christine Keeler was invariably photographed with a leggy young blonde named Mandee Rice-Davies who was also part of the party-girl ring that extended across the pond to New York City and to Washington D.C. A few of the other sex-for-sale ladies were East German spies, according to the FBI, named Ellen Rometsch, Suzy Chang and Mariela Novotny. As the scandal broke, they migrated to the United States.

As if on cue, Britain formally recalled one of its most prominent MI5 agents from his diplomatic post at the British Embassy in Washington, superspy Kim Philby. A leader of the old Cambridge Marxist ring that had earlier led to the defections of Guy Burgess and Donald McLean, Philby for some reason had continued in his post. He lunched often with American counterspy chief Jim Angleton which Angleton's CIA colleague William King Harvey could never understand, because Harvey was convinced that Philby was a Soviet spy. Once recalled to London and facing grueling debriefing, Philby kept going and wound up in Moscow where he was hailed as a defector. The New York Times called it the biggest double agent defection in history. Philby had been a Soviet spy working for British intelligence for 30 years.

KENNEDY ROMANCES IRON CURTAIN SPY

The same sex ring whose kinky bondage parties in London spilled over into the Profumo scandal would before summer's end cater to President Kennedy. The American president had taken intense interest in the unfolding overseas sexcapades, to the point that his ambassador to England was instructed to send him a daily update.

Near to the U.S. Senate Office Building in the Carroll Arms Hotel was a discrete new gentlemen's lounge called the Quorum Club that had been newly established by Bobby Baker, the longtime Senate page for Lyndon Baines Johnson. Baker was better known as the indefatigable secretary to the majority leader, namely LBJ. They were so politically close that Baker was nicknamed 'Little Lyndon'. Once he became vice president, Johnson openly disassociated himself as of 1961 from Baker's less savory activities, although a possible lingering problem arose from a bruising big business battle over a gigantic defense contract award. JFK's Secretary of Defense Robert McNamara and his Navy Secretary Fred Korth had determined that a joint Air Force/ Navy supersonic jet called the TFX-F111 was needed. The Pentagon solicited bids from Boeing, McDonnell-Douglas, General Dynamics-Grumann and all of the usual heavyweight aircraft defense contractors. The contract for 1700 fighter jets ran $6.5 billion, give or take a few hundred million- an historic high. The Senate infighting was worse than a Pier Six brawl. Before it was over Boeing's low bid had been rudely shunted aside in favor of General Dynamics in Fort Worth, Texas, the home state favorite of Lyndon Johnson. The losing bidders unleashed their investigative hounds and by Nov. 22, 1963 a certain witness named Donald B. Reynolds whose lobbying client had been edged was testifying before a Senate Committee that Bobby Baker had told him that an unopened attaché case contained $100,000 for LBJ as a reward for getting the contract for General Dynamics — a remark apparently tossed off by a needling Baker in jest since no one talked payoffs to the opposition – even if there were a kernel of truth to Reynold's wild talk. The last person Baker would cross was Johnson. The probe was dropped in the ensuing angst over JFK's assassination that occurred that very day. Some critics who claim Johnson must have killed Kennedy to quash the TFX probe totally ignore the fact that all of the Pentagon wheels who swung the contract to General Dynamics were appointees of President Kennedy – Defense Secretary MacNamara, Roswell Fitzpatrick, Secretary of Navy Fred Korth to name a few. The LBJ crowd including Texas congressmen beyond doubt were overjoyed that Texas-based General Dynamics won the fat contract. Nevertheless, it was the Kennedy team that had the juice.

The frayed nerves of disappointed lobbyists clearly needed soothing and Bobby Baker was just the boy to supply the balm. Baker sat on the board of directors of the exclusive Quorum supper club, bimbo bar and card room — an insider haven for lobbyists, legislators, lawyers and New Frontiersmen.

Baker was a charming South Carolinian with a soothing southern drawl. A power in Washington independent of LBJ, the majority leader's protégé was known as the hardest working page in the Senate during his years as LBJ's right-hand man. He also had his hands in a vending machine influence-peddling pie as a scandal would show. Sued in civil court by a vendor who was chiseled aside, Baker served a short prison term for positioning his Serv-U Corp. in partnership with lobbyist Fred Black, so that his vending machines – manufactured by a firm sponsored by Chicago racketeer Sam Giancana — won spots doled out by recipients of government contract awards.

The government aide on a salary of $20,000 a year made all kinds of side money as a lawyer, in real estate and banking, and as a partner in vending machine distribution and ownership. He parlayed all of his assets into a real estate partnership in Ocean City, MD where in mid-1962 he opened Bobby Baker's Carousel Oceanfront Hotel and Condominiums. Vice President Johnson and his wife were among a host of congressional guests, including a few senators. Baker described his resort as a getaway for the advise-and-consent crowd, a characterization given charisma because of Alan Drury's best-selling novel Advise and Consent which was published that year and made into a movie.

Always a fast one with the ladies, Baker hired a dozen girls and dressed them in brief costumes. Some said Baker was fixing up Washington folks with girls and throwing wild parties. However true, his main goal was legitimate real estate sales and rentals. The project grew to approximately 250 hotel rooms and some 50 condos.

He hired as bookkeeper Nancy Carole Tyler, a beauty queen who had reigned as Miss Louden County of 1957 outside Knoxville. Tenn. Miss Tyler was Baker's mistress and he bought her a $28,000 town house in a nice section of Washington. Expecting Baker to eventually marry her, she thought he would leave his wife and three children and was disappointed when he backed out. As one of the pretty Washington office girls active in a whirl of cocktail parties, Miss Tyler had once roomed with Mary Jo Kopechne, the Pennsylvania girl who in 1969 would drown in a submerged car in Chappaquiddick, MA driven by Sen. Edward Kennedy, younger brother of Jack and Bob Kennedy.

Miss Tyler and William O. Davis, a West Virginian pilot of a Waco biplane who had been staying at the Carousel for a week, crashed into the ocean and died a few hundred yards in front of the hotel on Sunday, May 10, 1965.

The couple had been drinking and the tipsy pilot was showing off and buzzing the hotel bar when he tried a flip and never came out of the roll. Broken-hearted over loss of his loyal friend and lover, Baker took her body back to the girl's parents in Tennessee. Her death was due to her happy-go-lucky lifestyle and had no sinister overtones, not even a scheduled meeting before any investigating committee. Baker clearly loved the woman.

Baker hired three European lookers as hookers, hostesses and waitresses at the 'Q' or Quorum Club. One of them was a buxom German cocktail waitress named Ellen Rometsch, 27, whose fishnet stockings and lacy décolletage caught the eye of President Kennedy. The president maintained a getaway suite in the Carroll Arms just as he did at the Carlisle Hotel in midtown

Manhattan in NYC and another near the Sears Tower in Chicago, his father's landmark spire.

Kennedy had an intermediary contact Baker who arranged for Rometsch to provide call girl service for JFK. Baker revealed in his autobiography Wheeling and Dealing published in 1978 that the president called to thank him for "the best time I ever had". He said it wasn't the only time he had accommodated JFK, and RFK as well. "It went on for awhile", Baker wrote.

Among the charter members of the Quorum Club were Democratic Senate stalwarts Daniel Brewster of Maryland, Harrison A. Williams of New Jersey and Edward 'Ted' Kennedy of Massachusetts. Several Republican congressmen were members as well.

Two other call girls at the Quorum Club were Suzy Chang and Czech beauty Mariel Novotny. The two and Rometsch were part of the Stephen Ward party girl ring of good-time girls and prostitutes active in sex romps among the aristocrats and government ministers in London. Novotny and Chang were pricey prostitutes in NYC, patronized by Jack Kennedy for a ménage a trois on occasion. Novotny was a stunning, statuesque blonde. When he was not engaged with the girls in his suite at the Carlisle Hotel or their apartment, Kennedy was not shy about being seen with them. The president dined openly with Miss Chang at the famed '21 Club' on the West Side of Manhattan in New York City on several occasions.

Both Chang and Novotny were East German espionage agents with ties to the Stasi, according to FBI investigations.

The FBI was already in all-court press mode and all the more so because the 'espionage summer' had given the KGB a big lead with two monumental coups, Profumo and Philby.

For J. Edgar Hoover, JFK'S Elly Rometsch Affair stretched belief. It was déjà vu, Kennedy's Inga Binga spy ring thing tarted up for a revival a quarter century later. JFK was still reckless and spoiled, lacking any shred of good sense or decorum, Hoover told his confidantes. This time even liberal Bill Sullivan, chief of the FBI Counterintelligence Division, had to agree.

The FBI investigations had pinned the three doxies down. All three were interviewed and investigated by FBI Division Five security agents who classified them as likely spies. They were definitely security risks, counterintel experts ruled. Rometsch had been a consort of Walter Ulbrecht, Communist president of East Germany; Novotny was a niece of a government minister in Czechoslovakia, an East bloc satellite of the Kremlin. Elly Rometsch, born in the east sector, was married to a sergeant in the West German army who divorced her for "inappropriate conduct as a wife" in West Germany after he learned of her sideline as a prostitute. Across the Berlin Wall in East Germany, the Stasi ran an intelligence service rife with wiretaps, interrogations and files on everybody and everything. It was unthinkable to believe that skilled Stasi agents would ignore the potential gold mine of information, influence and extortion into which honey traps Ellen Rometsch, Susy Chang and Mariel Novotny could draw the amorous leader of the western world.

Hoover had already begun his counter-attack during the summer by feeding columnist Courtney Evans information about the invasion of the East German call girls. He had never imagined that President Kennedy would push the envelope by mixing with suspected spies.

Kennedy sent word to Hoover that he would appreciate it if Hoover swept his indiscretions with Rometsch under the rug. Hoover refused.

Instead, he placed a call to Iowa where his old friend Clark Mollenhoff was pleased to get inside information on a shaping story – and a big one at that. It hinted at a national scandal that could sway the next presidential election. Mollenhoff reported on Oct. 26, 1963 in the *Des Moines Register* that the FBI had established that "the beautiful brunette had been attending parties with congressional leaders and some prominent New Frontiersmen from the executive branch of government. The possibility that her activity might be connected with espionage was of some concern because of the high rank of her male companions."

Almost at once New York Republican Governor Nelson Rockefeller would commission a Gallup Poll that showed him far ahead of all other candidates in Minnesota. It tipped off that billionaire Rocky might challenge front running Senator Goldwater for the GOP presidential nomination.

Already alerted that Hoover was on the warpath over the 'sexpionage' problem, Attorney General Robert Kennedy had already dispatched his agents to pick up Rometsch and ship her back to West Germany. It cost her husband a choice spot as a military attaché at the West German Embassy in Washington.

Seeing the *Des Moines Register* item, Bobby Kennedy put teeth in his cover-up. The very next day he sent his emissary LaVerne Duffy to Europe to pay off Rometsch to sign papers denying that she had ever had sex with any American official. For the lush payoff in hush money, Elly would have denied anything asked of her, skeptics now note.

RFK persisted in his campaign to dissuade the FBI bulldog. He nagged him to drop the espionage tack because to do otherwise would jeopardize "the best interests of the United States government." Embarrassing high officials could only help the enemy, Bobby Kennedy preached. The attorney general was waving the red, white and blue flag in the FBI director's face.

Hoover paused, but the poker game was far from over. It was less now than a month prior to the fateful day in Dallas. Hoover had many more arrows in his quiver, the sharpest being his symbiotic relationship with Walter Winchell whose Sunday night radio broadcasts to "Mr. and Mrs. America and all the ships at sea" and syndicated newspaper gossip columns from Winchell's flagship *New York Mirror* reached millions, often with devastating impact.

Still under Hoover's hat was the biggest blockbuster of all, Kennedy's conspiracy with Georgetown divorcee Mary Meyer to undermine American foreign policy by using LSD to soften the minds of American government leaders.

He called for a huddle with the Senate's senior leaders, Democrat and Republican. Hoover's private meeting with Majority

Leader Mike Mansfield and Minority Leader Everett Dirksen lasted for hours. None of them disclosed the gist of the confab but it was beyond doubt that it concerned both the Kennedys and weighty matters of state.

FBI ROOTS OUT UTOPIATES AND SEXPIONAGE

It was an intoxicating brew that staggered the White House in 1963, a heady distillate of new terminology. Inventive portmanteau words were needed to define sophisticated new mega-crimes: drugs that induced visions of utopia became 'utopiates'; sex mixed with espionage became 'sexpionage'. Only New Frontier verbiage could describe Jack Kennedy's unconventional – if not daffy – lurches into initiatives unknown and strange to the masses of America.

We are left to speculate how deeply the President's tilt toward James Bond spectacularism subsumed the romantic Kennedy's common sense. Surely he had a quixotic fascination for Ian Fleming's secret agent 007, the James Bond of Dr. No, which in 1962 became the first of an eventual 23 James Bond films spanning nearly a half century.

The James Bond series grossed $6 billion and claims to have been seen by one quarter of the world's population. It was easy to watch as manly, sophisticated Sean Connery good-humoredly outwitted, outfoxed, outmaneuvered and slickly out-romanced agents of Spectre and other evil empires.

President Kennedy made no secret of his fascination with James Bond and Unconventional Warfare. He gloried in his 'green berets', Special Forces commandoes sent out of Fort Bragg, N.C. to Vietnam with the expectation that they would wrap up that Vietnamese guerilla war in a New York minute.

He invited author Ian Fleming to the White House for brandy, cigars and brainstorming on how best to cope with jungle wars. Out of southeast Asian mythology to the Pentagon had come General Edward G. Lansdale, prototype for Colonel Hillandale in Burdick and Lederer's *The Ugly American*, the only character in the book who knew how to 'win the hearts and minds' of the peasants in the rice paddies, not only with gunplay and dynamite, but by strumming a uke in singalongs and telling fortunes in village gatherings. Kennedy dubbed General Lansdale 'my own James Bond" and made Lansdale the Pentagon chief of Operation Mongoose funded at $50,000,000 a year to get rid of Fidel Castro in Cuba. Few doubted that the secret agent who had given us Magsaysay while Americanizing the Philippines and who had blocked off Ho Chi Minh while saving the southeastern half of Indochina would have much trouble removing Castro.

Jack Kennedy, also, was acting without any degree of discretion. His sexpionage exploits courted danger, as if he needed to live on the edge, mere sex and seduction no longer being thrilling enough. He was on a Walter Mitty roll, playing secret agent 007, outfoxing zaftig women secret agents while he tracked villains before tossing the beauties aside like so many wilted petals. He was spending all of his free time with whores and spies, or a combination of both.

IRISH MAFIA ERECTS GREEN WALL

In all of his undertakings, he was shielded by the so-called Irish Mafia from Boston, all of whom felt that Jack could do no wrong. When Jacqueline Kennedy was out of town, Kennedy's faithful friend and retainer, Lem Billings, would handle arrangements for the president's dates with Mary Meyer. Jack Kennedy and Billings had been roommates and crew members at Choate. They were threatened with expulsion from the prep school for misbehavior until JFK's father intervened. Billings studied advertising at Princeton while JFK went there with him for a semester, until sickness forced him to drop out, later finishing at Harvard. Billings, a bachelor, actually had his own room in the White House and was helpful to the president's wife and to JFK himself. Gore Vidal, the talented gay author, did not like Billings. "He's basically your White House gay," Vidal said in describing Billings' presence. Not everyone agreed with Vidal, even though Billings was never known to date anyone. His one purpose in life was to serve Jack Kennedy, whether to go get cigars, drive a car on an errand, check the ball game scores.

Key to the Irish Mafia was Kenny O'Donnell, who handled all of the schedules and policed access to the president. You could not get in to see President Kennedy unless O'Donnell gave the okay, according to Larry O'Brien, who served as diplomatic bridge between JFK's youth legions and the old political pros around the country. The son of the Holy Cross football coach, O'Donnell had been a star quarterback at Harvard and a classmate of Bobby Kennedy. Bob Kennedy caught one of O'Donnell's touchdown passes before Kennedy had broken a leg. O'Donnell insisted on having his own private life and avoided Hyannisport, although he wanted not a word said against Jack. O'Donnell said there were plenty of women around the White House but Jack never laid a hand on them. He was known for his unemotional and unbiased views, neither liberal nor conservative. Dave Powers was seven years older than JFK, while O'Donnell was seven years younger. Powers had been a Navy man with Claire Chenault's Flying Tigers during World War II. He was far more worldly than O'Donnell and spent time seeking out women for Jack Kennedy, liaising with New York call girls and party girls. While lounging with office girls in the White House pool on one occasion, according to 19-year-old intern Mimi Alford, Jack Kennedy told her she ought to service Dave Powers because he seemed so tense. She had heard her master's voice and did as she was told, Alford wrote in her memoirs.

It was O'Donnell, the ultimate loyalist, who scheduled events for JFK's campaign trips to Chicago, Miami, Tampa, Houston, Fort Worth and Dallas as JFK's reelection campaign got underway in November 1963. He spoke to Secret Service supervisors and police to ensure security.

PAPA JOE'S MAFIA SITDOWNS

It had become relevant in January 1960 when old Joe Kennedy, father of Jack and Bobby Kennedy, sat down with his old Mafia pals to line up money and support for Senator Jack Kennedy's presidential race. The two consecutive sitdowns were held in downtown Manhattan in New York City at Felix Young's, a popular corner bistro at 63 Greene Street. The first Manhattan sitdown was attended by New Orleans Mafioso Carlos Marcello who also brought along Dandy Phil Kastel, the slot machine impresario of Cajun Town who had been identified by the Kefauver Rackets Committee in 1949 as the partner of Frank Costello, boss of the biggest and richest New York mob, the Lucky Luciano family. "I helped make Joe Kennedy rich," Costello often said, referring to their bootlegging days and other deals together.

The New Orleans and Sun Belt hoods agreed to help Jack Kennedy.

The second meeting within a month at Felix Young's would bring in the first team to sit down with Papa Joe. It was like family. The top echelon of the Chicago Outfit gathered for the political powwow. On hand was Joe 'Big Tuna' Accardo, the head man; Sam Giancana, gambling boss; John Roselli, Las Vegas/Los Angeles swingman; and Murray 'The Camel' Humphries, accounting whiz. "Sure we'll help out,' the boys told Pop Kennedy, figuring they could raise $500,000 for the cause, most of it cash that would help persuade impoverished but proud fundamentalists in West Virginia's give-me-a-reason-to-vote pivotal Democratic primary to go for a rich Catholic Bostonian.

"Hold it up a minute,' said Murray the Camel. "Not so fast." He expressed misgivings about the president's brother, who he feared was on some kind of cleanup crusade. He explained that they would like to see pressures eased, not tightened by too much reform zeal.

"Don't worry," the elder Joe Kennedy assured one of the most lethal gang of killers ever gathered in one place. "It's just Bobby's business – he gets a little carried away. Jack's the boss. It'll be all right." The tourists from Chicago glanced at one another. "If you say so, Joe".

What no one mentioned since only Giancana himself knew was that Giancana was in Jack Kennedy's corner for a negative reason. His daughter, Antoinette, had gone out with and been date-raped by the son of Bebe Rebozzo, chief moneyman behind Vice President Richard Nixon.

BOBBY'S FLAGPOLE FLIP

The Kennedys may not have totally antagonized Sam Giancana at the Senate Rackets Committee hearing but the same could not be said about Jimmy Hoffa.

As president and boss of the International Brotherhood of Teamsters, Hoffa was a cult figure, a rock star worshipped by a huge majority of the trucking union's 1.5 million members. From the day he became president of the Teamsters on Jan. 1, 1958, the union got stronger by the day despite Bobby Kennedy's interference in union business. In 1957 Kennedy stuck his neck out, promising to climb the Capitol flagpole if Hoffa were not convicted of a pending witness tampering charge. Hoffa was acquitted, whereupon he offered to fetch a ladder for Bob Kennedy to start climbing.

While routinely taking the Fifth, Hoffa at one point was needled by Bob Kennedy for allegedly coddling two Communist-led union locals, one of them on the West Coast led by flaming socialist Harry Bridges.

"Don't you go saying that," Hoffa exploded. "Don't you go attacking my patriotism. I don't want to hear that from you." He said the locals elect their own leaders, not the international. Bobby Kennedy mumbled an apology. Jack Kennedy had signaled him to back off.

Bob Kennedy was roundly criticized by college law professors and legal experts as a fumbling interrogator, a bully and, at times, a vicious McCarthyite. At the same time, he had his own fan club among hardliners who admired his spunk and determination. A Yale law professor denounced Kennedy as unqualified when he was appointed as US attorney general by his brother in 1961. As time would tell, the critic was not far wrong. Had Bobby Kennedy been a loafer or taken the job as little more than a sinecure, everyone would have been content, Instead, a hotheaded zealot was set free to rattle every cup in the china closet and to smash more than a few.

The blood feud between Bobby Kennedy and James Riddle Hoffa did neither of them any good. Once he became attorney general, RFK formed a Justice Department task force called the 'Get Hoffa Squad', which struck legal purists as the worst case of selective prosecution against a legitimate labor leader in history. Sen. McClellan and Counsel Bob Kennedy had already wasted the full year 1959 harrying the United Auto Workers, AFL-CIO. The inquiry demonstrated it was the best union in the country and under Walter Reuther the cleanest. Hoffa would win acquittal for extortion in Memphis in a federal courtroom on Nov. 22, 1963, only to be convicted a year later of jury tampering based on testimony of a Louisiana labor leader whose testimony was allegedly suborned by a Kennedy operative. Hoffa was in Lewisburg Federal Prison in Pennsylvania the day Robert Kennedy was assassinated in Los Angeles in June 1968, only minutes after RFK had defeated Sen. Eugene McCarthy, D-WI, a liberal intellectual, in the California Democratic presidential primary. A delusional Palestinian immigrant man named Sirhan Sirhan who said he objected to RFK's pro-Israel position was arrested and charged with the murder. Pardoned by President Nixon in 1971, Hoffa was infuriated to learn that he was barred by conditions of the pardon from resuming the union presidency, to say nothing of his successor's unwillingness to relinquish the spot. Whether due to his tug of war with former subordinate Frank Fitzsimmons or the Senate Church Committee's subpoena for Hoffa to testify about the JFK assassination, Hoffa on July 30, 1975 was rubbed out in what remains an unsolved abduction and disappearance.

HOFFA SIGNALS SUNBELT DONS TO KILL JFK

Years after the deaths of two sunbelt dons who were longtime

Kennedy haters, one of their attorneys who also represented Teamster boss Jimmy Hoffa said he relayed to them Hoffa's message, "It's time to kill Kennedy."

The story came from Frank Ragano, a Washington D.C. lawyer.

He said neither of the dons said anything. They simply eyed one another. The dons were Tampa boss Santo Trafficante, second-generation operator of the Cuban numbers racket who had also been the luckless owner-investor in the Tropicana Casino Hotel in Havana confiscated by Fidel Castro in 1959. He was thrown in jail by Castro and was slated for a firing squad until an intervenor bailed him out. The pardon was presumed to have put Trafficante in Castro's debt, but how deeply no one seemed quite sure. They did remain in occasional contact at a distance. The other don was Carlos Marcello of New Orleans, who had sworn to kill Attorney General Robert F. Kennedy. The grudge was personal since Bobby Kennedy had directed his men to brush aside legal proceedings to kidnap the chubby tomato king, owner of a farm called Churchill Downs and the Town and Country Motel, hangout of Marcello torpedo Nunzio Pecora, who ran strip clubs and slot machines. Marcello was an associate of rackets boss Dandy Phil Kastel, an oldtime former 'bucket shop' swindler for legendary Arnold Rothstein, and with New York City underworld gambling czar Frank Costello. Kastel lost out after his New York City partner Costello abdicated in 1958. The ex-lower eastsider from NYC, Kastel, died in his room at the Claiborne Hotel in New Orleans in mid-August, 1962 of a gunshot wound that was ruled a suicide. It left Marcello in charge.

One of four brothers, Marcello had fended off deportation using New Orleans attorney G. Wray Gil, surviving seven court hearings which were to lead to a trial in the third week of November 1963. Acting on orders from the AG, Justice Department strongarm men grabbed Marcello off the street and flew him south to Guatemala where they landed him in the wilds without a cent in his pocket. Marcello was forced to take a long hike to Guatemala City. He was quickly able to get new clothes and money, enabling him to hire a private plane for a return flight to New Orleans.

The return flight of a private plane from Guatemala City to New Orleans was piloted by David Ferrie, a charter pilot and contract soldier-of-fortune for the New Orleans base of the CIA-funded Alpha 66 ant-Castro Cuban group. Ferrie was the strange-looking fallen gay priest portrayed by actor Joe Pesci in Oliver Stone's movie JFK. His private investigating business and air charter service called United Air Taxi were hired regularly by Marcello, and he was doing leg work for the defense team on the fatal day. Ferrie was mixed up in the Cuban Revolutionary Front and engaged in training guerillas at a CIA-funded camp at the north end of Lake Pontchartrain in Louisiana. He was an open critic of JFK's timidity at the Bay of Pigs, once said offhandedly that Kennedy should be shot and had animatedly outlined a plan for assassination by crossfire during a drinking session at a bar in the French Quarter where those present included Lee Harvey Oswald, a friend of Ferrie's, and Clay Shaw, the director of the New Orleans World Trade Center and the man who would be unsuccessfully prosecuted by New Orleans District Attorney James Garrison four years later.

FERRIE TIED TO NEW ORLEANS MOBSTER

There are theorists who contend that Ferrie acted for Marcello in furthering the assassination.

A multi-talented adventurer who worked as an investigator for Marcello's attorney at the immigration trial, Ferrie was seen in New Orleans – 499 miles from Dallas – at the Marcello trial on the day JFK was assassinated. The perfect alibi was reinforced when it was shown that Ferrie was among those celebrating Marcello's court victory that came in shortly after word arrived that the president had been shot. Ferrie was fingered in 1966 by private investigator Joseph S. Martin, who claimed he had seen a Mannlicher-Carcano rifle in Ferrie's apartment prior to the JFK assassination. Martin was the same man who had told Garrison that he had been pistol-whipped the afternoon of the assassination by Guy Banister, the right wing retired SAC of the Chicago FBI office, who threatened Martin to keep quiet about all of the Cuban gunmen he'd seen frequenting Banister's private investigating office all summer during 1963.

The Garrison case, initiated with Ferrie's detention as a material witness, faltered after Ferrie mysteriously died after being quizzed by New Orleans District Attorney Jim Garrison in 1967. He died from a blow to the head or a heart attack or suicide, a natural death according to the coroner. The demonstrative Ferrie had predicted to Garrison that by putting him on the spot Garrison was sealing Ferrie's death warrant. His sloppy bachelor pad was devoid of much of anything except a dozen cages of mice. He had been conducting experiments injecting cancer into mice, Garrison's staff learned. There was speculation Ferrie wanted to find a way to cause Castro to die from cancer without it being traceable as murder. As time would tell, the CIA/Mafia team up in the early 1960s involving William King 'Two Gun Bill' Harvey, a CIA hardliner, and John 'Hollywood' Roselli, a hit man from the Chicago mob, had explored every conceivable murder scheme including exploding cigars, food poisoning additives and contaminating scuba diving equipment. The CIA itself would later retrospectively count nine separate assassination plots while Castro came up with a tally of 25 or more.

Indeed, Castro was like Hitler in thwarting or escaping assassination. It was as if the two wily dictators had a partnership with Satan. Both had paranoid personalities, their paranoia justified by reality. People were in fact trying to kill them. Both dictators had a sixth sense, an ESP for danger unmatched by their stalkers.

The 'Valkyrie' plot to assassinate Hitler in the summer of 1944, by a weird twist of fate – the devil's hand moved a briefcase containing the time-bomb three feet to spare Hitler's life – prolonged the European war by nearly a year at a cost of at least a million lives. The near miss would delay V-E Day long enough to rearrange the map of Europe to follow military deployments in such a way that much of the 40-year Cold War to come – with all of its worldwide heartache – would be nothing less than inevitable.

FIDEL'S LOST GOLDEN CHANCE

Some animists believe an endless concatenation of events starts from a pebble dropped in a pond. The fall of a leaf brews a hurricane a dozen time zones away. For want of a nail, a shoe is lost. The massive violence of the 20th century? Chekhov's 'piece of string'.

Marxist or not, Castro in 1959 during the first year of his ' revolutionary government' had legions of admirers in the United States. Conditioned by films such as *Viva Zapata* brilliantly scripted by John Steinbeck and portrayed by Marlon Brando, a romanticized tale of an idealistic young selfless liberator from the pastoral countryside, revolution was not far from the American ethos. Valiantly leading a peasant guerrilla army in fatigues from the mountains far from Havana, 'Dr.' Castro held hope in the palm of his hand. He was acclaimed by a sympathetic journalist from the *New York Times*, romanticized in American magazines, paraded before a massive audience on the Jack Paar television show. Castro was welcomed with open arms, a relief from Cuban dictator Fulgencio Batista who had been opening Cuba to mobster infiltrated luxury casino hotels. This utopian wanted more than pots of gold brought by tourists, manna the common folk might not share. In the United States, high government officials, including an impressive number of liberal CIA men, regarded Fidel as a breath of fresh air.

Was Castro a hero to his people?

Here was a man who could not handle success, any more than Jack Kennedy could handle success.

Life was a bowl of cherries. The world was Castro's oyster.

Yet within a year Castro's monumental ego would blow it all apart.

He began by quibbling about American 'interference' in his revolutionary plans. His 'nationalization' of entire industries and confiscation of lands and wealth for redistribution to the masses was 'misunderstood'. Owners wanted their property. People didn't want the state to take things away. Owners wanted to be paid for their losses. It was like the kulaks being wiped out all over again as they had been in Russia following the revolution.

Everything began shifting once Castro met adversity by blaming "the colossus to the north". His anti-American rant was music to the Comintern's ears. In no time, Soviet negotiators and technicians began pouring into Havana, signing long-term loan agreements, shipping in agricultural equipment, sending grain to Cuba at once-in-a-lifetime prices. A troublemaker in the underbelly of the United States? Life was good for Khrushchev, the Ukranian bully with the farmhand touch.

When precisely did Cuba turn Communist? At what point did the Kremlin swallow up supposedly free Cuba? When was liberated Cuba betrayed?

The United States may have been slow on the uptake but the Cubans themselves were not. Many of their best citizens began voting with their feet. By Castro's second year, the emigration floodgates were wide open. Five thousand a day poured into New Orleans, ten thousand a day into Miami. Thousands fled to Mexico, other Caribbean Islands, Central and South America.

Militant anti-Castro mini-cities flourished and festered in Miami, Hudson County, N.J., New Orleans. Many expatriates were merchants, people of means, the middle class, aristocrats. Many were of Spanish blood like Castro, himself a Galician. They did not appreciate a dictatorship of the proletariat, a peasant police state. Many Batista henchmen faced firing squads, shot personally by Che Guevara. To prove himself above Fidel Castro's suspicion, ex-Batista cop Frank Fiorini, who would later change his name to Frank Sturgis and play an active role in JFK's assassination, personally executed more than 150 condemned prisoners.

JUDY BAKER'S SUMMER FLING WITH OSWALD

It will be recalled that a young woman from Bradentown. Fla.

named Judyth Vary Baker summered as a cancer researcher from May to August of 1963 during which time she was nominally employed at the Reily Coffee Company in New Orleans. Lee Harvey Oswald was listed as working there at the same time, as their Social Security W-2 records proved. Now living in Holland, Mrs. Baker said she met Oswald in a post office line and was impressed when he chatted her up in Russian. Although she was engaged to a University of Florida man, she had a torrid summer affair with Oswald who was doing confidential intelligence work instead of merely bagging coffee. Baker said she had won a national science foundation award in high school, which landed her the research job from Dr. Alton Oschner, the 67-year old head of the honored Oschner Clinic in New Orleans. She was promised free tuition by Dr. Oschner at Tulane Medical School after her summer internship. She was assigned to work with Dr. Oschner's assistant, the brilliant Dr. Mary S. Sherman of Tulane University Medical School, Baker wrote in her 1994 book, Lee and Me, but most of her actual work was done at the private apartment of a man named David Ferrie, who had mice in cages in his apartment. Baker wrote that she soon learned that the experiments were intended to develop a galloping cancer virus that was part of a CIA project to eliminate Fidel Castro. By the end of that summer of 1963, they had developed the toxic strain. She said that her lover Lee Oswald had told her that he was pretending to be a Communist so that by going through the Cuban Embassy in Mexico City he could get a visa into Cuba to deliver the virus to a doctor who would inoculate Castro.

The project leader, Dr. Sherman, had her own secret lab where she used a specialized new type of scientific equipment called a linear particle accelerator (linac). Invented by nuclear physicist Leo Szilard, the linac generates radiation and charged electrons that are useful for medical purposes, sterilization and in advanced quantum mechanics.

OSWALD AND DR. SHERMAN

The Judyth Vary Baker disclosures are further proof that the Warren Commission and the authorities had Lee Harvey Oswald as oversimplified as a cardboard cutout.

At the same time, they shed no light on the means, methods or motives of the assassination itself.

"News is merely the first draft of history," the late Phil Graham, publisher of the *Washington Post*, often quoted an earlier sage as saying.

In Dr. Mary Sherman, orthopedic surgeon and professor at Tulane University, we learn of a tragic peripheral figure in the Kennedy saga. She had been called as a witness to the Warren Commission in 1964 as commission staffers made half-hearted inquiry into Lee Harvey Oswald's activities a summer earlier.

Dr. Sherman, 51, had she told her full story, would have blown the Warren Commission findings about Oswald to kingdom come. She may also have opened the door further to another enduring mystery which is irrelevant to the JFK saga but nonetheless of monumental significance for another day.

OSWALD AND FERRIE SEEK CARCINOGEN FOR CASTRO

She did not testify because she was found murdered in her apartment in the early morning hours July 21, 1964 – hacked to death with a kitchen knife, according to the coroner's report. The orthopedic surgeon had unexplained burns on one side and an arm was missing. The coroner said death was caused by a stab wound in the heart. The murder remains unsolved. Besides the bizarre research project mentioned in Judyth Vary Baker's book, *Lee and Me,* a New Orleans researcher named Edward T. Haslam in 1995 wrote a medical thriller that has been retitled and reissued as *Dr. Mary's Monkey.*

The book says Dr. Sherman's main research aimed to produce an antigen to Simian Virus 40, the monkey virus contained in contaminated Salk polio vaccines injected by the millions in the 1950s and 1960s to stamp out a devastating polio epidemic which had crippled thousands and imperiled thousands more. Involved in her research was the much maligned and enigmatic David Ferrie, the defrocked priest and fired Eastern Airline pilot, whose arrest by New Orleans District Attorney Jim Garrison in 1967 appeared to lead to his untimely death. Two suicide notes in Ferrie's hand, both unsigned, were found in his apartment. He had died from a blow to the head from all appearances. Garrison believed Ferrie was murdered. The coroner, noting the suicide notes, was content with a ruling of suicide.

Haslam wrote that Ferrie at one point had as many as 2000 test mice in his apartment that he told apprehensive neighbors he needed to find a cure for cancer. Be that as it may, he was also seeking a way to inject galloping cancer, Baker reported. He had been using a microscope, surgical instruments and other medical equipment.

That the team had devised the cancer-causing virus by 1963 summer's end meant it would have been available in plenty of time to test it on Jack Ruby when in 1966 he won reversal of his conviction for murdering Oswald. The reversal also set up a change of venue for a new trial away from Dallas, where Ruby would be free to talk. Ruby told relatives a prison doctor had inoculated him. On Jan. 3, 1967, a few weeks after getting the shot, he died at age 56 of a galloping cancer.

Judy Baker said Oswald had been tasked by use of double agentry to get a visa to Cuba where he was to deliver the cancer-causing virus to a doctor who had turned against Castro and would inoculate the dictator with the toxin. That mission was the reason for Oswald's mystery trip to Mexico City where he was said to have contacted both the Soviet and Cuban embassies without immediately achieving his goal of getting a visa. The Oswald lore centers on a nest of double agents at the Luma Hotel in Mexico City. The Mexican capital was the CIA's headquarters for Latin America and a crossroad for spying and espionage. Intelligence agent Nagell met Oswald there. Nagell in September of 1963 wrote to J. Edgar Hoover in Washington informing the director of plans afoot to assassinate JFK. When he received no reply, he worried that he was being set up to take a fall and countered with an ironclad alibi. He casually walked into a federal bank in El Paso, Texas, fired two shots into the ceiling and sat on a curb until authorities took him away to prison. He had his perfect alibi. He was in a federal prison when Kennedy was shot.

"WHAT HAVE I DONE?"

With Attorney General Robert Kennedy stunned by his brother's murder, he was heard to mutter, "My God, what have I done? I've killed my brother." He did not specify what he had in mind from among a wide range of possibilities including spearheading a Justice Department wiretapping and electronic bugging of dozens of Mafia bosses, unseen in annals of the bureau. Was he ruing his firing of CIA bigwig Bill Harvey? What about his kidnap roust to Guatemala of New Orleans mafia boss Carlos Marcello who was in federal court fighting deportation on the day of the assassination? Was it a backfire of initiatives to assassinate Cuban dictator Fidel Castro using the CIA and a special Harvey-Mafia killer team? Had he gone too far with his assertion to lifetime FBI Director J. Edgar Hoover that he, Bobby Kennedy, as attorney general was in charge of the FBI? Was it the bitter fruit of his alienation of Cuba Libre anti-Castro firebrands who blamed the Kennedys for the invasion defeat and capture of approximately 1200 Brigade 2506 CIA-backed commandos at the Bay of Pigs in Cuba in April, 1961? Had he erred in the recent arrest at Lake Pontchartrain, La. of a dozen CIA-backed regrouped commandos by the FBI on RFK's orders; or any one of a number of zealous actions undertaken under color of authority acquired as attorney general, acting boss of the CIA and underboss to the president of the United States?

GRAND DIVERSION FRAMES OSWALD

Whatever prompted Robert Kennedy's odd remark soon did not matter because Lee Oswald was wearing the horns.

The grand diversion immediately caught fire. Hoover's FBI troops across the nation, after being advised by the director and his counter-espionage chief, William E. Sullivan, to drop everything because the culprit had already been caught, fell silent. Nicholas Katzenbach, with his boss in tacit agreement, promptly wrote a memo on yellow-lined paper addressed to Bill Moyers, aide to President Lyndon Johnson, outlining the need to blame Oswald. FBI Agent James Hosty "round filed" a note that had been written to the FBI by Lee Harvey Oswald. The contents of the trashed note remain a mystery. When Agent Hosty later raised the issue, he was shipped off to the Kansas City Field Office, an approximation of Siberia for career-minded agents. In New Orleans, the SAC couldn't remember anything significant about Lee Harvey Oswald's personal visit to his office for a fairly lengthy talk about flyers Oswald had been circulating to spotlight his one-man 'Fair Play For Cuba' campaign backstamped with ex-ONI Agent Guy Banister's local private eye address.

Outside the inner circles in Washington D.C. there was little common knowledge that JFK was a compulsive womanizer, reckless and indiscreet, shielded by a conspiratorial press corps.

The scapegoating of Lee Harvey Oswald as a Marxist kook who single handedly caught JFK in a crossfire without a motive started falling apart by Sunday when people across the nation, glued to their television sets, watched in awe as a burly gunman hustled forward to shoot Oswald in the stomach while the self-described patsy was being escorted in the basement garage of the Dallas Police Station. It was widely seen as a professional hit. Nightclub girlie operator Jack Ruby had snuffed out Oswald. Not only had JFK been assassinated, a suspect had also been assassinated. Something was fishy.

THE TEXAS LYNCH MOB

The Texas menfolk conceit is that they are tougher and, yes, a lot meaner than anyone else.

They'll rope a steer, jump a bi-plane off a field of cacti, stare down a possible flush with a pair of one-eyed jacks and drop a leaping jackrabbit in mid-air just in time for vittles.

One of the ways Lyndon Johnson liked to test his ranch guests was to hand him a gun to see if he was squeamish when he shot an animal.

Was that the real Lyndon Johnson?

The knock on LBJ in Washington was that he was an uncouth son-of-a-bitch. He was smart, shrewd and the most persuasive Senator in the Capitol. He loved horse-trading, logrolling and pork-barreling. When he couldn't get his way, he'd come at you again the next day with a new angle. Talk about pressing flesh. He'd make his point by squeezing your arm and pleading until you saw it his way.

Unlike JFK, he was not an uncontrollable womanizer. He prided himself on control but there were exceptions. Johnson's Washington secretary was his workplace mistress. His primary mistress was Madeleine Brown, an Austin advertising executive. JFK preferred variety. Both were male chauvinist pigs by today's standards. They had anatomical pet names. JFK called his JJ. LBJ's was Jumbo.

Asked about her husband fooling around, his wife Lady Byrd Johnson had the perfect squelch.

"Lyndon loves everybody," Mrs. Johnson said, "and half of them are women."

Then why do so many people think LBJ killed JFK?

Few people know it but JFK and LBJ genuinely liked one another.

It was based on good-natured ribbing. It had started in the Senate, when LBJ was Senate majority leader, ruling the roost, and JFK was the playboy absentee boy wonder.

IT MIGHT GO LIKE THIS:

LBJ: Meet any nice new virgins today, Mr. President?

JFK: No, been too busy going over election returns from Wazoo County down near the Texas border. What did you win by, 87 votes? (Mock call to aide Dave Powers) Dave, Landslide Lyndon is here. Got any more bags of votes from Wazoo for Lyndon's election last month.

LBJ: Heh heh heh. Seriously, Jack. Can't we do something about that knucklehead McNamara? He thinks the war in Indochina is winding down.

JFK: All depends on who you talked to last. I sent Vik Krulak and that brain, what's his name, over to 'Nam to find out first hand. Marine General Krulak says we're winning. What's his name says we're losing. I asked them, you sure you guys visited the same country?

LBJ: That's a good one. What I came to see you about, you can do me a favor, Jack. All these jerkoff Irishmen you've got surrounding you. No offense, but who the f___k do they think they are? Bunch of snickering assholes. It makes me look bad, Mr. President. You gotta tell them to lay off. You see 'em alone, one on one, they're okay. Get them together, they're like a pack of f____n' hyenas. Old Lyndon this, old Tex that.

JFK: Who? They don't mean anything. Who said what?

LBJ: Bobby. I don't even want to start about Bobby, he's your brother, with all respect. He thinks you walk on water and he's the canoe. You could tell him to just ease up a little. But it's those others. Those horses' asses couldn't get elected dogcatcher.

JFK: We're thinkin' of runnin' them but the opposition is too strong.

LBJ: Now you take this f____n' Kenny O'Donnell. He thinks you're the queen of Sheba. I come up and say I got to see Jack, he jumps up and says do you have an appointment. The fuck is ready to call security. That rotten sonofabitch actually thinks we're supposed to genuflect and then ask to kiss your ring. He ought to be working for the Pope.

JFK: Oh, Kenny. He's okay, Lyndon. You just got to know how to handle him. You ever hear this one about Kenny's loyalty? The boss comes in, draws his thirty-eight, shoots this crippled woman dead. Guess what Kenny says? ... She deserved to die.

Lyndon cracks up laughing.

A WORD OR TWO HERE, A WORD THERE

J. Edgar was across the street, looking for a grassy spot to heel his dog. He saw Lyndon coming out of the town house, waving for his driver. A couple of Secret Service guys were skulking around, trying to look invisible. The jist of their talk:

"Lyndon. Got a minute?"

"What's up, Edgar?" Johnson said, flinging his hands up in mock surrender. "You got me. I'm innocent. What did I do?"

Hoover chuckled.

"No, this is serious," Hoover said, "Come close – I don't want this overheard". He glowered through his eyebrows at the security men.

"You're not going to believe this. Guess who charm boy is f____ing now?"

"Not the nuns down at the convent."

"Worse," said Hoover. "You know this blonde divorcee, Mary Pinchot, Cord Meyer's ex. The president is not only balling her in the White House every time Mrs. Kennedy leaves town, they're cooking up a druggie takeover, juicing the wives to brainwash everybody in town. Acid. LSD."

"Everybody?"

"Only people who count. Cabinet heads, a couple of Supreme Court judges, two senators, a few congressmen, law enforcement bosses. Who knows where it ends."

"On the level? " said Johnson. "He's gone bonkers."

"Got to be stopped," Hoover said. "I can't just walk in and say, you're under arrest, Mr. President, for treason. How would that look? Not only that, Bobby's in the way. He's AG, you know."

"He's ten times worse than Jack," Johnson said. "The president went slaphappy screwing those Profumo broads from East Germany. What does he think this is, the Ziegfield follies? What are we gonna do, Edgar?"

"You're close with Cord Meyer over at CIA. Could you say a word? He doesn't like Jack Kennedy to start with. He could get a few spooks from the covert side going on this. We can't just let this hang. It's our duty to take action. We've already got an affidavit from a wife who gave formal information. A squealer. There's more coming."

"Let me talk to a few people," Lyndon Johnson said. "Maybe there's more ways to skin a cat than one."

"Keep it on the Q.T.," Hoover said.

EDUARDO'S DIAGRAM

When superspy E. Howard Hunt on his deathbed outlined the chain of command of the mutiny he jotted down a few names. He then drew arrows to show who dealt with whom. At the top he placed the name Lyndon Johnson with an arrow pointing to the name Cord Meyer. The next arrow pointed to Frank Sturgis with whom Hunt said he met in a Miami motel room. Sturgis broached assassination. "We're going to kill Kennedy, " Hunt recalled Sturgis saying. David Sanchez Morales, a CIA hit man, had discretely stepped outside, a tradecraft precaution to ensure that no one could ever establish a three-man conspiracy.

Sturgis, a native of Cuba who had once been a Havana police boss, had worked with Hunt on other Latin American projects. He knew Hunt to be an outspoken critic of JFK infuriated by the president's handling of the Bay of Pigs debacle, which Hunt would later spotlight in his book Give Us This Day. Hunt's cover during his CIA career was a spy story novelist. Having had a dozen novels published, it stamped him as a chess master capable of circular strategies, the most noteworthy being his imaginative role in plotting the overthrow of the Arbenz regime in Guatemala in 1954. It had been the CIA's first great success story, the generational seedbed for an old boy network that spread its wings around the world for a dozen years.

Hunt said Sturgis confided that they were going to kill the president. "Are you with us?" Hunt quoted Sturgis.

"If you're set up already," replied Hunt, "why do you need me? Who else is in?"

"Bill Harvey's on board, "Sturgis said. Harvey was the CIA's point man based in Miami for the massive Operation Mongoose anti-Castro task force, directed from The Pentagon by General Edward G. Lansdale. He also teamed up with the Mafia's Johnny Roselli to plan the assassination of Fidel Castro, meeting often with Roselli of the Chicago-Las Vegas mob at the posh Fontainbleu Hotel in Miami Beach. There they would talk about contacts in Havana, Castro's weekend getaways to swim and scuba dive, his girlfriends, guns and explosives and poisons while lavishly dining on steak, lobster and prawns washed down in a sea of scotch, bloody marys and cuba libres. The Fontainbleu, a first class tourist hotel on Collins Avenue patronized by the rich and famous, was also a vacation magnet for wealthy mobsters wearing fat Palm Beach ties and loud shirts. In a holiday atmosphere, the big city sports threw big bucks around like confetti, some of the mad money going for generous tips to waiters or pretty cigarette girls and femme photographers who might accidentally or deliberately relay scraps of useful gossip back to Havana, where Castro's

Soviet-trained Cuban KGB had big ears. The Fontainbleu was like Grand Central Station. The only excuse for the two prominent would-be assassins to be conspicuously seen and overheard lunching and dining in plain sight would have been cocky overconfidence – a hubris drawn from too much power.

Hunt's initial reaction was that he would have nothing to do with the off-the-shelf bandit operation if Harvey was involved because in his view Harvey was an "alcoholic psychotic", he recalled telling Sturgis.

ALL SIGNALS GO

Overcoming initial reservations, E. Howard Hunt, code named 'Eduardo', eventually joined Sturgis to participate in the assassination in Dallas that he referred to as the "Big Event". He said he and Sturgis were "bench warmers" in Dealey Plaza. "There were so many plots – thank god one of them worked," he said without a twinge of regret.

Hunt's deathbed confession was no more than what the CIA brass always referred to as a "limited hangout." He did not elaborate on the active role of David "El Indio" Morales in executing the plot. He also made no further mention of William King "Two Gun" Harvey, whose scapegoating by RFK was the raison d'etre for the vigorous Miami-based 'Operation 40' assassination agitation that mushroomed into the Dallas ambush. It was Bobby Kennedy's controversial demotion of Harvey that had led to a boozy testimonial dinner in Harvey's honor by colleagues during which Harvey loyalists cursed the Kennedys, toasted their colleague and sank into dark and murderous vows to "get rid of the Kennedys". Harvey was slated to soon leave for his new assignment as Rome station chief. Canned by RFK in late '62. Harvey became the centerpiece for a testimonial dinner in honor of his career. It became the launching pad for the 'old boy' network to dust off the familiar format used as paradigm in Latin America, specifically in killing Dominican strongman Raphael Trujillo in

1962. Harvey would indeed fly to Rome, but he did not sever ties to nor physically leave the old stateside stamping grounds.

Pointing to dozens of loose ends to be tied up in Florida and Washington, Harvey reappeared in Miami where he continued to plot Castro's assassination using unofficial courtesies extended by his old buddy CIA Miami station chief Ted Shackley, the West Palm Beach native known informally as 'master of a million Slavic tongues' and the 'blonde whiz'. Shackley had been Harvey's backup man in West Berlin and owed his career to Harvey. So did David Sanchez Morales. Harvey was Morales' first boss when Special Forces paratrooper 'El Indio' was recruited into Harvey's counterintelligence network in West Berlin. 'El Indio' was good at killing, earning him a reputation as the Agency's "top assassin in Latin America" after he had been posted at the American embassy in Caracas, Venezuela.

CIA'S CORPORATE INNOCENCE

The CIA directs a vast international empire from headquarters in Langley, VA involved in collecting and digesting information of daily intelligence significance, and long, short and intermediate term economic trends, financial estimates, surveys of oil and gas reserves and natural resources, weather changes, oceanic movements, nuclear technology, military buildups and capabilities. It recruits on college campuses, seeking the cream of the crop for jobs as analysts, interpreters, scientific experts and agents. It is generously funded annually by Congress, which as recently as the beginning of Century 21 was budgeting 33 billion a year on "intelligence", at least $3 billion of which was earmarked specifically for the CIA. A dozen years later the CIA earmark was reportedly $14 billion against an intelligence appropriation of $50 billion.

These were enormous sums. It was a big world, attending to which was an enormous job. People could and did talk all night about whether it was worth it. The CIA correctly contended that it was hamstrung by its code of secrecy that left it unable to tout achievements, while slipups and setbacks drew disproportionate notoriety. There was a wall of honor at Langley that memorialized CIA gold star heroes who had lost their lives in service to the country, usually without fanfare or true recognition of how superb their sacrifices were. Yet the institutional CIA has left no stone unturned to cover up the role of what it only reluctantly conceded —- under withering scrutiny —- were "rogue agents" involved in the events of the early 1960s surrounding the JFK assassination. The CIA's Richard 'Dick' Helms, head of covert activities as deputy director of plans, routinely and predictably denied that the CIA had ever operated an 'executive action' project or that the agency had anything to do with the Kennedy assassination. Among the most admired sphinxes among old-time CIA veterans, Helms was an old World War II OSS hand from West Orange, N.J. who was not only an accomplished ballroom dancer, but a man who knew how to waltz around questions posed by congressional inquisitors. As far as anyone can figure out, Helms while heading the agency and its covert service for 20 years, give or take, and working the spy business for forty years, never was aware of anything out of order. As such, his biography titled *The Man Who Kept The Secrets* obviously fit him perfectly. Helms was indicted for testifying falsely to Congressional investigators in the late 1970s, after his retirement. He never served a day in jail.

During its Executive Action era, CIA determinations of 'extreme prejudice' were never the subject of memos or formal communication. A few mumbled words to a subordinate or to a faceless protected telephone line were enough. The covert service was more subtle than a Mafia family, more efficient and a lot more deadly when it was 'necessary'. No Mafia family could faintly approach the CIA in effectiveness or, in the words of longtime CIA secret agent, David 'El Indio' Morales, in ruthlessness. It took one to know one, Morales himself being a world-class assassin.

There is an issue of semantics when people point a guilty finger at the CIA. The tons of assassination literature spoke of the CIA as if it were a monolithic unity, moving in syncopated rhythm toward harmonic crescendo. Would it be fair to say, for purposes of comparison, that the State Department was a monolith, each embassy necessarily aware of what other embassies were doing? Did the Postmaster General expect a Postmaster in a New Jersey town to know the mail routes in Orange County, California? Was the fact that a fugitive from Bowling Green, Ohio was seen in Memphis, Tenn. mean that the fugitive was "linked" to the mayor of Memphis? Investigators were forever making sinister suppositions that were imaginative fictions tenuously strung together, conclusions reached from a false starting point interwoven with a string of associative coincidences and geographical loci. The CIA was widely construed as ubiquitous and creepy, sometimes with good reason, more often for little reason at all.

The CIA employed 'case officers' who were managers and stage directors in charge of what on an analogous corporate level were thought of as branch offices. They relied heavily on newspapers for fundamental information. The main power of case officers grew out of bundles of cash, payrolls, paid informants. They hired tipsters and indigenous personnel, contracting for finite periods of time with sources considered superior prospects. They bought loyalty needed to access and control foreign political entities and leaders.

HIRED SNIPERS HANDLED HITS

The payroll power extended to professional class agents money useful for propaganda, strong-arming, information mining, and spying.

In many instances, spies and hired hands had only a vague idea for whom they were working since Case Officers deviously propped up a third party to do a job or handle an assignment, using a code name or nom de guerre as an untraceable starting point. Often activity went on in a shadow world, a hall of mirrors, money being the lingua franca.

When a Case Officer hires an airport reservations clerk to a side job keeping him informed on people arriving and departing, who is the spy? Is the 'indigenous contact' now a 'CIA agent' or merely a routine information source? Undoubtedly both are spies, yet nothing about it is sinister. By the nature of their jobs, journalists are ideally positioned to 'spy', yet very few of them would acknowledge that their reporting was anything but noble.

In the Kennedy case, CIA action "agents" came not from original CIA recruitment, but from the ranks of military Special Forces. There is bitter irony in the fact that the special forces which President John F. Kennedy so vigorously promoted and which bears his name at the Kennedy Special Warfare Center at Fort Bragg, North Carolina was the elite 82nd Airborne Division guerilla force where two of his killers got their feet wet as Special Forces paratroop riflemen. They were David Sanchez 'El Indio' Morales, who headed the Miami hit team, and James File, triggerman for the Chicago hit team. Morales was a U.S. Army sergeant first class throughout his CIA career while Files was a U.S. Special Forces Army veteran who had seen guerilla duty in Indochina. On Nov. 22, 1963, Morales was employed by the CIA, Files by the Chicago mob.

Neither was a 'marksman', which designated a poor shot, or a 'sharpshooter', which was only mediocre. They were 'expert', meaning they could group three shots near the target bulls eye at 500 yards using a Garand M-1, the best and only American military rifle widely issued to American soldiers and marines in the early 1960s. Only an 'expert' could qualify for duty as a sniper at the time.

Shortly before he died in 1978, Morales was contacted by Gaeton Fonzi, an investigator for Senator Richard Schweiker's subcommittee for the Church Senate Committee and also for the House Select Investigating Committee. Nicknamed "Ahab' because of his dogged pursuit of the identity of a spy who called himself 'Maurice Bishop' - revealed to be CIA Case Officer David Atlee Phillips – Fonzi caught up with David El Indio Morales who gave him this lowdown on the covert arm of the CIA:

"They are the most ruthless motherf___ers there are and if they want to get someone, they will. They will do their own people up."

The viewpoint was expressed by the Executive Action specialist who had a reputation as the CIA's leading hit man in Latin America. Due to be questioned by Congressional probers, El Indio had a hunch he was a marked man and he was right. Supposedly retired from his post as consultant to the deputy director of the Joint Chiefs of Staff and drawing the pension of a brigadier general, the Army sergeant kept getting called back to Washington until he died there from what was diagnosed as a heart attack at the age of 53.

It was no era to be called as a witness, since one way or another some very big names and some very important insiders would bite the dust amid the flurry of subpoenas and public reports that they were wanted for testimony about the Cuba/CIA/Mafia plots of the early 1960s. The suddenly deceased included Sam Giancana, Jimmy Hoffa, John Roselli, George deMohrensheid and David Morales. It was as if the Committee clerks were issuing death warrants.

THE COWBOY CONSPIRACY

An author and college professor named Carl Oglesby once made a penetrating distinction in an historical work that he called *The Yankee and Cowboy Wars.*

The Yankees were the northeastern liberal old money and big media crowd into which John F. Kennedy fell. The Cowboys were the frontier livestock ranchers and big oil tycoons into which H.L. Hunt fell.

True to form, Hunt saw Kennedy's campaign trip to Dallas as a trespass that he was not about to ignore.

While women across the country were oohing and ahhing about handsome Jack Kennedy and his cultured young wife in the pink pillbox hat, old man Hunt was kicking over card tables and privately ranting about JFK's selling out the country to commies and JFK's crazy talk about killing the oil depletion allowance his generation of Texans had fought tooth and nail to hammer in place.

Hunt, fortressed in the Mercantile Building in Dallas just around the corner from Dealey Plaza, had already declared publicly that "Kennedy should be shot". His words carried weight: he was by most yardsticks the richest man in the world.

There was no unanimity in the country's view of the Kennedy presidency.

While Kennedy bubbled along in polls, a non-fiction takedown called *JFK: The Man and the Myth* by Victor Lasky was sailing along on top of the *New York Times* bestseller list. The scathing expose had topped the charts for months, casting Kennedy's PT Boat 109 exploits as ineptitude more than heroism while characterizing his "theft" of the 1960 presidential election as the "crime of the century".

The tarnished halo that Lasky saw in his looking glass was a vision embraced by a spate of fulminating right-wing groups most of which seemed unwilling to settle for anything less than a second American revolution. Among the groups were the Minutemen, the Patrick Henry Society, the Thomas Jefferson Society and. most significant of all, the John Birch Society.

Conservative to the core, the John Bircher code of old-fashioned patriotism at first rang a few bells. It was named by founder Robert Welch, a millionaire Massachusetts candy manufacturer who yearned for the Republic of our founding fathers and wanted a tool to fight Communism. He named it after a fallen American soldier. Established in 1958 to promote Americanism, its inception coincided with emergence of an extremely popular ballad of the day called "Tom Dooley" which was widely credited with sparking the folk music boom that was about to sweep the country. The folk ballad recorded by The Kingston Trio shot to Number One on the Folk Music charts and won a Grammy Award, relating a sad and haunting true tale of a poor boy who was about to die in North Carolina for killing his girl friend Laura Foster for seeing other men while he was away fighting in the Civil War. Both the Birchers and Dooley ballad found especially fertile soil in the south in the late 1950s, even though the song and the society were unrelated.

Among the John Birch super patriots active in the Dallas area in the early 1960s was H.L. Hunt, funding source for the radio station 'Life Line' which daily spouted an ultra-conservative ideology. Another was evangelist Billy James Hargis who conflated fundamentalism, segregation and anti-communism to a wide spectrum of followers. A third key propagandist and leader was former Major General Edwin Walker, a fierce anti-Communist who had carried out General Eisenhower's orders in 1957 to integrate the school system in Little Rock, Ark. and regretted it ever after. Many blamed Walker, a war hero, for inciting the riot at the Univ. of Mississippi in the fall of 1962 arising from a student protest against admission of James Meredith, the school's first black student. He was also deeply involved in organizing a hostile greeting for U.N. Ambassador Adlai Stevenson by hiring a Dallas auditorium packed with an audience armed with noisemakers and mocking flash cards in early November 1963, the famous incident during which Stevenson was spat at and hit on the head with a placard just two weeks before JFK'S assassination.

Walker sued the *Associated Press* and a number of newspapers for libel asking $30,000,000 in damages and won a $3 million award against the A.P. at the trial level, The appeal would be reversed at the Supreme Court level by Earl Chief Justice Warren who expanded the exemption, adding public figures to public officials, and for more reasons than one. On Gen. Walker's front lawn from 1962 through 1967 was a sign: 'Impeach Earl Warren'.

You didn't need a PhD to grasp that Dallas was the OK corral where Wyatt Earp and the boys were coming gunning. It was no place for an unpopular Yankee to go slowly cruising in an open convertible into a macaroni curve which had been mapped for all to see in both major Dallas newspapers by Wednesday two days before the 'Big Event", as plotter E. Howard 'Eduardo' Hunt described the posse's ambush.

HUNT AND HUNT, INC.

E. Howard Hunt of the CIA and Haroldson Lafayette Hunt of the East Texas Oil Fields were not related, and may not have even known one another.

They are historically related, however, in that both were prominent in the assassination of John F. Kennedy.

H.L. Hunt was born in 1889 in Fayette County, Ill. He had no formal education but had a mind for numbers and was as shrewd as they come. By the age of 23 he was running a cotton plantation in Arkansas that was swamped out. Using $100 as a stake, he went to New Orleans and won $100,000. He went back to Arkansas where he invested in and ran an oil field. Kind to his employees, he was tipped off to a big oil find in East Texas.

He sat down with the owner in the Adolphus Hotel in Dallas, across the street from the deli over which Jack Ruby's Carousel Club would later become famous. Munching on crackers and cheese, H.L. Hunt negotiated purchase and long-term leases of the oil-rich East Texas Oil Fields which would lead a *Life* photographer in 1948 to snap a photo of Hunt on Commerce Street in downtown Dallas on his way to a poker game. The *Life* issue of April 5, 1948 would ask, "Is This the Richest Man In The World?" He had bought an 88-acre tract outright together with leases for $1,336,000. The key was that the deal granted long-term leases covering 5,000 acres that would allow Hunt to drain them dry of black gold long before the leases would expire.

Living with his large family in a Dallas replica of George Washington's estate at Mount Vernon, Va., the Hunts were seen by some as model for the Ewings of the popular long-running television series *Dallas*. Two of his sons led by Nelson Bunker Hunt cornered the world silver market before authorities cried foul. They also owned Libyan oil fields before Ghadafy nationalized them. Another son, Lamar Hunt, owned the Kansas City Chiefs and formed the American Football League which famously rivaled the immensely powerful National Football League, forcing a merger out of which came the Dallas Cowboys with superrich Lamar a shielded owner behind papa's bosom buddy, Clint Murchison, another fabled poker player who profitably sold oil-rigging equipment.

One of the elder Murchison's three sons, Clint Murchison Jr., later became the majority owner of the Dallas Cowboys during the franchise's winning Super Bowl class team of the 1970s and had nothing to do with the events of 1963. The elder Hunt and Murchison were spotlighted in a 1948 *Fortune Magazine* article among the Big Four, "richest of the big rich," together with Sid Richardson, known to have dined privately with the Roosevelts, and Hugh Roy Cullen, whose Cullen Foundation's $160,000,000 bequest to charity was described by the *New York Times* as "the single largest gift ever made by a living American".

They were among a breed of oil wildcatters who survived the "strike it rich or crash" culture that powered much of the Texas economy in the 20th century. A man would chance all on getting a stake and drilling, often coming up with a dry hole that broke him.

JFK in his budget message in January 1963 touched on a subject sacred to Texas Oilmen called the ' oil depletion allowance", a tax preference in the Internal Revenue Code. John Simken of the *Spartacus Education Forum*, tracing growth of the oil industry in Texas, included the fascinating fact that in the dog-eat-dog world of competing oil fields, Hunt's East Texas Oilfield was once targeted by Texas marshals under a declaration of martial law promulgated by then Governor Ross Sterling, former owner of Humble Oil, because Hunt's competitors were being undercut by Hunt's lower per-barrel sale price.

Simken's research said the original 5% oil depletion allowance put in place in 1913 was by political maneuvering raised between 1926 and 1930 to 27.5%. It allowed oilmen to spread a profit over ten years.

During the World War II years net profits were taxed at unbelievably high rates, soaring above 80%. It left people like heavyweight boxing champion Joe Louis staggering in debt. The take by Uncle Sam was gradually eased back to about 48% on the top bracket, but it was not until President Reagan with Senator

Bradley working the other side of the political fence that the top rate fell in 1986 to 28% for a year, then to 33% before being pushed back up to 39% a year or two later because the downdraft had overly lowered revenues.

A popular cry from the gallery was to eliminate the oil depletion allowance, a populist fixation based on the presumption that oil makes everyone in Texas a millionaire. This menace to their interests caused Texas big oil over the years to dig in its heels, fighting tooth and nail with lobbyists and legislators to fend off the barbarian hordes. Their placement of friendly legislators to key committee chairmanships and generous campaign donations to presidential candidates did the trick. Early in 1963 Kennedy had mentioned the possibility of eliminating the oil depletion allowance, but practically no one believed he meant to follow through nor could observers imagine there was the slightest chance that adamant Congressional opponents would go along. Every president had seemingly toyed with the crackdown idea only to lose interest once the big campaign contributions poured in. Not until President Jimmy Carter did the oil depletion allowance get scrapped.

Did Kennedy's blithe reference to the cherished tax break shake up the Texas big oilmen? It didn't enchant them, but it was not seen as a compelling alienating force, perhaps contributive but hardly dispositive.

EYES OF TEXAS

The hometown cronies with whom Vice President Lyndon Johnson caucused when he was not in Washington included a loosely federated coalition of conservative businessmen known as the Suite 8-F Group, a sort of super chamber of commerce. It drew its name from its meeting place, suite 8-F in the Lamar Hotel in Houston.

Anchored by Edward A. Clark, senior partner in the Austin law firm that represented LBJ and a lot of others in the group,

Clark was often accompanied by another lawyer from the firm, Alvin Wirtz.

George and Herman Brown of the Brown and Root contracting giants regularly sat in.

Lyndon Johnson represented the Senate side of the Administration partnered with Oklahoma congressman Albert Thomas, chairman of the House Appropriations Committee. Governor John Connolly of Texas was a member as was former governor William Hobby, owner of the Houston Post. Jesse H. Jones, chairman of the Reconstruction Finance Corporation, was usually on hand.

Three insurance industry executives regularly attended: Gus Wortham and James Elkus of American General Insurance Company and William Vinslow of Great Southern Life Insurance Company. Another member was James Cameron, owner of Cameron Iron Works, a Brown and Root affiliate.

The usual order of business centered on government contracts, underway and prospective, domestic and international.

The Suite 8F Group functioned as a cooperative super chamber of commerce to embrace the capacity to handle large scale multi-million dollar private and government contracts such as government housing and military construction.

ANYONE FOR A SOFT DRINK?

Clinton W. Murchison, 68 in 1963, had met FBI Director J. Edgar Hoover a couple of years after the end of World War II. It was a perfect symbiotic relationship under terms of which Murchison and fellow oil mogul Sid Richardson could casually impress people by reference to their friendship with America's top cop while the millionaire oil men could extend favors not otherwise available to payrolled government employees.

Murchison annually gave Director Hoover and his top aide, Clyde Tolson, a California vacation at a hotel he owned near his Del Mar Racetrack, where they enjoyed watching the thoroughbreds race while risking a few quid on the ponies. Horse racing was America's passion during the 20th century, the sport of kings until a flood of state lotteries from 1970 on and casino gambling once limited to Las Vegas and the Bahamas expanded to mainland Atlantic City, N.J. in 1976, inviting a Niagara of slot and blackjack joints to follow suit all across the country.

Privy to the Mary Meyer-Jack Kennedy LSD brainwashing caper, Hoover was backed into a corner. He was damned if he tried to prosecute and damned if he didn't. An enforcement move would entail use of Justice Department lawyers whose boss was Attorney General Robert F. Kennedy, the president's muscle man, who would protect his brother to the bitter end. If Hoover let the matter slide, he could be hammered for non-feasance, obstruction of justice and a cover-up. Something would have to be done off-the-shelf so he confided in his influential old friend in Texas, Clint Murchison Sr., a John Bircher together with close ally H.L. Hunt. Hoover also touched base with Lyndon Johnson and CIA Counterintel chief James Jesus Angleton, who already knew about it through his line-of-duty wiretaps at Mary Meyer's town house and security taps at the White House.

The Mary Meyer bugs were standard operating procedure to avoid leaks as an outgrowth of the "ex-wife problem", as CIA brass called it. Later in life Angleton would inferentially admit he knew of the Kennedy-Mary Meyer conniving by threatening to expose "the real Jack Kennedy" and by stating that Mary Meyer had the capacity to "influence American foreign policy". Angleton's wife was a fellow Vassar girl and best friend of Mary Meyer while Angleton was a dear friend who helped look after her two sons after their mother was murdered. He always claimed he was out of the loop about the JFK assassination. "I was not privy to who killed John," he would dissemble.

There was little mystery as to where H.L. Hunt stood about Kennedy.

"He should be shot," he was quoted as telling people. "I don't know how long we're supposed to take this."

LBJ'S EX-MISTRESS TELLS OF TEXAS PLOT

There was a Pepsi Cola bottlers' convention in Dallas just prior to the assassination attended by among other stockholders Hollywood actress Joan Crawford and former vice president Richard Nixon. Nixon spoke at the convention. The former vice president jetted out of Dallas to New York early Friday morning and was in a New York City taxi en route from LaGuardia Airport to his home when the news flash came that JFK had been assassinated.

Crawford and Nixon were among guests a night earlier for a reception and party sponsored by oil magnate Clint Murchison Sr. at a ranch in honor of FBI Director J. Edgar Hoover, according to Madeleine Duncan Brown, Lyndon Johnson's mistress, in her 1997 memoir *Texas In The Morning*. She said multi-millionaires H.L. Hunt, George Brown and John McCloy were present. She said Lyndon Johnson arrived late, whereupon a group of the men immediately retired to a side room for a short private confab. When LBJ emerged, he was red-faced, she said. He seized her arm in a vise-like grip and grimly rasped:

"After tomorrow those goddamn Kennedys won't have me to embarrass anymore. That's not a threat, that's a promise."

His foreknowledge of the assassination rankled to the point that she badgered him during a hotel tryst shortly before the New Year. He tried to brush her off but she persisted, "People are saying you had the most to gain. Did you do it? Did you have Kennedy killed?" She said he got red-faced, throwing a 'Lyndon Johnson fit', as people who knew him called his outbursts. Exasperated, LBJ said it was the same people she knew, her goddamn oil friends and renegade intelligence agents who did it.

Ms. Brown had been LBJ's mistress from the time in 1948 when he was celebrating his "landslide' Box 13 primary victory over former governor Coke Stevenson until 1967, when they broke up after she was hurt in an auto accident. She said LBJ fathered a son out of wedlock named Steven who learned from his mother that LBJ had sired him. It prompted him to file a paternity suit claiming part of LBJ's estate after Johnson's death in 1973. Lady

Byrd Johnson denied any knowledge and won in court. The son, a Navy vet, died at Bethesda Naval Hospital while still a young man from lymphatic cancer under what Ms. Brown considered mysterious circumstances. She wrote her book after that and creditably supported it on a YouTube video. She died in 2002 at age 77.

As time went by, support grew for the view that Johnson had overnight foreknowledge of the assassination plans and did not intervene because he had always wanted to be president anyhow. He had in 1960 been strongly supported for president by H.L. Hunt, who had met in Los Angeles with Ambassador Joseph Kennedy, where he had reluctantly agreed to back JFK so long as Johnson was the vice presidential candidate.

"We lost the battle, but not the war," Hunt always said. Madeleine Brown knew H.L. Hunt well and on a slow weekday afternoon would play cards with him in the hotel opposite Jack Ruby's Carousel Club, she said. Jack Ruby was running around carrying a diagram of the motorcade route days before it was published in the city's two big dailies. He kept on talking about where JFK could be ambushed, she said. Before the 'wanted for treason' ad went in the newspapers, Hunt showed her the black-bordered ad in leaflet form, she said.

When it was over, she said, Hunt, a notorious braggart, remarked, "Now we've won the war."

FINGERPRINTS IN SNIPER NEST

LBJ had a strongarm man named Malcolm 'Mac' Wallace who was known as a henchman for Big Oil causes. He had beaten a murder rap and was a suspect in several seedy cases. He was supposedly in Houston on Nov. 22, 1963, an alibi that no one was challenging until Wallace's fingerprint was dusted from a sixth-floor packing case in the Texas School Book Depository. The finding was shuffled aside just as the Mauser rifle recovered from the Sixth Floor of the TSBD by police disappeared with the suggestion that someone had made a mistake.

More certain as a gunman or spotter from the Dal-Tex Building who was apprehended by a Dallas County sheriff's officer right after the shooting was Eugene Hale Brading, a Los Angeles career criminal who was on parole at the time. Found wandering around with no good explanation, he was arrested and taken in by the sheriff's officer. He claimed he had gone into the Dal-Tex building just before the shooting to make a telephone call, except that there was no telephone on his floor. He gave the name Jim Braden, an alias that no one checked out. In California, he had been arrested more than 30 times for bookmaking, burglary and embezzling funds. He called his parole officer in California from police headquarters while being detained following the assassination.

Braden and a man named Morgan Brown had arrived in Dallas a day earlier and checked into a suite at the Cabana Hotel, overlooking the presidential parade route. The Cabana Hotel was down the road from Dealey Plaza on the route to the Trade Mart so it was not involved in the assassination fireworks. Brown had flown back to L.A. by the time police went looking for him. Braden told interrogators he was in town on oil business. There was an element of truth, since he had been seen on Thursday in the lobby of the Mercantile building where H.L. Hunt's oil firm was headquartered. Others spotted there were Jack Ruby, Lee Oswald and CIA man Maurice Bishop, later identified as the alias of case officer David Atlee Phillips.

Although he had been "acting suspiciously", Braden was released without charges. Was Braden a patsy nominee, a shooter? No one followed up. It did develop that he had stature in the mob, being a Los Angeles contact man for mob sophisticate Meyer Lansky and a board member of the lavish LaCosta Country Club and golf course in California funded in part by the Teamster Central States Pension Fund.

Oilman H.L. Hunt was using Lee Harvey Oswald who was implicated in the arcane maneuvering whether he liked it or not. Oswald appeared to be spying while being set up as a possible cat's paw as he played out his Herb Philbrick triple agent scenario. He was also trying to make some money and Hunt was spreading money around. After the assassination, a note mysteriously surfaced from Oswald that was addressed to 'Dear Mr. Hunt'. The note writer said he was just asking, but he needed "further instructions". In Moscow, KGB experts claimed the note tied big oilman H.L. Hunt to Oswald and the assassination conspiracy. The FBI countered that the note was a fake planted by a Soviet spy.

GANG SKIPS TOWN

Oilman Hunt watched the motorcade pass below his office from an elevated floor as it wound into Houston Street at Dealey Plaza. After the shooting was over, oilman Hunt and six others immediately went to an airport and flew out of town, according to several sources. Some say they flew to Mexico City, others say New York. The prevailing view is that they flew to Washington D.C. where J. Edgar Hoover gave them cover, hiding them incognito until the heat died down.

LBJ mistress Madeleine Brown was not the only Texas insider who blamed big oil and suspected involvement by LBJ.

Barr McClellan, an attorney who was hired in 1966 by the prestigious law firm of Edward A. Clark in Austin, blamed Clark and LBJ in a book published in 2003 called *Blood, Money and Power: How LBJ Killed JFK*. At the time, coincidentally, McClellan's son Scott McClellan was press secretary for President George W. Bush, which was neither here nor there, the son being on his own and barely aware of what his father was doing at the latter's home in Gulfport, Miss.

Barr McClellan contended that Clark, the wily old senior law partner who handled virtually all of Lyndon Johnson's personal and business affairs, orchestrated and coordinated the assassination on behalf of LBJ. He had been hired as a junior law partner by Clark and had worked at the law firm for 14 years. McClellan said one of the other partners had told him Clark was implicated. In his own conversations with Clark, the senior partner had signified through primarily non-verbal communication an acknowledgement of a $2 million fee. McClellan spoke of covert glances, raised eyebrows and body English being a tipoff. His book pointed a finger of guilt at Malcolm 'Mac' Wallace, who was implicated in two prior murder investigations. Wallace, a big and hearty college graduate who was popular in some quarters, was a lover of LBJ's sister who in a fury had admittedly murdered a rival for her affections. His light five-year sentence was suspended by the judge thanks to powers associated with LBJ, McClelland wrote. He also said Wallace murdered U.S. Department of Agriculture agent Henry Marshall, a prober into the pending Billie Sol Estes grain-storage fraud case, whose death was ruled a suicide despite five bullet wounds. McClellan claimed Mac Wallace was a triggerman at Dealey Plaza. As proof, his book offered among scads of lawyerly exhibits Wallace's fingerprint which had been lifted by police from a crate in the 6th floor 'sniper's nest' of the Texas School Book Depositary where Harvey Lee Oswald had supposedly acted alone to pull off an unmotivated one-man blaze of multi-origin gunfire to kill Kennedy. A veteran fingerprint expert consulted by McClellan detailed 14 print features matching prints on file from Wallace's murder-case file, proving the FBI had dropped the ball by allowing it to be discarded as a "smudge". McClellan said even Warren Committee investigators in private notes had expressed "alarm" about the Wallace fingerprint.

THE ANTI-HISTORY LOBBY

His impugning of Clark and Lyndon Johnson stirred up a hornet's nest once it became part of a television documentary series called *The Men Who Killed Kennedy* aired in November, 2003 on the History Channel. Clark was an icon in Texas, a philanthropist who had served as assistant attorney general, aide to a governor and, from 1963–65, ambassador to Australia by appointment of LBJ. He had endowed the University of Texas and Southwestern University. Nor was Lady Byrd Johnson docile while her late husband was being accused of assassinating John F. Kennedy. She and influential Texas friends refuted various claims while mounting tremendous pressure against the television channel. Former presidents Gerald Ford and Jimmy Carter chimed in with their support of Lady Bird's effort. Their protests and lobbying persuaded the History Channel to retract and to apologize in April 2004. Ford would die two years later at age 93 and Mrs. Johnson would pass on in 2007 at age 95. The station promised to never again air the Johnson part of the series, which had been packaged as a nine-part video documentary by British producer Nigel Turner.

The fifty-year epic struggle between the Warren Commission Cult (WACC) and the Post-Assassination Truth & History Squads (PATHS) begs for clarity.

Between fixed loyalty to a fallen totem and adventurous pursuit of unproveable realities is a necessary consensus deserved by history. The lies must die, they argue.

There are many who sympathized with the slain president's descendents who nevertheless conceded no special entitlement or degree of empathy so extreme as to grant censorship over historic events which exploded in everyone's face on November 22, 1963 and which remained buried in secrecy. There was obvious preference by discomfited insiders to let sleeping dogs lie out of a sense of sympathy and compassion. The wish for silence, repose and respect, however, had to yield to the greater good of public understanding of one of the most dramatic episodes of the 20th Century, to find answers to riddles unacceptable at inception and proliferated insidiously by major media, economic and political nostrums ad infinitum.

The Kennedy hagiography is considered to be insufferable by many sincere researchers who legitimately question why history should be undermined year after year by obfuscating and pricey coffee-table photo albums as if anyone had ever disputed that Jack and Jacqueline Kennedy and their brood were anything except a photogenic family?

There was revulsion over perseverance of the monomanic myth that a man named Lee Harvey Oswald singularly and without motive supposedly had mounted a military-style ambush replete with crossfire and – according to one technical expert's estimate that eight or nine shots were fired in six or eight seconds – in defiance of laws of time and motion governing use of a single-shot, bolt-action, cheap mail-order imported rifle with a bent sight fired by a poor shot. The very idea was an insult to the intelligence of scrupulous observers unafraid of brash reality. The weight of evidence including mea culpas from conspirators now shows that the martyred president was not necessarily an innocent victim of dark and sinister forces who had nothing better to do than to promote evil and discord. The theory was always banal on its face and essentially preposterous. There had to be reasons that powerful forces ganged up to get rid of this one particular president.

Why do so many believe that John F. Kennedy was a model family man whose instincts were any finer than those of the next guy? Doesn't history show that JFK's own ambiguities, his inconsistencies, his contradictions created the toxic brew that boomeranged to destroy him? Doesn't history show that John F. Kennedy needed more than money, good looks and a gift of speech to run a nation? Doesn't the era demonstrate that JFK was in a job he neither wanted nor measured up to, and that he would have been happier pursuing a career better suited to his indisputable talents, rather than fashioning a power tour de force inflicted upon him by an overly ambitious father? The line from Ibsen's Ghosts comes to mind: "The sins of the father are visited on the son."

JOHN F. KENNEDY: A GREAT LIFE

"Live fast, die young and have a good looking corpse."

Jack Kennedy did all three.

The classic motto of Chicago slum kid Nick Romano in the Humphrey Bogart film noir 'Knock On Any Door' released in February, 1949 probably motivated JFK more than we know.

Freshly elected to Congress, home from hell on the high seas, beset by health problems, recovering from his broken romance with movie queen Gene Tierney, the 31-year old Kennedy did not miss a good movie and never failed to grasp a magic line. It might also remind him of his brother, Joseph Kennedy, who died over the English Channel during the last year of the war.

Neither a slum kid nor poor, JFK would in no way identify with the victim of society portrayed by John Derek, on trial for murder and defended by lawyer Humphrey Bogart. Bogart produced it based on a book by Willard Motley, a black author, from a script owned by the late Mark Hellinger.

Yet the line itself captured an existential spirit brought home from an entire generation of World War II survivors, many of whom doubted that they would ever make it home safe. Many had fixed their mindset on the prospect of a short life.

Was John F. Kennedy a satyr, a sinner, a saint?

There was overwhelming indication that during his presidency he was less a monogamous Catholic than something of a polygamist who courted and kept at least four 'wives', mistresses, concubines, or whatever you want to call them.

It happened, also, that his 1,034-day presidency coincided with his 43rd to 46th years of age which somewhat fit the clock of male menopause and a period when many ordinarily prudent American family men — as women and psychologists like to describe it – go "middle aged crazy". JFK did not change so much as proliferate his penchant for pursuing female sex partners. There was seldom any serious romance involved, from his point of view. His satyriasis ran to excesses that qualify as sickness.

A Sunday front-page story in the *New York Post* on Sept. 8, 2013 told of 'sex demons' experienced by Robert F. Kennedy Jr. as revealed in his diary recovered by his wife before she took her own life as their marriage fell apart. By-liners Isabel Vincent and Melissa Klein wrote: "The diary is laced with Kennedy's Catholic guilt over his infidelities, which follow the same pattern of affairs pursued by his uncles, John F. Kennedy and Ted Kennedy, as well as his own father."

RFK Jr.'s diary kept a scorecard showing a V for victory for every day he notched without having sex, which at least proved he was trying. A soft-spoken, charming and articulate man, the environmental head of Riverkeepers had far more days when he graded his sex activities as other than V. RFK Jr. said he was most serene while he was in jail in Puerto Rico for an environmental protest against Naval test shelling of Vieques, because there were no women around. He finally left New England and went to California to try marriage for the fourth time.

In the Catholic eschatology, adultery was a sin, no ands, ifs or buts.

Many married men cheated at one time or another, confessed or made their peace and went on, hoping the transgression would not warp their marriages, cause emotional rupture or be discovered by the wife.

Serial adultery as in JFK's case was another matter.

Kennedy was an armband Catholic, one who courted and gloried in the magnificence of the faith to the extent that he and his family consulted and privately socialized with the highest Roman Catholic prelate in New England, Richard Cardinal Cushing, who helped allay Protestant and Jewish fears that John F. Kennedy if elected might take orders from Rome. Cushing delivered the invocation at Kennedy's inauguration.

As a lad, Kennedy had attended catechism classes prior to making his communion and confirmation, as Catholics call those informational hurdles toward grace. The key was the Ten Commandments, universal teachings by Buddha, Christ, Mohammed on spiritual rules for life. The 7th Commandment stated, "Thou shall not commit adultery". One of the four apostles, Matthew, in his book in the Bible went so far as to preach that he who looks with lust at another man's wife has committed adultery. Matthew could not have envisioned an urban plaza peopled by mini-skirted young career women sporting spiked heels, spicy décolletage and a wedding ring on the third finger of the left hand. With all due respect to the Good Book and the clergy, this was regarded as a little hard to take by many practicing and especially fallen Catholics in contemporary America. In fact, it is impossibility, say experts who point out that lust is not volitional. Alluring half-dressed women were thrust at the male population daily in newspaper, magazine and television ads – an urban sex-driven society that the reclusive mystic could not have envisioned more than 2,000 years ago when he wrote about lusting in the heart. Former President Jimmy Carter referenced the phrase from Matthew in an article in *Playboy Magazine* and was widely and unfairly mocked for restating it.

OF POLYGAMY AND PROSTITUTES

Early in JFK's presidency, President Sukarno of Indonesia visited the United Nations in New York City where *Time Magazine* reported the State Department was directed to supply the Moslem dictator with a redhead, a brunette and a blonde for his sexual pleasure. Sukarno was a great stump speaker, a revolutionary hero who wore a black fez. He had led a native uprising which overthrew colonial rule and in 1948 established a Constitutional government in the former Dutch East Indies, a sprawling chain of southeast Asian islands stretching from Sumatra and Java to Bali and Tinian dotted by more than 100 active volcanoes and loaded with natural resources that had attracted the Japanese expansionism that triggered World War II.

As a Muslim he was entitled to four wives. He had four residences spaced far apart where he housed his wives: Japanese, Russian, Chinese and an out-islander thought to be from Bali. Indonesia was on the verge of being torn apart by internal war among Sukarno's Army-backed administration, Communists supported by Moscow and Peking, and the Air Force backed by the United States and CIA. A British colonial commando colonel in Malaysia, where Sukarno had threatened to invade, claimed Sukarno had progressive syphilis that was rotting his brain. In late 1965 an anti-Communist purge led by the armed forces killed 500,000 PKI members and sympathizers and imprisoned up to a million people. Sukarno was ousted in 1966 at age 65 and replaced by Army General Suharto who ruled for the next 30 years. Sukarno divorced his first wife, from Bali, and his second wife, with whom he had five children. In the Muslim tradition, he married several times more. Was he sinning by taking on the hookers bought for him by the State Department?

Polygamy was popular in many non-Western countries where its limits were practical and financial; satisfying multiple wives took management skill and money, even if the society found the practice unobjectionable. The influence of missionaries who spoke against polygamy cut back the practice in Third World Muslim countries. In the United States, Mormons in the Western territories were enthusiastic polygamists who also allowed four wives until Utah became a state and eventually banned multiple marriages prospectively, subjecting offenders to bigamy laws. Nonetheless, under the Muslim faith, polygamy was not sinful.

JFK was not a practitioner of Islam but of Christianity. He violated Christian sex morays as a way of life, qualifying him as a Hall of Fame adulterer and a first-rank sinner. Adultery was a mortal sin, which most transgressors wish could be reclassified as no more than a venial, or lesser, sin, but who were they to quibble with timeless rules for living codified thousands of years ago? JFK's good efforts presumably outweighed his deplorable record for adulterous behavior and, one hopes, took him to heaven after a brief stay in purgatory for a refresher course on the Ten Commandments.

The late 20th Century Western World trend toward secularism unfettered by religious orthodoxy introduced moral relativity into the cultural mix, making flexibility in private sex choices dependent less on morality than on economics.

Those who can afford courtesans take them for granted, yielding an exaggerated sense of entitlement. Thinking like that, Jack Kennedy saw no great harm in patronizing prostitutes or in having agents and panderers round up for his tasting a smorgasbord of pulchritudinous delicacies from the gardens of Hollywood stars and starlets, the pages of girlie magazines, the hardwoods of burlesque and showgirl stages, the casting lines of secretarial pools and the glittering wannabes of state and society receptions.

Money and access were not a problem for Jack Kennedy, a matinee idol as politicians went.

F. SCOTT FITZGERALD'S RICH BOYS

"Let me tell you about the very rich," Lost Generation author F. Scott Fitzgerald wrote in his 1925 short story *Rich Boy* collected in the 1936 anthology *All The Sad Young Men*. "They are different from you and me. They possess and enjoy early, and it does something to them..."

"Yes, they have more money, " fellow novelist Ernest Hemingway is said to have curtly commented. Fitzgerald, who restated the punctilio in his masterwork *The Great Gatsby*, never liked Hemingway's oversimplification since it was his observation that the rich born continued to think themselves better than others even after they had lost their fortunes.

Was JFK a harem keeper like Arab sheiks?

On a Garruta Airlines flight over Malaysia in 1963, two beautiful airline stewardesses told of an invitation they had received from an elderly sultan known as the King of Kuwait, then reputedly the richest man in the world.

On a recent flight, he had urged the duo to be his guests for as long as they liked. They had politely declined. Being treated like royalty just wasn't worth it.

"The girls who go – they never come back," explained Lucy of Penang, a delightful blend of Malay and Chinese. Added her voluptuous black co-hostess, grinning broadly, "he adds them to his harem. He puts them in his salon and won't let them go."

Jack Kennedy's harem was less restrictive. He never locked them up and preferred a revolving door approach, seldom forming attachments. When money changed hands it was handled by others, since Kennedy did not carry money with him.

CAESAR'S WIFE

It was said of Caesar's wife that she must avoid not only sin but even the appearance of impropriety. The Caesar's wife rule was part of the Puritan ethic and Victorian tradition that society applied as America entered the twentieth century. Politicians might play but they would pay if discovered – especially in the White House.

There was always the chorus of apologists who sang a strange song of permissiveness as if the White House were a flophouse devoid of monastic sacrificial needs. During the crisis Kennedy years, and ever afterwards, nuclear dangers hung like a sword of Damocles over the nation and the world. Was it too much to ask that the hand that held the nuclear 'football' refrain from indulging extracurricular sexual dalliances and dangerous diddling during his term of office, whether it be for four or eight years or any lesser span? The people who elected him expected no less, personal abstemiousness being a small price to pay for the presidency's emoluments, fame and riches.

A SOLDIER'S SACRIFICE

In those days, as during much of the 20th Century, self-sacrifice was endemic. Where was all the wailing for America's soldiers and sailors and marines who while serving in and between wars shelved their sexual needs and love life during endless months of training and combat duty? Take such a fundamental regimen as U.S. Army basic training for 16-weeks at Fort Dix, N.J., with mustering time stretching the monastic stint to a third of a year, during which a raw recruit age 18 to 22 had not the residual energy from grinding drills, the opportunity nor the money to avail himself of sex. It was widely believed that Army chow was spiked with saltpeter, which killed the sex drive. Then there was shipment to overseas duty, perhaps combat or garrison duty where meager pay barely above subsistence level left little more than cigarette money or a beer in the PX, let alone money for a date which almost certainly did not end up in sex. The lucky ones were those who didn't die for their country, where people would paradoxically later describe dereliction of duty regarding sex as a personal and private matter, as if White House duty were exempt from the constraints placed upon people in lesser stations of life.

During World War II literally millions of American servicemen sacrificed the best years of their lives for abstemious military service. Were their sex lives a private matter, consisting of circumstance cut off from any possible wholesome sexual outlet? The Korean War was just as demanding, depriving draftees for a full year in the frozen Chosin of any private sex life while trying to survive the coldest winter in East Asian history. During WWII at least a million draftees were denied any private sex life for three years – approximately the duration of the Kennedy presidency. Then came the war in Vietnam, where draftees over a span of two to ten years risked the danger of land mines and firefights in the bush and spiked mali in the rice paddies, without anyone even once arguing that they were entitled to a private sex life while on duty.

Apologists protest that JFKs private sex life was no one's business but his own. As we have seen, Jack Kennedy's compulsive 'sexpionage' stoked fires of revolt and mutiny that led inexorably to his elimination. That made his private sex life while in office everyone's business.

THE HONEY TRAP

SEXPIONAGE – The missing link as to why America's watchdogs favored elimination of JFK.

BRAINWASHING MISTRESS
"Our own Potomac cell"
Mary Pinchot Meyer
LSD DRUG PUSHER

GERMAN STASI SNITCH
"Best sex I ever had"
Ellie Rometsch
QUORUM CLUB CALL GIRL

HOLLYWOOD HONEY
"Happy birthday, Mr. Prez"
Marilyn Monroe
PAL OF RED SPY

CZECH BONDAGE QUEEN
Ulbricht's naughty niece
Maria Novotny
PROFUMO PARTY GIRL

HITLER'S OLYMPIC PET
JFK/Inga scandal
"Inga Binga" Arvaad
WW II NAZI SPY

LONDON SEXPIONAGE PRO
"Meet me at 21 Club"
Suzy Chang
NEW YORK CALL GIRL

Jack Kennedy had satyriasis – a compulsive and insatiable need for sex. Its counterpart in the female of the species is nymphomania. He was the first to admit his sex mania, according to memoirs by such notables as British Prime Minister Harold MacMillan, U.S. Senate Administrator Bobby Baker, Vice President Richard Nixon, Sen. George Smathers, D-FL, *Time* co-owner Clair Booth Luce and others.

Sex was never far from his mind. Concupiscence obsessed him from his early teens, relieved when his father took him to visit a prostitute, until two weeks before his death, when he called his young White House intern and body servant to his love nest at the five-star luxury Carlyle Hotel overlooking Central Park on E. 76th Street in New York City for a tryst before going on the road.

As she wrote in her memoirs fifty years later, Mimi Alford told the president that things had changed. She was no longer the 19-year old White House intern hired as a favor for her wealthy parents from Red Bank, NJ. Without ceremony at the first opportunity, Jack Kennedy had made the virginal college girl from the Jersey shore his sexual servant in the connubial bed that Kennedy normally shared with his wife. Alford wrote that she was glad to oblige the president even though Kennedy never kissed her. She was new to sex and fellated him whenever he wished, dallying in his 2nd floor pool afterwards, sometimes playing with the yellow toy sailing boats that replicated the actual sailboats that were his lifetime hobby.

The girl told Kennedy at the Carlyle that their sex activity had to end because she was engaged to marry. Kennedy's response was that he would like to see her again once he returned from Texas, Alford wrote.

The sexual use of the underage White House intern, statutory rape at the time, was seen by many as just one case of JFK's reckless disregard of the law. His exploitation of sexy young secretaries working for the government in Washington D.C. was a carryover from his Senate days when a clique of fortyish junior senators kept bachelor pads and partied with a secretarial sorority of free and easy stenos. Almost every Friday was a fraternity party.

SEX REVOLUTION

The 1960s saw an explosion of free love and casual sex.

Hugh Hefner's *Playboy Magazine* in the 1950s had built a magazine cult featuring scantily clad girl-next-door types centerfolded along with ads for pricey sports cars, Bell & Howell Polaroid cameras and such sartorial style-setters as jockey shorts and Hickey-Freeman charcoal gray suits. Starting with Marilyn Monroe, Hefner's parade of playgirls was no racier than the line-drawn Vargas girls who as far back as World War II had been featured in trendy and sophisticated *Esquire Magazine. Playboy* pontificated about something which Hefner named the 'playboy philosophy' which had he not spawned an international chain of popular Playboy Clubs may well have been eclipsed by stunningly bold and artfully portrayed mature beauties en deshabille exhibited monthly by publisher-photographer Bob Guccione in *Penthouse Magazine,* a slick sluice gate for a virtual torrent to follow of porno periodicals which left nothing to the imagination. What was new was that girlie magazines were for the first time openly displayed on magazine racks in candy stores, available to horny, sex-starved adolescent boys. The sex explosion of the early 1960s mushroomed exponentially with mass marketing of 'the pill', a contraceptive epiphany that suggested that female chastity had been conditioned less on virginal purity than by practical fear of pregnancy. The use of 'bennies' and amphetamine pills took root by the 1950s, commonly used as stimulants to fight off dozing on college campuses while cramming for exams and by over-the-road truck drivers. These subtle inroads into a shaping drug culture were trivialized by nothing less than an underground revolution in the 1960s when marijuana swept into latchkey society, feeding an after-school subculture during which teenagers merrily puffed away on grass in secret while swearing to their parents and guardians that they would never touch the stuff in a million years. Hard drugs, particularly addictive heroin, reached out to needy and nervous types, infiltrating the untotemic ghettos and unhopeful dead enders. Sugar cubes laced with LSD suddenly were discovered in the mix as the calendar turned into the 1960s. Self-developing Polaroid cameras heralded a monumental cultural shift; no longer was it necessary for saucy snapshots to risk censorship or confiscation at remote regional film-processing labs such as the one operated by Kodak in Rochester, N.Y. Film images materialized presto — right before your eyes.

SENATE FRAT PARTY PACK

As a young congressman with seemingly unlimited funds and an undemanding flexible schedule, Jack Kennedy when not ailing enjoyed the thrill of the chase. He could hit on the steno pool or couple with his secretary, Pam Tunure, who would later move up to become press secretary for her lookalike, Mrs. Jacqueline Kennedy. He could take the shuttle to New York City to an Eastside brothel or jet to Havana to frolic with lusty and busty Cuban senoritas of el noche.

By the time JFK won the presidency, the KGB and East German Stasi knew his weaknesses. The bait was spread, the honey traps set. Call girl rings brought themselves to his attention, inviting his patronage. They were not disappointed. There was a call girl circuit from New York City to Miami, with summer and convention hustles in Atlantic City. The same girls often plied their trade in all three cities, often driving up and down the Eastern seaboard in small sleek convertibles until they accumulated enough money to open a boutique or night club concession.

In the 1960s an influx of European prostitutes came to American cities. It was not long before diligent FBI and police investigators, some of them fascinated by the comely entrepreneurs, noticed that some of the visiting ladies of the night were mixing the second oldest profession in the world with the oldest profession, which was prostitution. The second oldest, espionage agents got a kick out of saying, was spying. The East German Stasi, an intrusive Communist super-bureaucracy which wiretapped everyone, had children reporting on parents, encouraged neighbors to inform on neighbors, stored millions of file folders, interrogated endlessly and often resorted to torture and murder, carried the KGB torch in Europe. It was unthinkable that the Stasi would overlook interrogating and keeping in touch with European and East German call girls who managed to get visas to the United States and keys to the digs of the rich, powerful and blackmailable. It was not remotely possible that the clever spymasters would miss the chance to plant bait in the form of a voluptuous pro in New York City or the nation's capitol in Washington D.C. In the espionage world such a lure was called a 'honey trap'.

The Profumo scandal girl-in-the-middle Christine Keeler, after professing innocence for years, later in life admitted that she had been a honey trap who conveyed secrets to her KGB handler.

HOOVER GOES ON WARPATH

J. Edgar Hoover felt constrained to crack down on Jack Kennedy's reckless patronage of dangerous women. Had the president seen too many James Bond movies? Why did his whores have to be security risks and honey traps? Hoover refused to be part of it. By leaking tidbits to trusted columnists who planted veiled exposes, Hoover knew he had crossed a line that declared war on the Kennedys. They would retaliate before long, seek to dump him as they had dumped Allen Dulles and his two top CIA men, Richard Bissell and General Cabell. What could he do? He could notify other gatekeepers, clucking disapproval, shaking his head in dismay. He commiserated with Lyndon Johnson, Cord Meyer, retired CIA chief Allen Dulles, retired Pentagon brass, Washington old timers. He called his old friends in Texas, oilmen Clint Murchison Sr. and H.L. Hunt. Murchison was planning a party, a sort of rally, in Hoover's honor and would keep him posted on when and where. Hoover would abdicate his presumed protection of the president, wash his hands. He would allow the Bureau to run itself, interfere not at all. He would not lift a finger to help the Kennedys.

The details of the party for Hoover at the Murchison ranch are hazed by time. Fifty years later, the Oswald-acted-alone chauvinists went to the extreme of seeking out domestics, in their nineties if not deceased, in hopes of proving that the party described by Johnson's mistress did not occur. The recollections of LBJ mistress Madeleine Brown set forth in her memoirs were direct observations from an inside witness, written long after Lyndon Johnson's death at a time when Brown was antipathetic towards LBJ's estate guardians.

In her book and in interviews she said she attended the November 21 party thrown by a longtime friend, big Texas oilman Clint Murchison, in honor of FBI Director J. Edgar Hoover. It fit because Hoover needed support due to a crisis in Hoover's dealings with the White House stemming from the bureau's planted news leaks about New Frontiersmen risking espionage by dillydicking with suspected East German honeytrap spies. Hoover had dropped all pretense of servility to the crown. Lese majesty was a sound rule for ordinary protocol but JFK's recent follies, foibles, indiscretions and abuses went far beyond the pale, forfeiting deference, as Hoover saw it.

While FBI agents were investigating call girl rings involving foreign-born prostitutes for espionage crimes – as Britain's Scotland Yard and MI5 had hounded Dr. Steven Ward, party girl Christine Keeler and a lordly circle of oddballs in the Profumo sexpionage scandal the previous spring and summer — Hoover's tolerance level for JFK's private peccadilloes had been exhausted. He had covered up for young Jack Kennedy in the Inga Binga German spy case 23 years earlier as a favor to old Joe Kennedy and FDR, but it seemed some people would never learn. A United States case as big or perhaps bigger than the Profumo scandal was already brewing when the FBI was double-downed by a blockbuster whistleblower complaint investigation. President Jack Kennedy and his mistress, blonde divorcee Mary Meyers, had puffed up pillow talk to new levels. The president was, at the very least, a tacit conspirator in her project to 'brainwash' top-level Washington government officials by use of LSD and drugs she called 'utopiates'. The purpose was to defrost the Cold War, to change attitudes; the customary noble purpose that Justice

Department prosecutors always contended was legally irrelevant under the statutes. More than a conspiracy, the project was going like gangbusters when a newly recruited member of Mary Meyer's 'cell', as she called it, "snitched", Mary's word to describe the breach of confidence resulting from her recruiting error, or as she told LSD researcher Dr. Timothy Leary, "I f__ked up".

By Indian summer of 1963 a full-court press by the FBI was underway. The criminal information that had been filed by the wife of a prominent official started whistles blowing and horns honking, especially in the Division Five counterespionage branch. The usual confidentiality applied as agents obtained wiretap warrants, tailed and photographed witnesses and suspects and fanned out to discretely interview informants without telling them that President John F, Kennedy was among possible targets. Mary Meyer was the focus, of which she quickly became aware. She flew in desperation to New York where she warned Dr. Leary about the investigative crackdown, as Leary's autobiography made clear. Agents filled the special file with the usual FD-302s, the field form for reporting information that might eventually be used as testimony. The secret file remains unreleased, fifty years after the fact.

ESPIONAGE EXERCISES

At issue was the general Espionage Act of 1917 of the U.S. Criminal Code's Title 18, modified in the late 1940s when much of Title 50, War, was moved to Title 18, Crime. The McCarran Internal Security Act of 1950 provided a statutory base under Title 18 with USC793 and USC798. These and sequential statutes criminalized breaches of national security in both war and peace, targeting actions inimical to the best interests of the United States.

Legal scholars and purists could and often did find fault with the espionage statutes, but as a general rule they were upheld by higher courts and applied strictly by the Justice Department, whose lawyers took the cases to grand juries and trial courts.

There was obviously a problem in any matter concerning John F. Kennedy, since even beyond his position as the highest elected official in the land he was supported 100% by his super loyal younger brother, Robert F. Kennedy, the U.S. Attorney General, who appointed and controlled most of the Justice Department staff lawyers. The inevitable expectation was that a dance of fancy footwork would ensue which would contend that the president could be put on trial only by impeachment, a divisive process of Constitutional dimension virtually unworkable in practice, and symbolically impossible in time of war or major hostilities. The insurmountable practical hurdles did not dissuade trained investigative bloodhounds from following the scent. Hoover saw the futility of pushing the case in court, where RFK's Justice Department lawyers would sabotage any move against their boss. He would have to find another way.

Until someone figured a way out, hostilities between Hoover and the Kennedys broke to the surface in the form of digs and slams back and forth in the press, usually unattributed and unsourced by their respective partisan press contacts. The pre-assassination party in Hoover's honor thrown by his old friend Clint Murchison Sr. involved two men who were born a year apart in the mid-1890s. Murchison and Hoover had been close friends since the 1940s.

Murchison, who made his fortune selling and leasing out oil rigs and technical equipment, was a poker playing pal of H.L. Hunt. Both men thrived on big poker games at the Four Deuces Club in Dallas. Many top Washington insiders bragged about having played poker with Clint Murchison.

Active in advertising, Madeleine Brown knew and had dealt with many of the people present at the Murchison party. She knew both Murchison and Hunt well and had handled advertising for both tycoons. She in fact often lolled away time playing cards with Hunt in the hotel opposite Jack Ruby's Carousel Club. Her book's recollection of the party rang true and was unchallenged.

The lavish party featuring roast quail and champagne was held at the Glad Oaks Ranch, a 22,000 square foot mansion located 75 miles southeast of Dallas near Palestine, Texas which Clint Murchison Sr. after suffering a stroke in the late 50s had turned over to the oldest of two sons, John, who lived there with his wife Lupe. At the behest of Clint Murchison Sr., the son had turned over the place for the night to grandly accommodate the guest of honor, J. Edgar Hoover, researchers said, which was not a problem since John's wife Lupe preferred to live in another of their houses anyhow, researchers said.

A chauffeur who was tasked to pick up "the bulldog" at the airport and return him that same night said he learned that the man referred to as bulldog was FBI Director J. Edgar Hoover. No one had bothered to tip him, he complained.

A maid for the Murchisons told researchers that the family "was joyful and happy' about the assassination. "It was champagne and caviar every day for a week", she said, adding that she was the only one who did not join the celebration.

LAWYER FINGERS SENIOR LAW PARTNER

A book fingering the two Texas oilmen and a cowboy cartel that was written by Barr McClellan, a prominent and successful Texas lawyer who worked for the prestigious Edward A. Clark law firm in Austin that represented Lyndon Johnson, would later add fuel to the fire. McClellan amassed an impressive array of facts, citations, quotes and commentary to make a case blaming Johnson while contending that McClellan's former senior partner Clark had orchestrated and raised some $2,000.000 of what was estimated to have been a $10,000.000 rubout bounty. The two books by Texas insiders persuaded many that while Johnson may not have personally sent out a Texas posse to ambush JFK in Dallas, his big business friends played a big poker hand in clearing the way for LBJ and Hoover to prevail over a shaping Kennedy dynasty that was planning early retirement for both Johnson and Hoover. To the Texans, it was dog eat dog.

The irony of the oil depletion allowance that Jack Kennedy had passingly mentioned was not only that Kennedy did not have the votes to amend it, as he well knew, but that it was not that strong a protection against the wild swings of the oil market, as the oilmen always contended. Not until many years later was the oil depletion allowance reduced, but by then both Clint Murchison and H.L. Hunt, among the world's richest men in the world as early as 1948 according to Fortune Magazine, had both put their oil firms into bankruptcy, filing for receivership as the price of oil tanked.

J. Edgar Hoover did not fear the presidents who occupied the White House during his 50 year run as founding father and director of the Federal Bureau of Investigation, an agency whose headquarters in Washington bears his name. He had co-existed in relative harmony with all of them from Calvin Coolidge to Richard Nixon with the exception of Harry Truman and John F. Kennedy, two of the four Democrats among the eight presidents who passed by his portals. Late in his presidency, as Communist hunters swirled around Washington D.C. and paraded "fellow travelers" reds and "pinkos" before Congress, Truman had publicly denounced the FBI. He said Hoover and the FBI were too powerful and a threat to a free society. What President Truman did not know was that Hoover had a secret treasure trove of information culled from the Venona Intercepts that U.S. Army four-star General Omar Bradley had shared with the FBI. Neither Bradley nor Hoover ever told Truman about the transcripts of Soviet espionage derived from breaking the Soviet codes. The secret wiretaps supported the FBI's cases against convicted traitor Julius Rosenberg and State Department presidential advisor Alger Hiss, both ballooned into causes célèbre by Comintern propagandists. The Venona Intercepts remained a secret for a half century because the United States and Britain did not want Moscow to know their code had been broken, or how. Accredited liberal Sen. Daniel Patrick Moynihan, D-NY, as head of the Senate Intelligence Committee, in the late 1990s finally tore the shroud off of the deep dark secrets – which incidentally represented one of the biggest and best intelligence coups of the 20th Century.

Shortly after the JFK assassination, Truman from his retirement home in Missouri tipped off knowledge that the assassination story was a lie. He denounced the CIA. Truman said that when he signed legislation in 1947 creating the Central Intelligence Agency, it had never been envisioned that it would become a virtually autonomous superagency that would make its own rules, pursue its own policies and answer to no one.

In 1948 there was published George Orwell's futuristic political novel *1984* foreseeing a world split into three scary totalitarian superpowers each of which regimented its citizenry into robotic servitude to the state. The book's forebodings swept through the halls of liberalism and across college campuses in an intellectual tidal wave, inspiring a generation to dedicate itself to preventing Orwell's nightmare society from ever becoming reality.

AFTERWORD

MISSING FILES ON JFK/ MEYERS FBI INVESTIGATION

If the criminal information initiated by a woman "snitch" who exposed Mary Meyer's LSD brainwashing plot in league with President John F. Kennedy is ever released from the FBI file morgue in Washington, the 50th anniversary of the assassination would be the time to expect it.

There should be an accompanying flurry of FBI agent 302 field reports because FBI agents were shadowing Mary Meyer during that Indian summer of 1963, after her plot to influence foreign policy had been compromised. It may be argued that she was neither a Mata Hari nor a foreign agent, but she most certainly was involved in espionage.

Would the FBI even fifty years later want to uncork another genie from the bottle of official secrets? Open a Pandora's box at the bottom of which is the biggest secret of all: the godfather of the FBI, Mr. Law and Order J. Edgar Hoover, took the law into his own hands when he conspired to aid and abet the murder of a president he was convinced could no longer be allowed to continue in office.

BIBLIOGRAPHY

1 Alford, Mary; *Once Upon A Secret: My Affair With President Kennedy*, 2013 Random House Paperbacks

2 Arnett, Peter; *Live From The Battlefield*, 1994 Simon & Schuster

3 Baker, Bobby G; *Wheeling And Dealing: Confessions of Capitol Hill Operator*, 1980 W.W. Norton Co. Inc.

4 Bergstrom,Signe; *Wisdom Of JR&E Kennedy*, 2012 Harper Collins

5 Brown, Walt; *The People v. Lee Oswald*, 1992 Carroll & Graf

6 Blakey, Robert; *Fatal Hour: Assassination of John F. Kennedy by Organized Crime,* 1992 Berkley Books

7 Burke, Richard E; *The Senator: My Ten Years With Ted Kennedy,* 1992 St. Martin's Press

8 Burdick Eugene & Lederer, William J; *The Ugly American,* 1958 W.W. Norton Co. Inc.

9 Burdick Eugene & Lederer, William J; *Sarkhan*, 1965 McGraw Hill

10 Buckley, William F; *God And Man At Yale*, 1951 Regnery Publishing

11 Buckley, William F; *Spytime: The Undoing of James Jesus Angleton*, 2001 Mariner Books

12 Burleigh, Nina; *A Very Private Woman: Unsolved Murder of Presidential Mistress*, 1999 Bantam Books

13 Carroll, Lewis; *Alice's Adventures in Wonderland*, 1865 Macmillan

14 Crenshaw, Dr. C; *Conspiracy of Silence*, 1992 Signet

15 Condon, Richard; *The Manchurian Candidate,* 1959 McGraw Hill

16 Dalleck, Robert; *An Unfinished Life: JFK 1917-1963,* 2004 Morland Dynasty

17 Davis, John H; *Mafia Kingfish: Carlos Marcello & Assassination of JFK,* 1989 McGraw Hill

18 Deighton, Len; Berlin Game, Mexico Set, London Match; 1993 Random House

19 Drury, Alan; *Advise and Consent,* 1959 Doubleday

20 Dulles, Allen W; *The Craft of Intelligence,* 1963 Harper & Row

21 English, TJ; *The Westies: Inside the,* 1990 GP Putnam's Sons

22 Exner, Judith Campbell; *Judith Exner: My Story,* 1977 Grove Press

23 FBI Wiretaps; *The DeCarlo Tapes,* 1970 Federal District Court

24 FBI Wiretaps; *The DeCavalcante Tapes,* 1969 Federal District Court

25 Flammonde, Paris; *The Kennedy Conspiracy,* 1969 Meredith Press

26 Forsythe, Frederick; *Day of the Jackal,* 1971 Random House

27 Garrison, Jim; *Trail of the Assassins,* 1988 Warner Books

28 Giancana, CK & Sam; *Doublecross,* 1993 Skyhorse Publishing

29 Greene, Graham; *The Power & the Glory,* 1966 Simon & Schuster

30 Hersey, John; *A Bell for Adano,* 1944 Alfred A Knopf

31 Hinkle, Warren & Turner, William; *The Fish is Red,* 1981 Harper & Row

32 Hunt, E. Howard; *Give Us This Day,* 1973 Arlington House

33 Huxley, Aldous; *Brave New World,* 1932 Knopf Doubleday

34 Jennings, Dean; *We Only Kill Each Other: Life & Time of Bugsy Siegel*, 1961 Prentice-Hall

35 Kahin, George; *Mct Intervention: How America Became Involved in Vietnam*, 1986 Alfred A. Knopf

36 Kanter, Seth; *The Ruby Cover-Up*, 1992 Zebra

37 Kerouac, Jack; *On the Road*, 1957 Viking Penguin

38 King, Stephen; *1/22/63*, 2011 S&S Scribner

39 Knebel, Fletcher; *Seven Days in May*, 1962 Harper Collins

40 Knightly, Phillip; *The Second Oldest Profession*, 1986 Bantam Doubleday

41 Kurtz, Michael; *Crime Of The Century*, 1982 University of Tennessee

42 Lacey, Robert; *Meyer Lansky, Little Man*, 1991 Century, London

43 Lane, Mark; *Rush To Judgment*, 1966 Thunder's Mouth

44 Lane, Mark; *Plausible Denial*, 1991 Skyhorse Publishing

45 Lansdale, Edward G; *In the Midst of Wars*, 1972 Brassy's Inc.

46 Lasky, Victor; *JFK: The Man and the Myth*, 1963 Regnery

47 Lasky, Victor; *It Didn't Start with Watergate*, 1985 Dell Publishing Co.

48 Leary, Timothy; *Flashbacks*, 1983 G.P. Putnam's Sons

49 Lederer, William J; *Nation of Sheep*, 1966 W.W. Norton & Co.

50 Lifton, David S; *Best Evidence, Disguise & Deception*, 1981 Macmillan

51 Livingstone, H.E.; *The Great Cover-Up*, 1992 Carroll & Graf

52 Marrs, Jim; *Crossfire: The Plot That Killed Kennedy*, 1989 Carroll & Graf

53 Maas, Peter; *The Valachi Papers*, 1968 GP Putnam's Sons

53 Machovec, FJ; *Tibetan Book of the Dead*, 1972 Peter Pauper Press

54 Martin, David; *Wilderness of Mirrors*, 1980 Harper Collins

55   McMillan, Priscilla Johnson; *Marina and Lee*, 1978 London Book Club

56   Melanson, Phil; *Spy Saga: Lee Harvey Oswald and US Intelligence,* 1990 Praeger NY

57   Messick, Hank; *Lansky*, 1971 Robert Hale & Co

58   Moore, Robin; *The Green Berets*, 1965 Skyhorse Publishing

59   Moldea, Dan; *The Hoffa Wars*, 1978 Charter Books

60   Nixon, Richard; *Memoirs of Richard Nixon*, 1978 Grossett & Dunlap

61   O'Connor, Edwin; *The Last Hurrah*, 1956 Random House

62   O'Neill, Tip & Novak, William; *Man Of The House*, 1987 Random House

63   Orwell, George; *1984*, 1948 Secker & Warburg

64   Persico, Joseph E; *William J Casey, Biography*, 1991 Penguin Books

65   Posner, Gerald; *Case Closed*, 1992 Random House

66   Puzo, Mario; *The Fourth K*, 1990 Random House

67   Ray, Pamela; *Interview with History*, 2008 Author House

68   Reeves, Richard; *Kennedy: Profile of Power,* 1994 Simon & Schuster

69   Reeves, Thomas; *A Question of Character,* 1991 Atheneum House

70   Roemer, William FJ; *Man Against the Mob*, 1991 Ivy Books

72   Russell, Dick; *Man Who Knew Too Much,* 1992 Carroll & Graf

73   Shaw, Irwin; *The Troubled Air*, 1951 Random House

74   Sheehan, Neil; *A Bright Shiny Lie*, 1988 Vintage Books

75   Shute, Neville; *On the Beach*, 1957 Heinemann Publication

76   Summers, Anthony; *Conspiracy*, 1980 McGraw Hill

77   Teresa, Vinny & Renner, *Tom; My Life in the Mafia*, 1973 Doubleday

78   Turkus, Burton; *Murder Inc.*, 1951 DeCapo Books

79 Warren, Earl; *Warren Commission Report,* 1964 US Government

79 Warren, Earl; *The Witnesses, WC,* 1964 US Government

80 White, Theodore; *Making of the President,* 1960-1961 Atheneum House

81 Wright, Peter; *Spycatcher,* 1987 Viking Penguin

82 Wylie, Philip; *The Disappearance,* 1951 University of Nebraska

Bibliography Notes

CREDITS TO BIOGRAPHERS, BLOGGERS, DIARISTS, DISHERS, LIBRARIANS

This book is uniquely my own but the brew owes its aroma to discoveries, research, investigative skills, tenacity and selfless courage by a multitude of mythbusters to whom with awe and gratitude I exercise my precious pup, doff my tattered cap and wave my Irish blackthorn stick in salute.

The blogosphere is a wonderland of biographies that were indispensable in my resolution of the Kennedy case. The amalgamation enabled me to break entirely new ground that placed Washington at the hub of the conspiracy wheel and JFK's sexpionage liaisons at roots of why World War II Cold Warriors authorized his execution. Google is the search engine that opened all doors. Appreciation accrues first to Wikipedia, then to Spartacus Educational, where John Simken's research is excellent. The Mary Ferrell Foundation was a fount of insights. DocuWiki and marysmosaic and crimemagazine uncovered many of the president's ladies while indyweek dug out tons of intel. Updates came from wherechanged, findadeath, infowars. Medical info on JFK abounded in doctorzebra. Such blogs as jfkmurdersolved, nypost, dailymail, Ufoconspiacy, histclo helped. Assassination-research fit pieces together. So too did bottleofbits, proparanoid. The unsparing blog cwporter bared all. Despite assuming too much at times, it consolidated vital research. Here were others from a list that is not all inclusive, omissions from which we sincerely apologize.

Wikipedia
http//en.wikipedia.org/wiki/
Spartacus Educational
http//www.spartacus.schoolnet.co.uk
Mary Ferrell
http/www.maryferrell.org/wiki/index.php/confessions

Online Journal
http//rense.com/general76/hunt.htm
Larry Chin, asst. editor
National Radio
http//www.prisonplanet.com/articles2007/300407
Confessed Assassin of JFK
http//www.themurdersolved.com/confession2.htm
Online Journal
http//federaljack.com/wp

My references included dozens of documentary films aired on The History Channel, the Discovery Channel, The Military Channel, networks and various other cable channels. I informally consulted weapons experts Vincent Walker of Tampa, a former U.S. Army armorer; retired Police Sgt. Joe Micci of Florida, a Vietnam veteran and crack pistol and M-16 shot; the late Conrad Foerter of Edgewater, Md., a former air navel cadet familiar with exploding rifle and shotgun bullets from his boyhood on a farm in New Jersey; and James L. Plosia, a U.S. Army combat infantryman in the Korean War. The writer was qualified as an expert rifleman in the U.S. Army during the Korean War at Fort Dix and at Fort Bragg, NC, using a Garand M-1.

My reading research was assisted over the years by the able and cheerful desk ladies, who through the public library's interloan syndication with most of the other libraries in Bergen County's 70 municipalities enjoyed a wide reach. Curiously, they had to go outside Bergen to Montclair in neighboring Essex County to borrow the key book in my research, Dr. Timothy Leary's *Flashbacks*, published in 1983, a book seemingly rare as hens' teeth. His diary-type memoir revealed his amazing liaison with presidential mistress Mary Pinchot Meyer and their collaboration to brainwash a cell of Washington influentials by use of LSD, as well as telling through Mary's frightened disclosures of a crackdown by angry federal agents in the Indian summer of 1963. It sounded preposterous. Yet it was the Rosetta Stone which unlocked the heiroglyphics of the JFK saga, confirmed by the careful, restrained documentations about presidential mistress Mary Meyer in a very fine 1999 biography *A Very Private Woman* written by investigative journalist Nina Burleigh and fortified by several authors who had reviewed White House Secret Service logs, notably by, among others, Richard Reeves, Seymour Hersh and Robert Dalleck. I found by careful tracking and side-by-side reading of the Tim Leary memoir and the Burleigh biography that the pieces fit neatly together. Burleigh's book focused on the strange, unsolved daylight murder of Meyer in Georgetown in 1966, which coincided with release of the Warren Commission Report. The report would later prove to be a whitewash, officially diverting focus of the assassination away from evidence of a broad murder conspiracy. Unfortunately, Ms. Burleigh skipped blithely past the importance of JFK's secret drugging and acid tripping with the president, almost as if it were of little consequence. Sexpionage, brainwashing and oddball behavior were raw meat for FBI pros, especially when it involved the main man, the guy who carried the nuclear football. The FBI and longstanding insider security apparatus was dumbfounded by what the "snitch" told them and bounded after Mary and the president like hounds at the hunt. It was little less than an unseen national emergency, and so it would be treated, it's disposition shielded by 50 years of national security secrecy.

JFK: SATYR, SINNER, SAINT!

www.ingramcontent.com/pod-product-compliance
Lightning Source LLC
LaVergne TN
LVHW051544070426
835507LV00021B/2405